Kurdistan

Kurdistan

Crafting of National Selves

Christopher Houston

Oxford • New York

First published in 2008 by
Berg
Editorial offices:
1st Floor, Angel Court, 81 St Clements Street, Oxford, OX4 1AW, UK
175 Fifth Avenue, New York, NY 10010, USA

Berg is the imprint of Oxford International Publishers Ltd.

Library of Congress Cataloguing-in-Publication Data
Houston, Christopher.
    Kurdistan : crafting of national selves / Chris Houston.
      p. cm.
    Includes bibliographical references and index.
    ISBN-13: 978-1-84520-268-2 (cloth)
    ISBN-10: 1-84520-268-6 (cloth)
    ISBN-13: 978-1-84520-269-9 (pbk.)
    ISBN-10: 1-84520-269-4 (pbk.)
  1. Kurds—History. 2. Kurdistan—History. I. Title.

    DS59.K86H68 2008
    956.6'7—dc22

                    2008010967

British Library Cataloguing-in-Publication Data
A catalogue record for this book is available from the British Library.

ISBN 978 1 84520 268 2 (Cloth)
ISBN 978 1 84520 269 9 (Paper)

Typeset by JS Typesetting Ltd, Porthcawl, Mid Glamorgan
Printed in the United Kingdom by Biddles Ltd, King's Lynn

www.bergpublishers.com

Contents

Acknowledgements

It is a pleasure to record my thanks to a host of people that have facilitated the writing of this book. First I wish to express my heartfelt gratitude to the staff at the German Oriental Institute Library in Istanbul, in particular to Ercüment Asil and Tomas Wilkoszewski, both for their good-natured responses to my never-ending requests for library material and for their fine friendship. I also wish to thank Barbara Pusch and Christoph Herzog for setting me straight on many issues of Ottoman and Turkish history. The book could not have been written in a better place.

I am also deeply grateful to Macquarie University in Sydney and to the Department of Anthropology there. Chris Lyttleton and Kalpana Ram have been supportive departmental heads through the process of the book's composition, and the University facilitated research leave in Istanbul. Ian Bedford read the manuscript and made many helpful comments: no doubt it would have been a better book if I managed to incorporate all his suggestions! The departmental seminar provided lively feedback on different chapters. And my undergraduate students suffered through varied versions of the book in tutorial discussions.

There is a third group of people who I am very glad to mention, individuals who in a myriad of ways, often without their knowing the true import of their contribution, have added their defining touches to the shape of the book. These are Joel Kahn, Kenan Cayır, Ugur Kömeçoglu, Claus Schönig, Fırat Bağdu, Aruz Yumul, Ferhat Kentel, Terry Austrin, Banu Şenay, Kirsty Bell, Alev Çinar and Zehlia Eliacık. Mark Hurst and Dean Falconer made constructive comments on my golf swing.

Finally I am privileged to name my family, to thank them for their support during the book's writing, and for ever before and for ever after. Humble thanks to my Mum and Dad, to my brothers and sister, and most importantly to Esma Çalık.

This book is dedicated to my two sons Raphael and Gebran, beautiful, challenging and beloved in their own unique ways. In its small arena, I hope the book might contribute to the crafting of a Turkey in which they would be fortunate to live.

Introduction

Many writings about the Kurds, most often but not only by Kurds themselves, begin in a commonsensical manner by compiling references to Kurds in various older manuscripts or even by reviewing archaeological remains of their past activities. Such textual and archaeological research is the invariable prelude to a more pressing endeavour: not merely to demonstrate the age-old existence and vitality of the Kurds but more ambitiously to construct a connection, however conceived, between Kurds in the past and Kurds in the present. In general these historical references are tendered as proof of Kurds' *legitimate* and *contemporary* presence and, like all good signs, they possess an ambiguity of meaning – thus allowing multiple use to be made of them in identifying the Kurds' enduring essence.

Kendal Nezan's introductory essay to the book *Kurdish Culture and Identity* is no exception: after briefly reviewing population estimates for Kurds in various countries, he proceeds by asserting the feelings of Kurdishness that they share. To prove how long-standing this sense of Kurdish identity is he quotes the sixteenth-century poet Melaye Jeziri (Nezan 1993: 10):

> I am the rose of Eden of Botan,
> I am the torch of the knights of Kurdistan.

By contrast, Müfit Yüksel is more specifically concerned to demonstrate the Muslim character of this historic Kurdish identity, noting its loyal allegiance to Islam:

> It is undeniable that the Kurds are one of the foundational communities of the Islamic Middle East. History shows that after Hz. Omer conquered Iran and Mesopotamia the Kurds like the Persians were introduced to Islam and in a short space of time became Muslims. During my research in the Bitlis area on grave inscriptions I have happened upon Muslim graves that date from 60, 70 or 80 years after the Hegira. (Yüksel 1993: 29) (my translation)

Somewhat differently Rohat Alakom, explaining the reasons for his book *Eski Istanbul Kürtleri* (*Kurds of Old Istanbul,* 1453-1925), writes that

> Up until now, Kurdish society has usually been analyzed from a political viewpoint. However Kurds in Istanbul have rarely been examined from an 'Istanbul perspective',

that is to say from the perspective of an important urban centre like Istanbul... This work, prepared on Kurds in Istanbul [during the Ottoman Empire] has been written in the hope that it will contribute to a greater understanding of the Kurds today, for whom migration has become almost a way of life. (Alakom 1998a: 7–8) (my translation)

Yet why do so many writings about Kurds or on the Kurdish situation demonstrate the urgent necessity of recollecting and affirming a historic continuity? The answer is clearly linked to the foundational practices of nation building and state formation in the Middle East after the First World War, as well as to their constant re-enactment by elites thereafter as key political resources in the present. This book brings these two processes together: the production of knowledge about Kurds and the ceaseless instituting of the nation by the regional states of Iraq, Iran and Turkey.

To do so the book is divided into two roughly equal parts. Its first half aims to elucidate some of the important ways in which, since the establishment of those states, individuals, groups and political associations have imagined Kurdistan and Kurds. They have not imagined them existing in splendid isolation: one important interlocutor of this emergent knowledge is the Ottoman empire, or more precisely its historiography and its often nationalized accounts of Ottoman origins, conquests and legacy. The book's second half puts this discourse on Kurds in its proper context: the emergence of new centres of power concentrated in Ankara, Tehran and Baghdad. As with disputes concerning the distinguishing features of the Ottoman empire, so too have the political projects of these nation-states, particularly in reference to their Kurdish provinces, been interpreted and evaluated in radically different ways.

More precisely, then, Chapters 1 and 2 explore recent discourses on Kurdish identity that delineate and attribute particular interpretative importance to a number of key historical developments. These might be thought of as the standard highlights of a self-conscious Kurdish historiography. The first of these is the incorporation of much of the Kurdish regions into the Ottoman Empire in the years 1514–18, or the loss of their Kurdish territories by the newly founded Safavid state in present-day Iran. This 'first division' of the Kurdish areas also involved the institution of the Ottoman provinces of Diyarbakır and Kurdistan.[1] A second historical moment is the modernization heralded by the Ottoman *tanzimat* reforms in the long nineteenth century, in which new processes of centralizing authority transformed relationships between the imperial centre and its provincial peripheries. Similar impulses to modernization invigorated the Qajar dynasty in Persia. A third is obviously the

1. The term 'first division' is used by Abbas Vali (2002), and implies a prior regional and ethnic unity. Yet from the point of view of its inhabitants, Kurdistan was divided in numerous ways already, tribal sections facilitating and restricting access and usage to particular areas of territory, and ethnic and/or religious communities living in their own villages (Armenian, Alevi, etc.) or in their own homogeneous quarters of towns (Greek, Jewish, etc.). Further, space was divided on gender lines. Given the porousness of the imperial borders between the Ottomans and Safavids, these 'micro' spatial divisions were no doubt more significant for their inhabitants and users.

institution after the First World War of the nation-states of Turkey and Iran and then of Iraq in the territories where Kurds and other minorities lived, resulting in what Kurdish nationalists describe as the second division of the Kurdish region.

This exploration is not intended to provide a short version of the history of the Kurds. Rather it identifies the most commonly repeated landmarks of Kurdish historical experience and puts this historiography in its proper context – the social and cultural revolutions spearheaded by what I argue should be denoted as the Kemalist states of Turkey, Iraq *and* Iran after that war. Chapters 4 and 5 expand upon an idea of Bobby Sayyid, who labels as Kemalist the ideology and social programmes of *all* the secularizing, modernizing and nationalizing Ottoman successor states that mediated independence in Muslim-majority areas following decolonization in the Middle East. For Sayyid, Kemalist regimes are unified by their common rejection of 'the use of Islam as the master signifier of their political discourse' (Sayyid 1997: 70). This does not establish an 'atheistic' politics. Kemalism politicizes and instrumentalizes Islam neither by benign indifference, strict separation or implacable hostility but in a *Hobbesian* fashion; that is, the Kemalist state arrogates to itself the right to command the religious institution what doctrine it must preach.

Yet I also argue that Sayyid's definition of Kemalism is insufficient. In prioritizing its disenfranchising of Islam as its core component he minimizes its equally important homogenizing nationalist project and its constructing of new sovereign ethnic selves, Turkish, Persian and Arabic, in the three countries under consideration. He also posits a strong distinction between Kemalist and Islamist political orders, presenting them as binary opposites. It is typical of the political capital invested in the Kemalist project that not only Sayyid but other scholars too present either Kemalism or Khomeinism (Sayyid's paradigmatic example of Islamism) as the diametrically opposed and sole choice for the Muslim world. This binary is false: not only does it grossly simplify Islamism and conflate it with theocracy but it also takes the Kemalists' own self-representation at its word, assimilating their reforms to what is presented as a universal political development initiated in Europe and thereafter adopted by progressive elites worldwide. Obscured in this are important similarities – of course there are differences too – between Kemalism and Khomeinism. Most strikingly, both Kemalist (Pahlavi) and Islamist Iran have insisted on the 'denial of Kurdish national identity as a prerequisite of their national sovereignty' (Vali 1998: 91). Significantly, both Reza Shah in 1921 *and* the Islamist regime in 1979 began their rule with military campaigns designed to crush autonomist movements in the Iranian province of Kurdistan. The Islamist movement in Turkey, too, has consistently downplayed any important differences in the experiences of Kurdish and Turkish Muslims.

Sayyid's fault is not his alone. Many analyses of Kurdish society focus on Kurds in one country, or fragment their treatment by devoting separate chapters to the 'Kurdish issue' in different countries. At best, Kurds are studied in interrelation with that country's specific state. Few studies provide a proper comparative perspective able to connect the dominant political project (Kemalism) of the states of the region with the emergence at the same time of a non-unified but transnational pro-Kurdish discourse and its self-description of Kurdish difference. By contrast, the core chapter in this book (Chapter 4) elucidates a multitude of governmental strategies in Iraq, Iran and Turkey all informed by the Kemalist political paradigm, reforms made not only in what Kandiyoti calls the 'juridico-political and institutional realms' (Kandiyoti 1997: 13) but just as influentially in their explicit making of a cultural revolution. Here we examine the Kemalists' creation of a range of practices, including their revolutions in language or alphabets, their amplification or muting of selected musical forms, their programmes for women's education, their new festivals, folklore and theatrical performance (including radio theatre), their innovations in maternal training and even in sciences of household management.

Likewise Chapter 5 extends our transregional understanding of Kemalism by describing its founding or re-modelling of cities, or its creation of what I provisionally name the 'Kemalist City'. The constructing of Ankara, the demolition of Tehran, the monumentalizing of Baghdad: all were or are transnational strategies of Kemalist urbanism and architecture through which Islam is controlled and re-ordered and nationalism engendered and expressed. In the process, any equivalent crafting of a Kurdish national self is disallowed. Le Corbusier's famous comment summarizing the modernist architectural ethic – the 'house is a machine for living in' – applies equally well to the animating of cities as Kemalist by their statesmen and architects. The city, too, is a machine for living in and as we will see, the spatial organization of the 'Kemalist City' is calculated to 'enforc[e] a particular direction of action by virtue of the particular intention built into its construction' (Humphrey 2005: 43). The final section of Chapter 5 returns to the discourse and experience of Kurds and what it means for self-conscious Kurdish actors to live in a Kemalist built environment.

Chapter 3 presents the reader with a vital detour, an examination of some of the exemplary anthropological literature in English (and Turkish) on Kurdish society. Here the perspective switches from analysis of historical accounts of state power and its relations with Kurdistan to Kurdish society and the various ways in which ethnographers have represented it and the actions of those 'external' influences upon it. Examining ethnographic accounts also allows us to see how in their cultural revolutions, the Kemalist States of Iraq, Iran and Turkey themselves have been influential producers of ethnographic knowledge, as they collect and formalize an official folklore, music and material culture for their respective national ethnic group.

Kemalism is therefore a key concern in this book. It will be noted that the title of this book is *Kurdistan* and the subtitle *Crafting of National Selves*. By *Kurdistan* I mean in the first and uncontroversial instance the region denoted thus in the Ottoman administrative system, before its disappearance and renaming, along with much else in the Middle East, by those same Kemalist-states. The term *Crafting* draws attention to the social and cultural policies of these states that were designed to transform Kurdistan, while simultaneously seducing and mobilizing its population. *National* refers to the logic of social and political practice that these states require of their citizens, and *Selves* focuses on the personalized aspect of those practices, because state initiatives are null and void without individuals' subscription to them, in a process of self-institution. Appeals to Turkish, Persian, Arab and Kurdish national identities carry with them an ethical dimension, a claim and an orientation to virtue and it is in their projection of potential new ways of acting that their affective power lies.

If Kemalism is a key influence, there is still an unresolved question over the efficacy of the assimilationist drive of these political projects. For example, emphasis on the programmatic or semiotic power of architecture and urban planning needs to be complemented by examining how cities are reckoned with in this instance by their Kurdish inhabitants, in order to act in and upon them differently. One of the book's main presumptions therefore is the self-generation of individuals and groups as Kurds through these very processes of imagining and practising Kurdistan and in response to Kemalism's struggle against such self-conscious 'Kurdishness'. This Kemalist struggle involves the proffering of alternative self-understandings to the populations of these nation-states. As the first half of the book shows, one vital dimension of crafting a national self is the plotting and interpreting of historical events. Narrating the past enables subjects to become political actors of particular hue in the present. In her book on the Ottoman empire, Caroline Finkel writes that the task of the historian is to 'show how the past led up to the present, or to a present that is now past' (Finkel 2005a: xiii). The emphasis of the anthropologist is somewhat different: more to show how people's interpretation of the past – made partly through their refashioning of the labour of the historians – is a vital aspect of their present. Needless to say, although remembering the past, whether by reflecting critically upon it or by appropriating dominant understandings of it, is a primal act of human agency, it does not lead on to unconstrained self-creation. Personal and collective projects of change or stasis involve the constructing and narrating of history: but the agency of individuals and people is generated and suppressed through other social relations as well.

In reality the endeavours of the historian and the anthropologist are inseparable, though not easily brought together. So Balkan historian Maria Todorova notes how perception of the past – in this case the perception of the Ottoman period in Bulgarian historiography – is best understood as

> a process of interaction between an ever-evolving and accumulating past, and ever-evolving and accumulating perceptions of generations of people who are redefining their evaluations of the past. Whether in literary or historiographical works, this is a question not of reconstructing, but of constructing the past, with more or less allegorical motives. (Todorova 1995: 108)

She goes on to note the key actors in this process, in addition to the nation state and its 'Establishment': historians, poets, writers, journalists, intellectuals and politicians. In the Kurdish context we might add to these: pro-Kurdish social movements, although the writers of their pamphlets and the strategists of their tactics should also be classed as intellectuals. Conspicuously missing from this list of shapers of perceptions of the past are the narratives or testimonies of less educated people who do not print or broadcast their experiences or memories. Somewhat shamefully for an anthropologist, I must admit that on the whole their voices are missing from this book as well, given the focus in the first three chapters on textual representations of Kurdish identity, history and society. Nevertheless, regardless of whether individuals are highly literate or otherwise, like all of us their creation of self-identity through narrative imbibes something of this wider literary production. Even more influential, the vast majority of the younger generations of Turks, Iranians and Iraqis have been taught in nationalistic education systems that seek to stamp their embodied and gendered versions of ethical practice upon them. The young men have done long months of compulsory military service as well. Invariably today, popular histories, and even personal narratives and memories, are constructed in intimate relationship with the nationalist discourse of states.

Somewhat timidly, I do not usually seek to – indeed am not able to – assess the veracity of these variable constructions of the past. This seeming agnosticism vis-à-vis agents' appropriation and reordering of historical traces might disappoint those who stress the essential 'fact' of people's Kurdish inheritance, regardless of whether this heritage is significant for these individuals themselves. It may also gain the disapproval of those who continue to doubt whether this self-identification is genuine or important. In both cases my agnosticism is not meant to consent by default to the practical and ideological efficacy of Turkish, Persian or Arab Kemalism and its endeavour to assimilate Kurds. On the contrary, it is to take a position against metaphors of ethnicity that are basically genealogical, as if ethnic identity is genetically inherited on the one hand, or inexorably diluted over time on the other. By contrast, ethnic and nationalist identities are understood in this book as enlivened in specific social-historical situations by the cultural and political relationships of the period.

In other words, the different ways of imagining Kurds and Kurdistan that are discussed indicate that Kurdish ethnicity is a relational and creative act, something made by – not given to – every Kurd. The genesis, context and content of Kurdish ethnic or nationalist discourse may be historically explicable, but its assertion is not inevitable. In brief, because of the relationality of ethnic or national identity, this book is as much about the imagining and producing of Turkish, Persian and Arab identities as it is about those of Kurds. Consequently the authors of the multiform discourse on Kurdish identity explored in the study are not all Kurds, as these very Turkish, Persian and Arab identities constitute themselves through the censoring or despising of any Kurdish self-description of difference. Despite this, readers will find that I have devoted more space to Turkey. This bias might partially be justified by the brutality of numbers: approximately two-thirds of the Kurdish population live there (Özoğlu 2005: 14). The Turco-centric focus also reflects my own experience and limitations.

Nevertheless, I hope to have explored in part some of the ways in which Kurds in Iran and Iraq, too, have been participants in the crafting of national selves. Events in Iraq make that country even more important in the present, as the Kurdish parties in the north appear to be establishing the first Kurdish – and dare we also add – Kemalist Kurdish state in history. The 'netherworld' (Stansfield 2003: 181) in which Iraqi Kurdistan has existed since the withdrawal of the military and administrative forces of the government of Iraq in 1991 is slowly dissolving. But at the time of writing, the constitutional arrangements of a fractured Iraq are still unclear, as are the responses of the Turkish and Iranian states. For this reason, I have not extended the book to consider the new crafting of national selves in Iraqi Kurdistan currently under way. The importance of that topic requires a study of its own.

–1–

Nationalizing Origins

'Anthropologists rush in where historians fear to tread.'

'People adapt their memories to suit their sufferings', claimed Thucydides (cited in Barbir 1996: 100). Is history then made primarily in the present? The question seems counterintuitive given the endeavour of historical analysis to discern in the lineaments of our everyday condition the development and enduring influence of historically instituted social orders and forms. And yet this simple query is of great importance for this study, as it seeks to comprehend the narratives that people tell about themselves in their piecing together and enacting of a usable past. True, the efficacy of historically evolving state propaganda mechanisms, especially mass education, in providing cues and genres for subjects' personal confessions is very great. Yet, irreducible to these, people tell stories that concern the meaning of historical events, spotlighting events that gain their significance through this very telling; sometimes they move in opposition to more institutional accounts.

Since the emergence of the nation states of Turkey, Iraq and Iran after the Great War, historians and writers on the Kurds have attributed a specific range of meanings to what they 'remember' as a series of traumatic events. One of these has been the sixteenth-century incorporation into the Ottoman system of what is often described as Kurdistan. Some have interpreted the event as heralding 400 years of continuing external domination. Others have seen the resulting autonomy of the Kurdish principalities as a golden age of Kurdish independence, at least compared to what came later. Both of these summaries assume two key tenets of nationalism: first, that the social world is divided into groups on the basis of their nationality and, secondly, that those divided national groups have the right to self-determination.

Chapters 1 and 2 examine these and other interpretations more closely. This first chapter explores three issues of vital relevance to contemporary discourse about the Kurds. First, how have the distinguishing features of the Ottoman empire been identified and portrayed, particularly in reference to its political origins – is it Turkish, Islamic or something more hybrid? Second, how have selected writings on Kurds constructed the Ottoman history of the Kurds, as well as their Ottoman *pre-history*? And thirdly, how are these representations of Kurdish Ottoman history and prehistory articulated in turn to standardized components of official Turkish history, both to its account of the Ottomans and to its broader nationalist discourse

9

on Turkishness? To analyse answers to these questions, Chapter 1 deals exclusively with discourse articulating the Ottoman empire, Turks and Kurds. This is not because Turkey is the natural inheritor of the Ottoman mantle but precisely because how and in what ways the Turkish republic has come to claim that patrimony needs to be explored.

Genesis and Genius of the Ottoman Empire

In 1512 the newly proclaimed Ottoman Sultan, Selim Yavuz, grandson of Fatih Mehmet (the transformer of Istanbul) began a campaign against adherents of heterodox Shi'i Islam in Eastern Anatolia that would result in the extension of the empire beyond its 'core' provinces of Western Anatolia, Thrace and the Balkans and conclude with his occupation of Cairo five years later. In the process the Ottoman Sultan also became the Caliph of the Islamic world, while the Sherif of Mecca sent Selim the keys to the holy cities (Medina and Mecca). For the first time, the Ottomans were now rulers of much of the Sunni Arab lands of Islam, including Aleppo, Damascus and Jerusalem. Baghdad itself was to fall to the Ottomans two decades later. Somewhat by contrast, 'heterodox' Shi'i and nomadic elements (Turkish and Kurdish speaking) in central and Eastern Anatolia were disinclined to submit to the authority of a state proclaiming itself to be a defender of 'orthodox' Sunni Islam. These *kızılbaş* groups – so named for their red head coverings – were also courted by Shah Ismail, leader of the newly emergent Safavid Shi'i empire based in Tabriz, who was instrumental in extirpating Sunni Islam from what is now Iran (McDowell 2000: 27). This struggle throughout the sixteenth century between the Ottoman and Safavid empires for the dominant form of Islam in central and Eastern Anatolia, as well as for control of territory and population, was settled relatively early, at least in terms of an approximate border zone and frontier. Sultan Selim engaged Shah Ismail at Çaldiran (midway between Erzincan and Tabriz) in 1514, defeating him there and going on to occupy his capital of Tabriz. Selim's troops however refused to winter there (Imber 2002: 45) and Selim retreated to Amasya. Nevertheless for the next two years he suppressed Safavid influence in south-eastern and Eastern Anatolia, partially through war and partially through negotiation. To quote Imber, in 1515 Selim sent Kurdish notable Idris of Bitlis 'to secure the allegiance of the Kurdish chieftains of southeastern Anatolia and northern Iraq ... [B]y the end of the year, all except one had recognized Selim's overlordship' (Imber 2002). The Kurdish princes retained de facto control of their lands and some continued to mint their own coins. At the same time their recognition of Ottoman suzerainty formalized their barrier status precluding 'the Safavid empire from access to the Kızılbaş populations further within Ottoman territory to west and northwest' (Sinclair 2003: 121). The border between Ottoman Anatolia and Safavid Azarbaijan established by Selim's victory at Çaldiran 'persisted despite disputes, encroachments and invasions until 1914'

(McDowall 2000: 26). Viewed from Istanbul, the Kurdish regions were now vital frontier provinces of the empire, with all the insecurities such status involves. What the view of the Kurdish princes might have been, as well as their tribesmen, will be taken up in Chapter 2.

In respect of nearly all writings about Kurds, the 400 or more years of Ottoman rule (indirect or otherwise) over much of the Kurdish territory has to be given some sort of meaning.[1] One key way the relationship is represented and politicized is through debates or claims over the genesis and genius of the empire itself. This is an interpretative task, given both the lack of extant sources from the fourteenth century and the wildly varied assessments of its origins.[2] For example, in the final days of Britain's 'informal' imperialism in the Ottoman territories the historian H. Gibbons (1916) wrote famously of the empire's non-Asiatic roots. Twenty years later the Turkish historian Fuat Köprülü (1935/1986) was sketching out its Turkish ethnic core. In a key essay in the volume *The Ottoman City and its Parts*, Speros Vryonis (1991) notes the Greek influence upon the conqueror of Constantinople Fatih Mehmet, while both Brown and Inalcık argue in their respective essays in *Imperial Legacy* (1996) that the Ottomans were not a Turkish empire, despite this designation by Europe. Bernard Lewis (1961) hedges his bets by claiming that no other regime/people submerged their identity in Islam as much as the Ottoman Turks, although as Meeker (2002) notes such a position allows the nationalism of the Turkish republicans to be represented as a natural corrective to a somehow unnatural repression.

Although this may appear an arcane controversy, the arguments scholars and writers make vis-à-vis the Ottoman's political heritage are vitally important, connected as they are to a multitude of contemporary claims to identity and power.[3] As such, they have become part and parcel of many ordinary people's historical knowledge as well. This pertains not only to writings about and by Kurds but to a host of other historiographies that have emerged in the wake of the formation of nation states in the former Ottoman territories. Perhaps one of the most interesting recent books examining some of the important historiography on its early years, as well as presenting its own tentative thesis about the Ottoman State's historical evolution,

---

1. Most of the Kurdish regions of present-day Turkey, Iraq and Syria were included within the Ottoman Empire after 1515. See Chapter 2.

2. However see Runciman for a survey of Byzantine historians of the fourteenth and fifteenth centuries and a defence of their importance to fourteenth-century Ottoman history. His conclusion is that 'early Ottoman history is not well served by its Turkish sources' (Runciman 1962: 276).

3. Debate over the political heritage of the Safavids by contrast does not produce anywhere near the same heat. One reason for this is that the Iranian nation-state in the present and thus Kurdish intellectuals in Iran are not continually vexed by the question of its relationship to the Safavids. Secondly, with the victory of the Ottomans over the Safavids at Çaldiran, the majority of the Kurdish regions passed under Ottoman suzerainty. For these two reasons I will not explore in this chapter contemporary Kurdish accounts of Safavid rule.

is Cemal Kafadar's *Between Two Worlds: The Construction of the Ottoman State*. Kafadar draws attention to the uncanny similarities during the eleventh to fifteenth centuries between the two peninsulas at the opposite ends of the Mediterranean – Iberia and Asia Minor. In both regions he perceives a competition for political control 'between powers that saw themselves as members of different religio-civilizational orientations' (Kafadar 1995: 19). The last outposts of Christian and Muslim power, Trebizond (Trabzon) and Granada, were captured by the Ottomans and the Catholic King of Spain in 1461 and 1492 respectively. Kafadar goes on to note another similarity: like the Anatolian, Indian and Balkan cases, 'the Iberian one has been an ideological quagmire of modern historiography'[4] (Kafadar 1995: 20). He mentions but does not dwell on one further similarity: the denying by these historiographies of the decades and more of coexistence and mutual influence between Christians and Muslims in the early centuries in both Spain and Anatolia, before their transformation into representatives of Catholicism and high Islam respectively and the writing of their imperial origins by chroniclers with more orthodox sensitivities.

What are some of the contending theories that have made writing the history of Anatolia so ideological? And how do the underlying themes of these histories apply to the discourse on and by the Kurds? Gibbons' study of the origins of the emergent Ottoman state (according to Kafadar the first monograph specifically oriented to this problem) of course bears the stamp of its time (1916). For Gibbons the rise of the Ottomans and the demise of the Byzantines was not only 'illustration of the wrath of God upon the fourth generation of those who had hated and despised Him' (Gibbons 1916: 48), but also of the wrath of (Darwinized) History as well, the Byzantines proving themselves unfit in the struggle for existence. By contrast the Ottomans led by their founder and chieftain Osman were a younger, more dynamic force, especially after Osman's conversion to Islam. Yet what is interesting in Gibbons' account is his argument about the creation of a new people – the *Osmanlis* (Ottomans) – through the mingling of Turks and Greeks. In the place of the Byzantines was raised up a new 'race', 'by the fusion of elements already existing at the place of birth' Gibbons 1916: 49). Granted, these elements on the ground 'were mainly Greek', but these new Muslims 'were not averse to ... helping in the founding of a new nation to inherit Constantinople' (Gibbons 1916: 49).

Twenty years later Fuat Köprülü begins his work *The Origins of the Ottoman empire* by summarizing Gibbons' supporting theses – and then ruthlessly points out their flaws. His objections are expressed in the first instance via methodological critique, not only of Gibbons' use or misuse of sources but also of historical analyses that in place of the complexity of historical realities posit single causal explanations.

---

4. For India see the recent analysis by Rajagopal (2002) of the televised version of the Hindu epic *Ramayana*, and its representation of Muslims in India as descendants of an non-indigenous and invading force.

Particularly galling for Köprülü is what he claims to be the axiomatically asserted prejudice of Western historians, shared by Gibbons, that only Greeks and not Turks were able to create a state. By contrast, Köprülü argues that given the Turkish Selcuk legacy and the advanced level of Anatolian Turkish urban life in the early fourteenth century, it would have been easy for the fledgling Ottoman state to find experienced Turkish administrators. Although not denying the presence of Christian converts in the Ottoman population, Köprülü claims Gibbons exaggerates their numbers and influence. Accordingly the idea that 'this brand new race or people, completely separate from Turkish character, constitutes the nucleus of a great state is a fantasy' (my translation) (Köprülü, 1935/1986: 49). In brief, for Köprülü the Ottoman state was a creation of Turks. Moreover, some of its features might be traced back, via the Seljuks, to central Asia. Here the continuity of pre-Islamic Turkish culture within the emergent Ottoman polity is signalled, although not elaborated, by Köprülü. As we will see later, this is important for both official and more popular Turkish histories.

A third influential interpretation – indeed the explanation that according to Kafadar prevailed for nearly half a century after its formulation in academic circles outside of Turkey – is the so-called 'Gazi thesis' of historian Paul Wittek. Published in 1938, this maintained that the driving motivation of the first Ottomans, although sometimes overshadowed in later times by the demands of imperial *Realpolitik*, 'was the struggle against their Christian neighbours' (Wittek 1938/1958: 2).[5] In the fluid frontiers (named 'the Marches' by Wittek) between the more settled Selcuk and Byzantine populations in the late eleventh century and then again at the end of the thirteenth century, a special category of mainly Turkish-speaking 'March' warriors developed, living primarily from the booty captured from the more sedentary hinterlands but inspired too by an idealistic resolve to war against the infidel. These Gazi leaders, upon settling down in conquered districts, established Gazi emirates, one of which was the emirate of Osman, 'the nucleus from which the Ottoman empire later developed' (Wittek, 1938/1958: 34). It was this Gazi ethic that impelled the Ottoman state to continue its conquests, most particularly in the Balkans. Nevertheless, and somewhat contradictorily, Gazi bands were not closed entities, despite Wittek's emphasis on their ideology of holy war. Indeed two of their fundamental tendencies included 'conversion to Islam and the absorption of indigenous elements' (Wittek, 1938/1958: 49). Because the frontier zones produced similar cultural practices among both Byzantine and Turkish warriors, 'the mode of life imported by the Ghazis was easily assimilated by the autochthonous element, with which they had much in common... It was really only the Byzantine varnish that vanished, to be replaced later by an Islamic one' (Wittek, 1938/1958: 20). Combined with an emphasis on the Gazis' Turkish identity, mainstream Turkish historical scholarship accepts, explicitly or implicitly, the Gazi thesis.

---

5. Halil Inalcık puts it slightly differently. The intended aim of holy war was 'not to destroy but to subdue the infidel world, the *darulharb*' (Inalcık 1973: 7).

In brief, and despite those matters where the latter writers concede some of the formers' arguments, we might simplify again to note one key difference in the three interpretations presented above: the Ottoman institution was established either by ethnic Greeks, ethnic Turks or ethnically-mixed Muslims. This formulation neglects other dissimilarities of course, but at least indicates some basic faultlines of post-Ottoman nationalist historiographies.[6]

Taking a more general view, Kafadar discerns three underlying and still disputed currents energizing the debate over the building of the Ottoman state. First is the question of demographics, made controversial by the ethnic and religious categories with which the numbers are associated. How many local people (Greek or Christian) converted to Islam? How many 'real' Turks arrived in the form of colonizing Turkish tribes, and in this arithmetic who therefore formed, organized and staffed the new state and its institutions?[7] Second is the question of the violence or otherwise involved in the invasion (or migration) of the Turkish speaking groups or Muslims. Did local people welcome the more equitable social arrangements heralded by the emerging new polity? Or was Ottoman rule brutally imposed from above, including via forced conversion? The third live issue is the question of influence: the arguments about the origins of administrative models, of cultural traditions or practices (like the 'tree of life' motif prevalent on Anatolian carpets, or of puppetry and conjuring, or the game 'Blind Man's Bluff'). The possibility of their status as transnational phenomena is denied. Could rough-and-ready nomads really invent a food as complex as baklava?

We might add a fourth obsession partly related to this third: the evolutionary assumption that state founding in the first instance is a more developed form of socio-political achievement, attained (attainable) only by certain peoples. Prior to

6. There is a large and continuing literature examining the question of the beginnings of the Ottoman polity and its transformation into an empire. One recent study is that by Heath Lowry, based on his research on the Ottoman tax registers in the late fifteenth and early sixteenth centuries for the island of Limnos. Lowry implicitly dismisses both Wittek's 'gazi' and Köprülü's 'Turkish creation' theses (or combinations thereof), arguing that until the invasion of the Arab Islamic world in the early sixteenth century under Sultan Selim, the Ottoman's main policy towards its Christian subjects was one of toleration and accommodation. Claiming the primary motivation for expansion was the 'financial rewards of conquest', Lowry sees Ottoman policy as a 'reflection of the fact that the state which was forming was one in which an overwhelmingly majority of the inhabitants were non-Muslims, and that there simply were not enough Ottomans with the administrative experience or, for that matter, linguistic skills, to effectively administer the fiscal exploitation of the growing Balkan entity' (Lowry 2002: 43). In brief the Ottoman presence was a veneer, under which continued existing social and financial practices. In a second book, Lowry investigates the 'plundering confederacy' of the early Ottomans more systematically, seeing it as a hybrid polity including both high Islamic culture and administrative practices, and adoption of earlier Byzantine and Balkan practices. Accordingly, Lowry describes the early Ottoman entity as a new 'Islamochristian synthesis' (Lowry 2003: 137). Kafadar's position is discussed briefly in Chapter 2.

7. These questions still vex the minds of historians – see for example Kiel (2004).

the angst over *whose* achievement was the remarkable and durable Ottoman empire, is the assumption that state-building is in itself an evolutionary superior activity, and conversely that stateless people are to be presumed inferior because they are unable to develop such higher forms of social organization. That those groups may be well acquainted with processes of state formation but have decided against such arrangements, seeking by doing so to preserve social and political relations they deem to be more desirable, is not considered.

Are these radically contested constructions of the Ottoman state's institution also of importance for writers on Kurds? Despite Kafadar's siting of these disputes in the nationalist *raison d'être* of Ottoman successor states, discourse on Kurdishness is only partially invested in the first issue, namely the demographics and the ethnic composition of the founders of the Ottoman state. However the discourse is vexed over the question of violent conquest (although not forced conversion) and it readily speaks of a more generic oppression of Kurds by 'external' elements, including the Ottomans (Turks). Similarly the discourse is also concerned with the question of cultural influence, appearing anxious to defend the cultural autonomy of the Kurds. And equally important for much of the discourse on Kurdishness are the assumptions underpinning claims about state-founding or statelessness, especially as they are connected with the rise of civilization.

These differences then between the concerns of Kurdish nationalist histories and the issues identified by Kafadar as important for mainly European post-Ottoman nationalisms relate in the first instance to the ethnic Muslim status of Kurds.[8] But before discussing this and Kurdish constructions of the Ottoman interlude in more detail, it will be useful at this point to take a slight detour and sketch out briefly some of the ways in which the Ottoman *pre-history* of Kurds has been represented. That is to say, how do various recent narratives about Kurds construct the origins of Kurdish commonality?

Genesis and Genius of the Kurds

In his study of the debates conducted by Kurdish intellectuals in the Istanbul newspaper *Özgür Gündem* in the years 1994–7, Hirschler analyses one recent attempt at

---

8. It would also be interesting to compare differences and similarities between Kurdish accounts of the Ottoman experience with Arab nationalist writing on the Ottoman era of Arab history, especially given the Kurdish and Arab regions' parallel incorporation into the administrative structures of the empire under Sultan Selim. The lack of material on Kurdish perceptions of Ottoman rule stands in stark contrast to the much greater research on Arab historiography. Kafadar's critique of the nationalist historiographies that dominate history writing about Ottoman state formation and thereafter is directed towards accounts focussed on the Balkans and Asia Minor. He ignores the problem in relation to Turkish and Kurdish historiographies.

constructing a Kurdish pre-history.[9] He argues that the longest continuing controversy in the newspaper centred on the pre-Islamic period, involving in particular narratives of Kurdish 'ethnogenesis, homeland, resistance and national character' (Hirschler 2001: 152). The reconstruction of Kurdish *ethnogenesis* (or the 'when' of the Kurds) involved the claiming of a direct ethnic link to ancient peoples better attested in the near-Eastern literature and posited as the original inhabitants of the Kurdish regions. Meaningful in the context of Turkish nationalism's denial of Kurdish particularity – that is, in the light of the official claim that Kurds are of Turkish origin, hence members of the same ethnic group and therefore candidates for assimilation – the ancestral people of the Kurds are identified as the Aryans and/or the (Aryan) Medes. Along with this genealogical link, *homeland* narratives (the 'where' of the Kurds) sketch out a stable geographical reference for the Kurdish region, identified as eastern and south-eastern Anatolia but also sometimes as Mesopotamia. Hence present-day Kurds are direct descendants of the region's indigenous people before the invasion and occupation of their homeland by outsiders, including most importantly Persians, Arabs and Turks. *Resistance* narratives posit a consistent opposition to these projects and experiences of foreign rule, minimizing their influences on indigenous traditions and ensuring instead the uncontaminated continuity of Kurdish national character. The narrativizing of *national character* closes the circle of Kurdish history, with the Kurds – or their direct ancestors, the Aryans – constructed as producers of near Eastern civilization, including the domesticating of horses, wheat farming, building of settlements and temples, introduction of mathematical and geometric principles and the invention of the telescope (Hirschler 2001: 155). Civilization builders are contrasted with harbingers of barbarism, represented as uncivilized outsiders to the Mesopotamian region and its people. Central to the emerging schema is the idea that the Kurds did not come from anywhere else but have always lived in what is now called Kurdistan, even if known under different names. This narrative is in stark counterpoint to official and popular constructions of Turkish history and character, wherein Turkish genius is narrated as a history of migratory state founding. Thus we have Atatürk's famous phrase: 'The Turks have always moved from east to west.' In its earliest phase, Turkish nationalist historiography represented this migration not as the corrupting but as the bestowing of civilization, in this case the dispersing of state-building traditions to people with whom the Turks have interacted.[10]

9. *Özgür Gündem* (Free Agenda) has been subject to severe state censorship, and was closed down in 1994. The analysis is mostly based on its successor newspapers, which were also progressively banned. *Özgür Politika* is currently published from Germany. See Hirschler (2001) 148–9.

10. Although the major planks of this nationalist history were put together in the early 1930s, its reassertion, elaboration and refinement continues in many Turkish-language Turkish universities today. See for example Istanbul University's Ayhan Bıçak's recent study *The Idea of the State in Pre-Islamic Turkish Thought*, a book in which he seeks to explain the origin and structure of the Turkish 'system of thought'. Despite admitting the difficulties in such a task – such as the close relationships of Turks

In fact, the historical vista sketched out above is more properly the product of what Hirschler calls the *Monopolists* among Kurdish historians, whose work as we have seen posits the autochthonic creation of localized Kurdish cultural characteristics. Not surprisingly, their theses have been subject to revision by writers Hirschler whom identifies as *Inter-Activists* (Hirschler 2001: 150). Inter-activist narratives, although accepting the ethnic specificity of Kurds, expose Kurdish history to the possibility of 'outside' cultural influence. Outsiders accordingly are not necessarily barbarous. The most biting critique of 'monopolist' history and its resemblance both thematically and methodologically to Turkish nationalist historiography, is made by Gürdal Aksoy. In his book *Tarihi Yazılmayan Halk Kürtler* (*Kurds, The People whose History is Unwritten*), a title that comments more on the status of existing rather than absent texts, he analyses recent Kurdish history writing, including the work of many of the contributors to *Özgür Gündem*. He lists their most striking characteristics as:

> I. Nationalist-centralism... Historical events and personalities are examined from a Kurdish centre; II. Romanticism; III. Populism; IV. Their combining of history and myths; V. The dominance of the 'cut and paste' research method; VI. The over-influence of the mythology of the Aryan Race; VII. Reactiveness and an event-driven focus; VIII. Their *a priori* nature... Before examining an event properly, the historian knows what it means; IX. Methodological eclecticism... Rather than constructing a convincing synthesis, the historian incorporates whatever material they stumble upon; X. Captivity to and shaping by daily politics. (Aksoy 1996: 63) (my translation)

Yet are the themes mapped out by the monopolists also found in the work of other writers in their histories or analyses of Kurdish identity? The earliest reference to the Medes as possible Kurdish ancestors appears to have been made on linguistic grounds by Minorsky in the first edition of the *Encyclopaedia of Islam* (1913–36). Ninety years later a new book on Kurds in Iraq begins by repeating some of the same elements of the monopolist narrative. Citing an online *Encyclopaedia of Kurdistan*, it notes that

> the Kurds are native inhabitants of their land and as such there are no strict 'beginnings' for Kurdish history and origins. In modern times, Kurds as an ethnic group are the end product of thousands of years of evolution stemming from such tribes as the Guti, Kurti, Mede, Mared, Carduchi, Gordyene, Adianbene, Zila and Khaldi, and the migration

---

with other great civilizations, and their spread over huge geographical areas, without having left much sign of their presence there – he is confident that the Turkish conceptual system left its mark on those civilizations. In brief, 'it [Turkish culture] is a culture which spread throughout the largest continent, Asia, affected Europe a great deal, and made important changes in the basic values of the civilizations it had relationships with' (Bıçak 2004: 18). In the book he repeats an older nationalist claim that before conversion to Islam the Turks had independently arrived at a monotheistic religion.

of Indo-European tribes to the Zagros mountain region some 4,000 years ago. (Yildiz 2004: 7)

Other influential writings on the Kurds also stress their indigenous status, including Ismail Beşikçi who connects Xenophon's 'Karduklar' (Carduqi in English), mentioned in his book *The Retreat of the Ten Thousand* (400 BC), to the Kurds (Beşikçi 1969/1992: 106–7). Somewhat by contrast, Paul White claims that the [Kurdish?] *Kizilbas* are probably the descendants of the Dailamites, at the same time writing that *Kizilbas* should not be confused with ethnically Turkish Alevi sects, despite admitting the identical nature of their 'beliefs, rituals and traditions' (White 2000: 45). Here White seems to posit an ethnic origin for the followers of what is more usually seen as a form of heterodox Islamic practice. We might also mention the introduction by well-known writer Maxine Rodinson to the book *People Without a Country*, edited by Gerard Chaliand, whose work has been influential in the French context in introducing reflection upon the Kurds. Rodinson writes rather splendidly that

> The rights of the Kurdish people should be obvious to everybody. We have here a specifically defined people with a language and a culture all their own (whatever people may say in Iran), living in a geographically coherent area, and refusing *en masse* the cultural assimilation which others seek to impose upon them. For more than a century this people has demonstrated time and time again its consciousness of being a specific ethnic or national group whose vocation is to form its own political institutions and to make its own decisions autonomously. (Rodinson 1978: 4)

Other writers in this selective survey are more circumspect: Van Bruinessen casts some doubt on the sustainability of the connection with the Medes, but nevertheless begins his essay on Kurdish identity in the book *Ethnic Groups in the Republic of Turkey* by writing that 'most Kurds in Turkey have a strong awareness of belonging to a separate ethnic group... There is, however, by no means unanimity among them as to what constitutes this ethnic identity and what the boundaries of the ethnic group are' (Van Bruinessen 1989: 613).

He goes on to note that it might be more accurate to think of the Kurds 'not as one, but as a set of ethnic groups (for instance Sunni, Alevi, Yezidi)' (Van Bruinessen 1989: 614). McDowall too is rather careful: although Kurds have 'existed as an identifiable group for possibly more than 2000 years ... it was only in the early years of the twentieth century that they acquired a sense of community as Kurds' (McDowall 2000: 2). These varying statements can be brought together only by conceding that despite their appeal to common linguistic, cultural and religious similarities among Kurdish people, we would do better to focus on the various ways in which such similarities are or are not imagined as significant markers of a shared translocal or national identity. In that case the construction of Kurdish identity derives from particular narrative/discursive agendas, rather than from supposedly objective shared cultural traits.

Imagining Kurdish Ottomans: A First Sketch

Given then that very often discourse on Kurdishness attributes to Kurds prior to their incorporation into the Ottoman empire at very least an awareness of a Kurdish distinctiveness (recognized by themselves and others) and at most a consciousness of their own distinct national character, how is this incorporation and its afterlife imagined? And do Kurdish writers of an earlier generation who experienced first hand the demise of the Ottoman empire represent its political features in the same way? Almost in passing Hirschler notes that the so-called monopolists in *Özgür Gündem* summarily dismiss the Ottoman period as yet one more experience of an oppressing outside force. His comment on their position is worth quoting:

> The uncivilized Other is represented in the Islamic period almost exclusively by the Ottomans – a term used interchangeably with 'the Turks.' [For the monopolists], they [the Ottomans] built their society, in the framework of a 'plunder ideology', merely on military bases. After the external expansion had ended, they turned after Sultan Suleyman 1 (d. 1566) to internal plundering of the conquered territories. Consequently, the cruelty of the present-day Turkish army 'is a heritage of the Ottomans.' (Hirschler 2001: 156)

Here rather than presuming an Ottoman-Kurdish pact or even the possibility that the Kurdish princes may have wooed Ottoman statesmen in order to establish enhanced authority or new networks and supports, the monopolist stance towards Ottoman Kurdistan takes for granted the control and manipulation of its parts via a divide and rule policy of imperial Istanbul. The critique of such a policy is predicated on the assumption of the actually existing and morally desirable unity of the Kurds, if obstructed until now by the fragmentation inherited from the Ottoman ruling strategy. Put this way, the Ottoman experience is represented as an interruption, even an aberration, in the longer and still unravelling thread of indigenous Kurdish history. Yet not altogether extravagantly and perhaps more in line with the sentiments of the *Inter-Activists*, we might transfer Todorova's *bon mot* for the Balkans to Kurdistan: 'It is preposterous', she says 'to look for an Ottoman legacy *in* the Balkans. The Balkans *are* the Ottoman legacy' (Todorova 1996: 46).

Have many writers on Kurds conceived of Kurdistan as the legacy of the Ottomans? In the first instance the overwhelming interest in the long nineteenth-century dissolution of the empire has meant that in comparison the integration of the Kurdish regions into the Ottoman system in the sixteenth, seventeenth and eighteenth centuries has received much less historical attention. Yet it was under the Ottomans that Kurdistan became a relatively coherent entity, despite the Selcuk empire's creation of a province named Kurdistan (the land of the Kurds) in the mid-twelfth century. 'It was not until the sixteenth century ... that the phrase "Kurdistan" came into common usage to denote a system of Kurdish fiefs generally, and not just the [Selcuk]-created province' (Yildiz 2004: 7). Secondly, in this process the Ottomans re-established and in some places even brought into being Kurdish tribal confederations under the control of selected ruling families, who were allowed – or demanded – the exceptional privilege within the Ottoman administrative system of the time of hereditary succession. Thirdly and equally influential in terms of constituting Kurdish identities, the sixteenth-century sectarian struggle between the Safavids and the Ottomans, particularly in the formation of 'oppositional' Alevi and 'establishment' Sunni identities in the Ottoman Anatolian territories, still resonates and is imagined today.

What Hirschler does not add is that monopolist Kurdish *disinterest* in the Ottoman polity mirrors many Turkish historians' ignoring of Kurdish Ottoman history and the region's 400 year experience as part of the empire. Even the doyen of Ottoman historians, Halil Inalcık, does not mention Kurds in his discussion of Sultan Selim's eastern enlargement of the empire in his classic study *The Ottoman Empire: The Classical Age 1300–1600*. Revealingly, he describes the incorporation into the Ottoman empire of the region from Erzurum to Diyarbakır after the battle of Çaldiran in 1514 as a process whereby 'local dynasties and tribal chieftains' recognize Ottoman suzerainty (Inalcik 1973: 33). Here for whatever reason – a lack of historical sources, or a deliberate disinterest – the Kurdish history of the empire is made invisible. Even more problematic is the gloss put on the campaign by Feridun Emecen in his essay in the book *Osmanlı Devleti ve Medeniyeti Tarihi* (*History of Ottoman State and Civilization*), a massive two-volume work collectively authored by a group of Turkish historians. Talking about the defeat of the Safavids, Emecen writes that

> the victory consolidated Ottoman rule in eastern Anatolia. The lands of the Dalkadiroğlu (at Maras) were conquered in June 1515, and after Diyarbakır recognized Ottoman authority the rest of the cities in the region passed under Ottoman rule. Ever since the Selcuks, Diyarbakır in particular has been the cradle and centre of numerous Turkish states founded in eastern Anatolia... The Sunni-Shafi tribes in the region known as 'Kara-Ulus' remained loyal to the Ottomans and played an important role in the struggle with Iran. (Emecen 1994: 29–30) (my translation)

Despite Emecen's claims, Diyarbakır has been as much a Kurdish city as a Turcoman one. In 1515 it was mainly a Kurdish city, and its inhabitants declared their allegiance to the Ottomans despite the opposition of its Safavid governor (see the *Sharafname* of Sharafuddin of Bitlisi below). The term 'Sunni-Shafi tribes' is a synonym for the obviously unspeakable word Kurds, who in fact did not 'remain loyal' to the Ottomans but negotiated a special arrangement with Istanbul. The

'Kara-Ulus' (Black People) by contrast were Kurdish nomads (see McDowall 2000: 29), not party to the arrangements negotiated by the resurgent Kurdish lords. There was not, of course, an 'Iran' for the Ottomans to be in conflict with. In fact these two volumes scarcely mention Kurds, clear indication that the particularity of Kurds as constructed by Kurdish discourse is rejected.

What also needs to be explained is a similar neglect of the Ottoman history of the Kurds on the part of non-Turkish scholars. The book *Imperial Legacy: The Ottoman Imprint on the Balkans and the Middle East,* for example, has nothing to say on the afterlife of the Ottoman period in 'Kurdistan', despite the shocking serial violence characterizing the region during and ever since the empire's dissolution. Even more striking, in the book's long list of 'Dates and Duration (Number of Years) of Ottoman Rule by Country or Region', Kurdistan is not mentioned. Thirty other places are, including Al Hasa, Crete, the Crimea and the Hijaz (see Brown 1996: xiv–xvi). Other texts appear more consciously biased: Justin McCartney's general orientation is discernible in his title (*The Ottoman Turks*) and the Kurdish princes' negotiation over recognition of Ottoman authority is not even mentioned.

Still, it was not only in the name of an enduring Kurdish national character that most of the participants in the *Özgür Gündem* debate about Kurdish history summarily dismissed the Ottoman 'interlude' as yet another encounter with a divisive external power. The newspaper itself and the writers gathered around it were not in general sympathetic to the Sunni Muslim history or Islamic enthusiasms of many Kurds. By contrast, other Kurdish writers and intellectuals who were either invested in Kurdish Islam or who were to some degree or other Islamic activists oppose what they perceived to be the laicizing endeavour of the newspaper and its contributors. Not surprisingly, their varying assessments of the Kurdish experience of Ottoman rule have been more positive. Kurdish Muslims' accounts of the period vary from standard Islamist analyses that attribute antagonisms between the Turkish republic and Kurds to the influence and infiltration of Western ideologies like nationalism that fatally infected the Ottoman polity, to more critical assessments of the historic *pax Ottomana* in Kurdistan on a variety of issues. For example, in the latter case some attribute what they describe as the unsatisfactory situation of Kurds under the Ottomans to the somewhat corrupted status of Ottoman Islam, particularly when compared with the exemplary Islamic polity of the *asr-ı saadet* period. As a solution to the Kurdish problem, other more religious Kurds have argued for the institution of an adapted or neo-Ottoman federal system that would obstruct the domination of any one hegemonic centre and ensure regional autonomy, a solution seen as Islamic in principle. Nevertheless, despite these differences of opinion between secular and Islamist writers, we should also note what in fact they share: both identify Kurds as distinct actors within the Ottoman system, regardless of the interpretation of their colonized or integrated status.

Finally, do writers on Kurds from an earlier generation who experienced first hand the painful demise of the Ottoman empire represent its core features differently? Or do the themes distilled by Hirschler from the Kurdish history debates in the Turkey of the 1990s have a longer pedigree? Typically, we can find in the literature examples of both. According to Strohmeier, the editors of the first Kurdish newspaper *Kürdistan* (published in 1898) were particularly hostile, as was all the liberal opposition at the time, to the reigning Ottoman sultan, Abdulhamid. 'The issues of *Kürdistan* manifest an unabashed Kurdish self-awareness and attribute Kurdish suffering to a long history of Ottoman domination' (Strohmeier 2003: 22). But Strohmeier also notes that the influential Bedir Khan family, publishers of the paper, had personal cause to be antagonistic to the Sublime Porte, having been deprived of their lands and exiled in 1847 by the Ottoman government. By contrast, the writer of the first 'systematic' nationalist history of the Kurds Muhammad Amin Zaki, is more sympathetic to the Ottoman empire's last attempts to freeze its own dismemberment by formulating the notion of an Ottoman multicultural 'citizenship.' Indeed it was only after the

> replacement of the general concept of Osmani [Ottomanism] by the notion of Turani [Turanism, the mythical homeland of the Turks] in Turkey, [that] like members of the other millets, naturally I too took pride in my own roots within this [Turkish] community more strongly, and national pride impelled me to express my feelings on every occasion. (cited in Vali 1996: 32)

Vali notes in short that the reason Zaki felt impelled to write his two-volume *Brief History of the Kurds* (published in 1931 and 1933 respectively) was the emergence of Turkish and Arabic nationalism and not a conviction of the Ottoman exploitation of Kurdistan. When it was not possible to be Ottoman any longer, and in response to the nationalism of others, Zaki became a Kurdish nationalist.

In sum, more secularist accounts of Kurdish history, ironically perhaps if understandably, tend to conform to Turkish nationalist accounts that interpret the Ottoman polity as a Turkish empire. Accordingly, the control exercised by the Ottoman centre over the Kurdish regions, however minimal in practice, is understood as an experience of Turkish overlordship.[11] In other words, Kurdish accounts that presume the Turkishness of the Ottoman polity are in partial agreement with Turkish nationalist histories that laud the empire's Turkish core. Needless to say, the consequences and impact on the Kurdish region of the Turkish bias of the Ottomans is assessed very differently. Todorova describes a similar discrepancy between Bulgarian and Turkish historiography, in which the three hundred years of Ottoman rule over the region is routinely described by Bulgarian historians as the period of the 'Turkish Yoke' (Todorova 1995). The metaphor implies an imposed check on the pre-existing

---

11. White for example writes that the political significance of post-Çaldiran Ottoman control of eastern Anatolia was that the 'Kurds were divided from this point right up to the present day between Turkish and non-Turkish overlords' (White 2000: 54). Vali too uses the phrase, but more carefully writes of 'Persian and Ottoman overlords' (Vali 1998: 83).

Bulgarian nation's productive capacities, an artificial holding back of one nation by another that for a period waylaid its proper development.[12] Quite logically, the extent to which the Ottoman empire is presented as a Turkish creation influences the willingness of Kurdish writers to claim its history as one aspect of their own. Those who do so wish might start with the designations used by the Ottomans themselves. According to Caroline Finkel, the term 'Turk' was never used for the Ottoman ruling class; indeed in 'state rhetoric 'Turk' might be used to denote those who resisted Ottoman writ, such as the rival Safavid dynasty of Iran' (Finkel 2005). 'We are the Byzantines', says one Kurdish writer happy to identify with what he analyses as the multi-religious and multi-ethnic Ottoman polity. 'All we did was circumcise the city', pointing to the minarets above Hagia Sophia.'[13] The 'we' here are Muslims, but it is interesting to hear nearly a century later an unexpected Kurdish echoing of Gibbons.

Crafting Turkish Selves

Careful readers might remember historian Fuat Köprülü's gesturing towards the vital contribution of pre-Islamic Turkish cultural traditions in the founding of the Ottoman state, as well as his claims about the 'real' as opposed to the converted 'Turkishness' of its highest administrators and great men. Yet obviously he has not been alone in stressing the central Asian (Turkish) and Middle Eastern (Islamic) heritage of the empire, or in subordinating the Islamic element to the Turkish one in this new Anatolian synthesis. According to Kafadar, 'in Turkey, Köprülü's tribal-ethnicist views as well as his emphasis on the Turco-Muslim origins of the Ottoman administrative apparatus came to enjoy nearly the status of dogma and were eventually taken in a more chauvinistic direction as they were increasingly stripped of his demographic and sociological concerns (Kafadar 1995: 42). Directly related to this stripping then, readers will also have noticed in some of the previous sections my own gesturing to the category 'Turkish nationalist accounts' or 'official and popular national history'. In this final section of Chapter 1, we need to explore in more detail some of the key components of this 'chauvinistic' official nationalist history in Turkey, insofar as it is vital in influencing not just Kurdish writers' representations of Ottoman Kurdish history but their more general discourse on Kurdishness.

Hirschler makes the important point that nearly all the contributors to *Özgür Gündem* have been *educated* in the Turkish nationalist discourse. Taking this as our cue, and in order to condense and simplify a very complex landscape in which there are myriad producers of competing knowledge about Turkish history, it will

---

12. She also describes the outcry caused by a recent history that re-titled its examination of the period 'The Ottoman presence' (Todorova 1995: 115)

13. Mufid Yüksel, personal conversation.

be useful to track the nationalist ideology by looking in the first instance at the historiography taught in Turkish schools, especially as formalized in textbooks. Although there is serious debate over the process and efficacy of national education in inculcating younger generations with certain values and embodied dispositions, schools are still one key place where we see particularly clearly the promulgation of official Turkish nationalistic views of history.[14]

A recent study summarizing the qualities of current textbooks used in Turkish schools concludes rather grimly that they contain numerous passages in which

> certain groups of people are denigrated and discriminated against; sexist discourse is especially common, and gender inequality openly cultivated; xenophobia is not absent; pluralism and difference are seen as suspect values; an isolationist outlook nourished by the paranoia that Turkey is under 'internal and external threat' underlies almost all textbooks and goes hand in hand with a self-celebratory discourse of uniqueness; and, finally, death is exalted in many of them. (Ceylan and Irzık 2004: 5)

Nearly all these characteristics of the national curriculum can be seen as impacting upon, even negatively constituting, how Kurdish identity is imagined. But what do the school books actually say? First textbooks continually assert the ethnic difference and superiority of Turks, the Turkish language and Turkish culture: thus students read that 'the moral system and comprehension of our nation is very unique', a 'moral system ... that does not resemble the morals of other nations' (in the textbook *Studies in Religion and Morality*, cited in Bora 2004: 54). Similarly 'Turkish is the best language for the expression of sentiments ... the most beautiful, richest and easiest language of the world' (*Turkish Language and Literature*, cited in Bora 2004: 58). Armed with such powerful tools, and 'being one of the oldest and most fundamental nations of the world, the Turkish nation established many states in Asia, Europe and Africa in its thousands of years of history, and has created an advanced culture and civilization since ancient times. The Turkish nation has been a model for other nations. Many epochs through history were influenced by the Turks' (*General Turkish History 1*, cited in Boztemur 2004: 127).[15] 'Even where they

14. The Turkish primary and high school curricula are centrally developed, as are the school textbooks. *All quotes from textbooks are taken from textbooks in current use at the time of writing.*

15. We must make three important and related points vis-à-vis this discourse on Turkish superiority. First, according to Copeaux, this gifting of civility to other nations has also included a claim about the Turks' contribution to Islam. In this narrative of Turkish greatness, traceable back to the late nineteenth century, *hizmet* (service, helpfulness) has always been a key term. To quote the famous 1931 publication *The Main Lines of Turkish History*, 'the Turks provided very great services in the development of both the Muslim religion and Muslim civilization, which is wrongly reputed to be an Arab civilization; they produced the greatest scholars and philosophers of the Muslim world' (cited in Copeaux 1996: 101). Second, Copeaux also makes the point that despite a stressing of Turkish service to Islam in textbooks even in the 1930s, this claim has taken a magnified turn since around 1990, somewhat replacing the idea of service to the whole world. Accordingly two of the most striking ideas about this worldly service,

[Turks] remained a minority they appeared as the sovereign component' (*General Turkish History 2*, cited in Boztemur 2004: 127). The qualities of the states founded by such a nation are clear: 'Whatever their name, no matter what name is given to the person at their heads, all Turkish states in history have been shaped by the same state tradition. Some of the basic elements of this tradition are: independence; a conception of an everlasting state; devotion to customs under all circumstances; a sense of justice that incorporates the ideas of equality and freedom' (*Sociology for High Schools*, cited in Irzık 2004: 163–4). In brief, 'the culture and civilization developed by the Turks in Anatolia and the Balkans are among the most beautiful, the most superior, the most humanistic and the most elaborated civilizations of history' (*History of the Revolution of the Republic of Turkey and Ataturkism 8*, cited in Boztemur, 2004: 146).

Hyperbolic love of the national self is complemented by an implicit inscribing of the inferiority of non-Turks. 'In reality Turks both were more civilized than Byzantines and had superior racial characteristics' (*General Turkish History 1*, cited in Irzık 2005: 27). 'Turkish does not contain the consecutive y's or forceful r's of Italian, or the consecutively used 'sin's, resembling the hissing of a snake, and the lisping s's and z's of Greek... The superiority of Turkish is thus revealed' (*High School Linguistics 1*, cited in Gemalmaz 2004: 35). The inferiority of non-Turks is also combined with their hostility towards Turkey: 'During the reign of the Umayyads, who espoused Arab nationalism, the Arabs were applying all types of oppression against Turks who had converted to Islam... During their conquests [the Arabs] aimed to plunder the rich and civilized countries and to find new resources for their constantly expanding lands' (*History of Islam for High Schools*, cited in Gemalmaz 2004: 32). Arabs pillage, whereas Turks advance (into foreign territories). Armenians too 'were neither innocent, nor loyal to the state. Their activities concerning the state in which they lived after the end of the nineteenth century was beyond all tolerance,

---

the claim of the diffusion of Turks to the whole world in the Neolithic ages that resulted in the spread of civilization, and the idea of the Turkish origin of other languages, has disappeared from textbooks. Yet how this change has been discussed is instructive. Even a writer highly critical of the retrospective insertion of Turkish nationalist motivations or categories into historical narratives such as Kafadar asserts (thankfully) that such extreme historical claims are a thing of the past. Yet as our examples of the historical knowledge taught in schools shows, even as certain aspects of it are adjusted, there are still clear continuities with the 1930s. Third, we need to acknowledge that this nationalist self-praise is intimately connected in turn to the historic and continuing production of derogatory European or Eurocentric writings on Turkey and on the Ottoman *Turks*. Lord Gladstone's famous pamphlet *Bulgarian Horrors and the Question of the East*, also written in the late nineteenth century, gives some idea of the depths this racist hostility might reach: 'Let me endeavour very briefly to sketch, in the rudest outline, what the Turkish race was and what it is... They were upon the whole, from the black day when they first entered Europe, the one great anti-human specimen of humanity. Wherever they went a broad line of blood marked the track behind them; and as far as their dominion reached, civilization disappeared from view' (cited in Itkowitz 1996: 33, 34). See Pesmazoglou 1995 for a tracing and analysis of the relationship between Turkish and European historiographies.

fully treacherous and hostile' (*History of the Revolution of the Republic of Turkey and Ataturkism 8*, cited in Gemalmaz 2004: 35). As this enmity of non-Turks is eternal, 'it is the duty of us all for the future and security of our country to be aware of and alert to the external and internal elements that threaten it' (*Social Studies 7*, cited in Altinay 2005: 90), because 'to demolish and destroy the Republic of Turkey is the great dream of internal and external powers' (*History of the Revolution of the Republic of Turkey and Ataturkism for High Schools*, cited in Bora 2004: 64). This dream is often pursued under the pretence of minority rights or cultural differences: 'those who do not want Turkey to become great nation ... aim to divide the nation into groups that do not like each other and are mutually antagonistic, and then to take control of or exploit her without difficulty' (*Literary Texts: High School 2*, cited in Gemalmaz 2004: 40). But in reality, 'more than 95 percent of Turkey have shared the same fate for thousands of years and have blended with the same culture and goals' (*Studies in National Security*, cited in Altinay 2004: 129). (The remaining 5 per cent are the official non-Muslim minorities.)

These discourses on Turkish superiority, its inferior yet hostile 'others' and a paranoiac national security are sutured together through the 'myth of the military nation' (Altinay 2004). Here a Turkish national consciousness is posited as teleologically informing the actions of 'Turkish' states, whose military institutions are exemplary reflections of an unchanging or essential Turkish national character. Education merely 'reinforces the national security consciousness that naturally exists in all Turkish youth' and students become worthy of their ancestors by 'displaying the heroism that is naturally present in their character' (*Studies in National Security*, cited in Altinay 2004b: 80). Similarly, 'every Turkish citizen is an indomitable volunteer soldier in our army' (*Social Studies 7*, cited in Altinay 2005: 89) and 'military service is viewed as a sacred duty' (*Citizenship and Human Rights Education 7*, cited in Altinay 2005: 89). In that case love of homeland equates most perfectly (and reductively) with a readiness to die for it:

> The ideals of our century replace the selfless people of ages past who die for their god with heroes who die for the nation. The spiritual power which made people die by exposing themselves to x-rays in order to serve humanity ... lies in society. The phenomena which created religious heroes in the past are the same phenomena that created heroship for nationhood today. (*Sociology for High Schools*, cited in Irzık: 161)

Although not stated, the glorified spiritual power enabling heroes to die for the nation also legitimates their right to kill for it.[16] But even this spiritual power must be subordinated to the sovereignty of the state: thus the 'integrity of state and

---

16. Certain groups informed by an 'extreme' version of Turkish nationalism have indeed interpreted it as a duty to murder. For this reason Hamit Bozarslan (1996) describes radical Turkish nationalism as a doctrine of civil war.

nation means the loyalty of our nation to its state' (*Studies in Religion and Morality*, cited in Bora 2004: 68). Loyalty to the Turkish state means appreciating that it is because 'the state recognizes certain rights [that] we can participate in the country's governance and form political parties' (*Citizenship and Human Rights Education 7*, cited in Gök 2004: 113). Nevertheless, 'an institution with a politics of its own cannot move its politics away from the general policy pursued by the state; it must develop to the extent established by the state's general policy. Therefore "politics" is to be understood first of all as the policy of the state, which resides at the highest level' (*History of the Revolution of the Republic of Turkey and Ataturkism*, cited in Çayir 2004: 98).

In brief, the present textbooks used for lessons taught in Turkish schools reveal in starkest outline the systematic attempt by the state to indoctrinate students with a clear political subjectivity, or what Bourdieu would call a 'matrix of perception' (Bourdieu 1977). As the primary school reader for *Citizenship and Human Rights Education* insists, 'Education must *instil* the Turkish identity. Within this identity there must be our star and crescent flag, our holy land watered with martyrs' blood, our beloved nation, and the fundamental national and spiritual qualities' (cited in Gök 2004: 115, my emphasis). Intimately related to this 'instillation' is what Bora (2004: 53) calls the textbooks' 'semiological indoctrination', with their omnipresent national flags, maps of the 'Turkic world', Ataturk portraits and verses of the national anthem. The same visual landscape is apparent in the built environment of the schools.[17] 'We are Turks and Ataturkists', says the textbook *Turkish Language and Literature 3,* cited in Bora 2004: 52).[18]

Obviously 'Ataturkist nationalism' and its desired character formation are not meant to be confined to the classroom. And in fact it is not, but can be seen in partial or elaborated form in numerous sites of public debate, from the parliament, to the

17. My son's school, as approached by the students, has a large bust of Atatürk in the general courtyard, another smaller one at the entrance to the primary school with a plaque on the wall engraved with a saying of Atatürk. Entering the building, small Turkish flags with the face of Atatürk superimposed upon them are stuck to the windows in the stairwell, and at the top of the stairwell hangs a large panel of Atatürk and another of his sayings. An Atatürk photograph makes up the bulk of the large corridor clock face. Inside the classroom itself an Atatürk portrait presides over the lessons. The distilling is successful: parents waiting to pick up their children on Friday afternoons stand to attention in silence at the sound of the anthem.

18. The attempted depositing of a nationalist perceptual matrix does not cease with the end of primary and secondary education. University students too are expected to conform to clear guidelines concerning outlook and behaviour. The first two clauses of Article 4 of the Higher Education Law (No. 2547) define the purpose of higher education to be: '(1) To produce students who are loyal to Atatürk Nationalism through a proper understanding of his revolution and ideals. (2) To produce students who internalize the Turkish nation's morals, humanism, spiritual and cultural values, and who feel both honour and happiness to be Turkish' (my translation, cited from *Marmara University Student Handbook 2004*, distributed to students by Marmara University).

media, to the academy. Just as nationalist educators would hope, this nationalized 'cognitive blueprint' (Ceylan and Irzik, 2004: 3) creates conceptual categories to think with (and against). Amidst literally countless appropriations and strategic modifications of the blueprint, let me present just four eclectic yet representative examples, to give some sense both of how widespread the main theses of Turkish nationalism are and how people can apply and extend them. Witness first the speech made in parliament by Ali Topuz, Parliamentary Group Chairman of the Republican People's Party (CHP). Reported in an article published in *Radikal* newspaper (4 January 2004) entitled 'Islam in Turkish Identity' (*Türk Kimliğinde Islam*), Topuz states that 'Islamic culture is not our true culture. The cultural foundations of the Turkish republic rest on Turkishness. This is the culture of Anatolia. Influenced in its development by other cultures, Anatolian culture has acquired many diverse dimensions' (my translation).

The newspaper article goes on to note that the contents of the extended speech were 'identical' to the arguments of anthropologist Bozkurt Güvenç in his book *Turkish Identity: Cultural Historical Sources* (*Türk Kimliği: Kültür Tarihnin Kaynakları*), although parliamentarian Topuz does not reference this work. According to the article, Güvenç's more elaborated thesis divines Turkish national culture (*ulusal kültürümüz*) as beginning 4,000 or 5,000 years ago in Central Asia and two or three thousand years ago in Anatolia. Over time two other traditions merged with these sources, Christianity and Islam. These influences converged in Anatolia around AD 1000 to create a still-evolving *synthesis*, one of whose works was the birth of the republic of Turkey. Obviously the place and nature of the Ottoman empire and its inspiration by Turkish, Islamic or other sources becomes of key controversy here, as the rest of the article in *Radikal* indicates. For Güvenç, in comparison to the lasting influence of these Anatolian and Turkish traditions, Islam is only of minor importance in the shaping of contemporary Turkish identity. Accordingly, Islam should be understood not as an independent but as a dependent variable directed by the more influential streams of Turkish ethno-history. Two powerful currents in these streams are nationalism (*ulusalcılık*) and *laiklik*. Fascinatingly then, *laiklik* is represented as an ethnic trait or as a component of ethnic identity – true Turkish identity is essentially secular – rather than as a political system or procedure.

Our second example is an article by newspaper columnist Haluk Şahin, discussing the rise of a new nationalism in Turkey (titled 'Nationalism's Mutation'). In an extended analogy, Şahin compares the anxiety over the possible mutating of the bird flu into a more deadly strain, with similar potential transformations in 'popular' nationalism in Turkey. According to him:

> The social science literature distinguishes between different varieties of nationalism. It makes a rough and ready distinction between two main categories, positive and negative. Positive nationalism, and Ataturk's nationalism falls into this category, prefers to praise itself instead of criticizing others. (Of course, if this self-praise is exaggerated to a

chauvinistic degree in terms of national superiority it can develop into the other type.) Negative nationalism by contrast degrades other nations (people, ethnic groups). This approach defines itself (xenophobically) in terms of hostility to foreigners. Because it sees the world as full of enemies it desires either to conquer them or to isolate itself from them. When we examine the latest wave of nationalism in Turkey we see examples of all of these – national pride, chauvinism, hostility to foreigners and isolationism… Further, either internally or by combining with other currents we might see the development of dangerous or even deadly mutations. (*Radikal*, 10 February 2006) (my translation)[19]

Yet as we have seen in the taught curriculum in Turkey, Şahin's positive and negative nationalism is a spurious distinction, as is his attempt to quarantine 'Ataturk's nationalism' away from supposedly contrasting and more xenophobic strains. In fact, his two categories are produced by stressing different aspects of the same narrative, which points to the flexibility of the cognitive blueprint in enabling both different emphasis to be made and variable political practices to be pursued.

My third example is taken from a new book by Prof. Dr Tuncer Baykara, *Atatürk ve XX. Yüzyıl Türk Tarihi Araştırmaları* (*Research on Ataturk and Twentieth Century Turkish History*) (Baykara 2006). In an essay titled 'The Turkish Republic and the Republican Principles of the Turks' he attempts to prove that the essential principles of the republic already existed in nascent but unmistakable form in the Ottoman polity (and before). He goes on to substantiate his claim in seven steps:

i. The foundational feature of a Republic is a lack of distinction between individuals, so that society and its administrative structure issue in a population of equals. Despite the institution of the Sultanate, Ottoman society knew of no rank or distinction. Accordingly Ottoman society was essentially republican. Importantly, when we look at Turkish life as a whole, especially western Turks, the same thing is true: the rule of aristocrats based on select lineages was unknown. Even the roundness of the Turkish table symbolizes this principled equality.

ii. This same classlessness can be seen in the Turkish language. For example, there is no equivalent for the term 'princess'. Among the Ottomans no sultan's daughter ever claimed or desired noble status.

iii. Because Turkish people intrinsically possessed this characteristic [social equality], they always participated in government. For example, even if their views were not always clear, they found a way to choose between Sultan Fatih's sons. Similarly, the Turkish people prepared the way for the youngest son of Beyazid II to become Sultan. In fact, in Turkish society this type of election had a long history.

---

19. The express reason for his column was the murder in Trabzon (in February 2006) of an Italian Catholic priest by what he describes as 'mutant' Muslim nationalists. Şahin's model also allows him to qualify the products of popular culture: thus the recent novel '*Şu Cılgın Türkler*' (Those Crazy Turks) is positively nationalistic, whereas the film '*Kurtlar Vadisi Irak'da*' (*The Valley of the Wolves in Iraq*) is negative.

iv. Turkish society has always admired and followed virtuous leaders. They were remembered for their heroism, resolution, happiness, good fortune, gallantry, and trustworthiness. As leaders they aimed to make people happy.

v. In short, the foundational ideas of republicanism exist within the Turks. Further, the primary reason Osman's sons were accepted as leaders was because of their virtuousness, honesty and honourable governance. Thus Osman Gazi left few possessions as his inheritance. And everyone knows the behaviour of Murad II on the field of battle. Faced with almost certain death, he threw a handful of earth inside his shirt, saying let the dust touch my skin, and thus commenced fighting.

vi. Yet by the beginning of the twentieth century, Osman's dynasty had lost its virtuous qualities. Accordingly they lost the affection of the Turkish people and for this very reason their rule.

vii. With the collapse of the Ottoman regime, the question became: what now? Would a new dynasty be founded, or a real Republic? Would society's most virtuous person become the leader? General Mustafa Kemal emerged, heroic, blessed, and resolute. Here was a faultless Republic. And here was a faultless man. Those who made that revolution were truly virtuous. And those today who want a new republic according to their own sterile points of view should acquaint themselves with these great Turks of the past.

(Baykara 2006: 97–101, my translation and summary)

We hardly need to point out what this narrative excludes – for example, the Ottoman *devşirme* system (youth levy on mainly Balkan Christians) that produced the empire's bureaucracy; the slave military and their often influential role in deposing or installing the Sultan; the early sultans' marrying of Christian and other Muslim (never Turkish) princesses; the role of the queen mother in politics; gradations within Ottoman society and the very existence of Islam as a political imaginary. Still, Baykara presents us with a novel anthropology: essentially republican before the republic, how did the Turks as natural republicans rule themselves? A society of equals can only organize itself by consent, on the principle of virtue. In more classical anthropological terms – no less a narrative – Baykara presents the social relations of a nomad and stateless society (tribal and classless) as continuing on relentlessly into the present, despite the disappearance of Turkish tribes and the appearance of countless Turkish states. In that case republicanism, like secularism and nationalism for parliamentarian Ali Topuz, is an essential ethnic characteristic of Turks or Turkish culture, indeed their fixed and defining features.

Nevertheless, we hear only half the tale if we rest content with pointing out the anachronistic nationalism or gross historical error of such constructions. Baykara's anecdote about Murad II or the round Turkish table shows nationalism's power resides not only in its imagining of origins or of shared community but even more so in its imagining of that community's ethic. Being or becoming Turkish is associated with certain desirable ways of relating to others or ordering social relationships. These include social equality and denial of special privileges. Nationalism is thus an invitation to a new virtue. As we have seen, the discourse on Kurdish identity too brings with it an ethical dimension, constructed partially around the virtues of indigeneity and authenticity. The difference between the two is that after the institution of the republic, the Turkish nation-state is able to legislate virtue.

The fourth and last example, and one that is oriented towards a more 'popular' readership, is the book by researcher and writer Orhan Bayrak, entitled *Türk Imparatorlukları Tarihi* (*History of the Turkish Empires*).[20] Bayrak positions the Ottomans as the seventeenth and penultimate Turkish empire. He begins his book by writing that

> Turks have always established and been assured of their place in history as a nation that has established innumerable independent states. As the historian Hammer says, 'Turks are first class experts at founding states.' For this reason I must confess a certain excitement about writing about such states (empires), given the many peoples that within their wide borders have been under the authority of these Turkish states. (Bayrak 2002: 17, my translation)

Bayrak's identification and examination of sixteen other historic Turkish empires in his book, starting with the Huns, is no mere personal view: he includes the same sixteen independent states that are represented by the sixteen stars in the Turkish republic's Presidential *Forsun* (seal). His history then conforms closely to the official political (state) pre-history of the Turkish republic as taught in its educational institutions, including in its military high schools. This history is also symbolically embedded in the built environment of Turkish cities, although not without seemingly contradicting other historical narratives also generated through design of public space. In Maçka Park for example (Nişantaşı, Istanbul) busts of the sixteen founders

---

20. Hirschler makes a distinction between academic and popular history writing in Turkey (Hirschler 2001: 147), a distinction I think problematic although one that is rather widespread. For example the authors of an article entitled 'Turkish Social Anthropology since the 1970s' argue for a similar loose difference between popular anthropology and academic anthropology in Turkey (Erdentuğ and Magnarella 2001). Presumably Bozkurt Güvenç's work (see example one above), as befitting his status as professor of anthropology at Hacettepe University in Ankara, would be catalogued as academic. Their contrasting example of popular anthropology is a work by a certain Ibrahim Yılmaz detailing an alternative cultural fusion to Güvenç, one in which Islam plays a greater part in the historic development of a unique 'Turco-Islamic' culture. The cover of Yılmaz's book *Ecdat Kültürü* (*The Culture of the Ancestors*) gives some idea of his different emphasis: '*We set out from Ergenekon with Turkish blood in our veins/ We joined with the divine light of Islam in our hearts/ With countless martyrs, we reached the oceans and ruled the world.*' Why the author's use this as an example of popular anthropology (and not Güvenç's work) is unclear, given their mutual dependence on a nationalist theme. An alternative way of differentiating products and producers of historical knowledge in Turkey might be between academics trained overseas and working in private or English-language state universities, and academics trained locally and working in Turkish language state universities. This too does not reflect fixed boundaries or groups of scholars either, but at least indicates how historical knowledge and its production is also connected to the politics of a social and institutional field, that of tertiary education in Turkey.

of these Turkish empires are arranged in a semi-circle.[21] By contrast, citizens in Ankara encounter the Hittite symbols dotting parts of that city, including guarding the ceremonial approach to the Ataturk Mausoleum complex (Anıtkabir). The Hittites are not one of the sixteen empires represented in Bayrak's book nor is their founder memorialized in Maçka Park. Nevertheless nationalized public space in the capital encodes them as proto-Turks, or as Turks who had forgotten their ethnic roots.

Yet aside from retrospectively ascribing an essential Turkishness to these states, the defining characteristic of Bayrak's book is its extreme reduction of these varied imperial life worlds to three features: an account of their leaders, their victories or defeats in battle and the monuments (often mosques) commissioned by them. In other words, the study is deeply militaristic, sanctifying violence and its gains or losses as worthy of remembrance, and erasing as non-important all other forms of civil relations. The history of the Turks becomes the history of their military prowess, proof and illustration of the claim that 'the nation forms a whole with its army' (Parla 1998: 44). Bora notes a similar emphasis in the school textbooks, and argues that such a focus leads students to believe that military activity is the most important human pursuit (Bora 2004: 68). As for the Ottoman empire, in three of these examples it has been cut down to size, relativized as just one (and in many ways the most problematic) variant of a much broader species, the species of Turkish states founded by a free and equal people.[22]

In conclusion then, it is not surprising that contemporary Kurdish discourse is either uninterested in the Ottoman polity, or willing to see its virtues only as a reflection of its Islamic character. Indeed, since the institutionalizing of a nationalist Turkish history as one key component of compulsory education in Turkey, many aspects of Kurdish discourse can only be understood as constructed in the context of this imagining of Turkishness. For example, because dominant versions of Turkish historiography have stressed both the Turkish facility to found states and implied a

21. Thanks to Uğur Kömeoğlu for pointing this out.
22. Discourse on the existence and role of the Turks over millennia, for good or ill, has of course been produced by more than just Turkish Republican historians. One recent book is that of Carter Findley, *The Turks in World History,* published in 2005. In it he tries to mediate between some essence of Turkish culture continuing over time, and analysis of its historical transformations. The project resides on a knife edge: 'Turks [are] a group of people definable by their languages and by certain shared elements of culture and history but otherwise astonishingly diverse among themselves' (Findley 2005: 4). His concluding chapter attempts to identify the influence of these enduring cultural characteristics on Turkish social life in the present. But how do these cultural elements reproduce themselves? And if they are essential to Turkish culture why is so much conscious care taken by concentrations of power like the Turkish military to produce them as cultural givens? The book's identifying of three enduring (essential) influences on contemporary Turkish identity is anachronistic to say the least, as well as typically within the bounds of official Turkish nationalism. How for example is Turkish ethnic origin important for understanding the work of a writer nourished in Islamic thought? The idea of an alloyed identity, made up of different, identifiable and *continuing* components, is a staple of nationalist thought.

Kurdish inability to do so, Kurdish historiography is often engaged in identifying past independent Kurdish or proto-Kurdish states. Similarly it has also been concerned with identifying which revolts or uprisings against Ottoman or Safavid power were nationalist in character, or at least with clarifying the relative influence of Islamic or nationalist motivations within them. (See for example the difference of opinion between McDowall 2000, Olson 1996 and White 2000 over the nationalist aims or otherwise of the Sheikh Ubaydallah rebellion in 1879.) Some Kurdish histories are also concerned to rehabilitate historical personages such as Saladin as Kurds, although this seems to depend on context.[23] (See Hirschler and Strohmeier.) Further, Kurdish origin narratives are concerned to stress both the antiquity and culturally autochthonic nature of Kurdish society, in response to Turkish nationalist history, which stresses the civilizing influence of Turkish culture on (and thus the implied sterility of) other groups. Civil everyday social interchange in the present between Kurds and Turks is understood as threatened by the Turkish nationalism of the republic, and not only by malign external forces (as in official Turkish history).

On a different level, the question of individual or collective agency is often underplayed in Kurdish narratives as well, whereby claims regarding the oppression of Kurds and the Kurdish region by barbaric outsiders imply an absence of social relations unconditioned by this domination. Islamist Kurdish narratives, too, have not constructed a particularly nuanced presentation of Ottoman imperial power. Further, in much writing about Kurds there is a disproportionate focus on the centre/periphery political dimensions of Kurdish history, a concern that appears to mirror the reductionism of much official and popular Turkish historiography in which the non-military aspects of social life are also of little interest. Gender relations or Ottoman popular culture for example are rarely incorporated into the picture, as we will see in the next chapter. All of these echoes make us conclude that official history in Turkey, and much popular history writing too, as well as many of the histories written in the name of Kurds, is the continuance of nationalism by another means.

In brief, imagining the origins and essential characteristics of the Ottoman empire has provided the foundational myth for nearly all the nation-states that have been established in what was its geographical domain. Yet despite the respective teleological narratives relaying their long national suppression and awakening, the instituting of the Greek, Bulgarian, Turkish, Arab and other nation states on Ottoman territory was not inevitable. Or at least if it was, that 'inevitability' originated in the global system of nation states emerging in the long years of the empire's demise and not in the release from the imperial clamp of always existing but long denied nations or ethnicities, including the Turks. It is on the basis of this trans-historical nationalist logic that a certain discourse on the Kurds rues the lack of a similar outcome in

---

23. Bayrak in *Türk İmparatorlukları Tarihi* describes Saladin as being of Arabic origins, but Turkified, and thus counts the Ayyubid dynasty founded by him as one of the Turkish empires. By contrast Yılmaz in *Aşiretten Ulusallığa Doğru Kürtler* talks of the 'Eyyubi Kürt devleti' (1991: 27).

Kurdistan in the early decades of the twentieth century, viewing those years as a missed opportunity (see Kendal 1980: 38ff). Imagining the Ottoman empire and its pre-history has also been vital for discourse on Kurdishness, although the vaunted autonomy of the Kurdish principalities under the Ottomans has sometimes been presented as injurious to the formation of a proper nationalist consciousness (see Vali 1998). We have also seen how Turkish nationalism is produced in a number of selected social fields, including in textbooks, parliament, the media, the academy and in popular literary culture. By doing so I hope to have given readers a more vivid sense of what crafting the national identity in Turkey actually consists of. More importantly, Kurdish identity in Turkey in the present is constructed in the context of this reiteration of Turkish superiority. This same intimate relationship applies between discourse on Kurdishess in Iran and Iraq and those countries' official national histories, as we shall see later.

By way of concluding, let me make two points. Pre-modern imperialism as a political project (such as the early Ottomans') sought control of territory and extraction of resources, including taxes, from lands brought under the empire's juris-diction. But it was neither able to fabricate nor interested in fabricating culturally homogeneous imperial subjects, excepting perhaps on doctrinal grounds. By contrast, the political regime *par excellence* concerned with cultural standardization is the nation-state, both in its attempts to produce a new national and ethical identity and in its suppression of the recital or performance of unauthorized cultural difference. The reason is clear: the very basis of the state's legitimacy – that is to say, of its sovereignty in a world of nation-states – is its representation of its 'nation'. All the better, therefore, if that nation can be shown as existing in order to bring its benefits to other groups, as in the metaphor of the 'white man's burden'. This nation in most cases – as also in Turkey – is rarely seen as essentially multicultural.

How ironic, then, that stereotypical analysis of contemporary globalization frets about its recent production of (global) cultures of sameness. The concern is a century late. Yet equally out of time are contrasting theories of globalization that see as something peculiar, and paradoxical to the present era, the rise of particularistic identities as products of globalization itself. As a *global* ideal for more than a century, the construction of national particularity has ruled. Accordingly, it was the narrators of national liberation who first made the argument about the unnaturalness of social and cultural homogeneity, attributing to imperial formations such as the Ottomans and the Habsburgs the suppression of their own national diversity. This final point leads us on to our next chapter, where we will explore more extensively how imagining Kurdistan has involved interpretation of the significance of the assent of the Kurdish princes to Ottoman suzerainty. It has also involved constructing how relations between imperial (Ottoman) and imperialist (Russian, British) powers were played out in the empire's critical eastern provinces in the process of Ottoman modernization throughout the nineteenth century, resulting in the deportation of Armenians and questions over Kurds' involvement in it.

'Set aside from the Pen and Cut off from the Foot': Imagining the Ottoman Empire and Kurdistan

In this second chapter we will explore in more detail three processes or events that have been remembered as vital for varied presentations of Kurdistan and Kurdish identity. These are, firstly, the initial incorporation (or the 'first division') of the Kurdish regions into the Ottoman and Safavid spheres of influence in the early sixteenth century, and what the discourse on Kurds has stressed as its critical consequences. Secondly we will examine different Kurdish responses to what has been described as Kurdistan's 'second' incorporation and transformation throughout the long nineteenth century, resulting from the attempted centralization of Ottoman power and the change in relations between Istanbul and the Kurdish regions brought about in its wake. Indeed, not just in Kurdistan but all over the Empire new procedures aimed at asserting and monopolizing imperial authority reorganized the relationships between the Ottoman centre and its provincial peripheries. Similar impulses to centralizing control invigorated the Qajar dynasty in Persia, and impacted upon Iranian Kurdistan in turn. Thirdly, because the Kurdish uprisings in resistance against the new practices of Ottoman power often impinged violently on Christians in the region, we need to address one further element crucial for discourses on Kurdish identity: these discourses' (under)representation of inhabitants speaking other languages and following other religious traditions in Kurdistan. The extensive yet downplayed participation of Kurds in the Young Turks' murder of Armenians means that in many interpretations of the past, the memory of massacres carried out by 'forbears' appears to be repressed.

Ottoman Kurdistan: Historical Reconstructions

In Chapter 1 we sketched out some of the various strategies whereby the patrimony of the Ottoman empire is neutralized and nationalized – on the one hand selectively claimed for the Turkish nation by the republic, and on the other indicted as the cause of backwardness and oppression by Balkan and Arab states for much the same reasons. In the ten decades after its demise, Kurdish discourse, too, has been concerned to imagine the empire and its impact upon Kurds. In this first section of

Chapter 2 I want to narrow our focus so as to describe and analyse interpretations of the status of the region known as Kurdistan in the aftermath of its lords' assent to incorporation within the Ottoman sphere. As we have seen, more secular and monopolist Kurdish accounts of what is condemned as the Ottoman interlude incline towards a narrative of Ottoman exploitation of Kurdistan and ceaseless local resistance. By contrast, many Islamist narratives deny the alien character of the Ottoman system, sensing in its dissolution instead the origins of present-day problems in the region. The contrariness of these positions attests to the nationalist desire to uncover – as well as the difficulty of assessing – the relative influence of external and internal centres of power upon the identity of the region and its social relations. Kemal Karpat describes the perceived problem rather succinctly when he writes that Ottoman studies has usually treated the Ottoman borderlands 'in terms of their political relations to Istanbul rather than … view[ing them] as cultural-social units with their own identity and internal dynamics' (Karpat 2003: 1). This difficulty is not avoided if we reframe the analysis and talk instead of one single imperial social system, as we are still left with questions of historical change, regional variation, concentrations of power and processes of resistance. If as Karpat suggests historical analysis has tended to overemphasize the influence of the centre, anthropological analysis (as we will see in Chapter 3) has revealed a bias towards the autonomy of the periphery, minimizing the imperial constitution of society as well as transnational institutions and cultural practices that indicate much wider networks of social influence and relations. A related problem is how to connect political developments to the borderland or frontier economy, both to local relations of production and to the wider political economy of the empire as a whole. As we will see in this and the next chapter, in its narrative of Kurdish identity Marxist discourse seeks to theorize the particular impact of feudal under-development and exploitation in and of the Kurdish regions.

Clearly, everyone wants a reflected slice of the Ottoman empire's glory or else to distance themselves from its perceived brutalities. But this selective appropriation is not unique to the present. The Ottomans themselves were greatly interested in the origins of the imperial dynasty and in constructing and propagating certain versions of it. For this reason among others, study of the texts of the Ottoman historians (Ottoman historiography) has become as legitimate a topic of historical research as the empire's wars or conquests. These early Ottoman histories from the late fifteenth century are indirectly important for this chapter for another reason, because the Kurdish regions were integrated into the empire (1514 and thereafter) during a period when the writing of Ottoman history was intimately connected with legitimizing concurrent processes of state centralization.[1] Indeed Idris of Bitlis, the

---

1. Piterberg claims that in two critical periods, the latter half of the fifteenth century and the first half of the seventeenth century, 'the histories of the state and of the historiography are so closely related that they might be indistinguishable' (Piterberg 2003: 5). He argues, in part summarizing Kafadar, that the commissioning and writing of Ottoman historiography in Fatih Mehmet and Beyazid II's reigns

man charged by Sultan Selim to negotiate with the Kurdish principalities on behalf of the Ottomans in 1514, was also a notable historian. Selim's father Sultan Beyazid II (1481–1512) commissioned him in 1502 to write in Persian a definitive history of the House of Osman. Even earlier, with the 1453 conquest of Constantinople, most historians writing on the early Ottoman period agree that the struggle for the soul of the empire was resolved in favour of the centralizing party. Proof of this victory and the discontent it caused among many is seen in Sultan Fatih Mehmet's (1451–80) encouraging of the first chronicle histories of the Osman dynasty, which produced conflicting versions of what the chroniclers and the imperial elite must have perceived as the 'shady' past of the Ottomans. These sanitized accounts at the same time denied particular dimensions of its early state formation, while contributing to and symbolizing the transformation of the empire into a (more) orthodox Sunni Islamic state. As with the histories of the empire's origins constructed in the present, these late fifteenth-century works, written 150 years after the events they seek to represent, should be understood as intimately articulated with the politics of the time in which they were written.

Yet as we have seen, precisely because contemporary analysis of the formative influences at work in early Ottoman society and its state are so varied, so too are the arguments over the very qualities of its 'shadiness' that this historiography of the latter half of the fifteenth century sought to reinterpret or suppress. The differences between Kafadar and Lowry's theses here are instructive. Kafadar represents the early decades of the emerging Ottoman polity (in the fourteenth century) as a period of increasing tension between centralizing and centrifugal tendencies. The Gazi forces, both those which had participated in the heterodox and moving frontier of the early Ottoman expansion and those who had imbued or profited from that ethic, were gradually subordinated to the central administration. As part of this process the term 'Gazi' was contested and redefined, as the 'shady' Ottoman past of sufi or dervish Gazi and their unorthodox practices or beliefs were displaced by medrese-trained orthodox *ulema* (schoolmen). The struggle against the so-called *Kizilbaş* is intimately part of this process.[2] By contrast, Lowry reads the fifteenth-century Ottoman historiography as seeking to stress the legitimacy of the Osman royal line against the claims of the other (Christian) co-founders of the Ottoman confederacy. Here the 'shady' past is the 'religio-social hybrid Islamo-christian entity' (Lowry 2003: 142) responsible for the creation of the early Ottoman state. This past is cleaned up in the histories through the representation of the early Ottoman sultans

---

were key aspects of their concern to defend a newly emergent 'centralized, bureaucratic and dynastic state' (Piterberg 2003: 31ff). See Inalcık (1962) for a different emphasis on why histories of the Ottoman dynasty were so important during the reign of Beyazid II. In this article Inalcık describes Idris Bidlisi in passing as Persian.

2. It is only after this interpretation of the Ottoman state becomes standard knowledge that someone today can re-read back into the period claims such as the spy status of Mevlana for the Mongols against the 'Turks'.

as Gazis fighting for the faith of Islam. Although Kafadar sees Christian converts to Islam as one component in the fluidity of identity marking the frontier culture in the early decades of the Ottoman polity, they are minimized in his depiction of Gazi identity, which emerges in a 'Turco-Muslim' milieu (cf. Kafadar 1995: 95).

Despite their disagreement over whom this Ottoman historiography was seeking to disenfranchise, the work of both Lowry and Kafadar indicates that the primary integration of the Kurdish regions into the Ottoman empire (we will explore in the following pages how this has been interpreted) occurred in the years immediately following these first 'history wars', in the decades often described as perfecting the empire's 'classical' institutions or its political and cultural apogee. As the documents cited below show however, political and administrative arrangements in the Kurdish provinces did not conform to the classical standardized pattern. This Kurdish exception is extremely important, as we will see below. A summary of Inalcık[3] (1973) and Imber's (2002) snapshot descriptions of provincial administration in the sixteenth century will allow us to see the distinctions. We will then be able to better appreciate the reasons why these differences have been imagined and evaluated as important in the discourse on Kurdish identity.

According to Imber, Ottoman provincial government rationally 'divided the Empire into provinces, provinces into sanjaks [region or district] and sanjaks into fiefs' (Imber 2002: 206). The origins of the administrative boundaries often resembled pre-Ottoman divisions, especially in the immediate aftermath of their conquest. Nevertheless, boundaries were changed and standardized over time too, so that 'by the sixteenth century [the provinces] presented a rational administrative pattern of territories, based usually around the town or settlement from which the sanjak took its name, and with a population of perhaps 100,000' (Imber 2002: 184). The number of districts (*sancak*) within a province varied. Both provincial (*beylerbeyi*) and district (*sancakbeyi*) governors were appointed by the Sultan, and their tenure was non-hereditary. The major role of both provincial and district governors was to command the troops raised in the area under their control, as well as to maintain order. The majority of district governors were trained in the palace bureaucratic system and were transferred from *sancak* to *sancak* throughout their careers. In addition to the governors a second figure centrally appointed to each district represented the Sultan's legal authority, the judge (*kadı*) who was a member of the *ulema* and an expert in Islamic religious law (*şeriat*).

The most extensive category of land within districts was *miri* (crown land), or land that belonged to the Ottoman ruler or state. According to Inalcık, in 1528 87 per cent

---

3. Nevertheless, Inalcık has his biases: as a student of Fuat Köprülü he is inclined to claim the origins of various Ottoman institutional practices as central Asian (i.e. Turkish), and he describes the recipients of the special privileges negotiated by Idris of Bitlis in Kurdistan as 'tribal chieftains in some areas of eastern Anatolia' (p. 105). And like Köprülü, he also downplays the Ottoman synthesizing of Byzantine institutions. Further, his list of the extant Ottoman provinces in 1610 is organized according to their date of conquest, although it is debateable whether this is the appropriate term for Idris of Bitlis' 1515 administrative organization of the new provinces of Diyarbekir and Kurdistan.

of land in the empire was classified as *miri* (Inalcık 1973: 110). *Miri* land was organized according to the fief (*timar*) system. Indeed, 'the typical Ottoman province was one where the *timar* system was in force' (Inalcık 1973: 107). Carefully surveyed every 20 years or so by agents of the Land Registry Office, *miri* land was allocated by the Sultan or his representative (such as the provincial governor) to the military 'class' as fiefs or estates. Fiefs themselves were organized and distributed in three administrative units (*timar*, *zeamet* and *has*) according to their value or revenue-raising potential. The smallest fiefs and least valuable (*timar*) were granted to cavalrymen (*sipahis*), both as reward for military service and in order to facilitate their continued obligation to provide military service. Failure to appear upon the call to campaign with armed retainers would result in the revoking of the grant. *Zeamet* and *has* fiefs were granted to officers and district and provincial governors by the Sultan. All fiefs had farmers or peasants – the taxpaying subjects of the empire – tied to them, whose rights, obligations and dues were carefully codified as an aspect of the detailed land surveys (*tahrir*). As the productive members of the Ottoman society, their movement was restricted: if peasants left land uncultivated the legal code required them to pay compensation to the fief holder. As well fief holders were also expected to maintain order in their areas as well, although in major centres the standing army of the Sultan (the Janissary corps) also had garrisons.

In how many provinces did this system operate? As the empire expanded, so did the number of provinces. Following the massive increase of territory in the wake of Selim's military conquests, a 1527 list shows eight provinces in the empire. In addition to the much older administrative units of Rumelia (capital Edirne), Anadolu (Kütahya), Rum (Amasya) and Karaman (Konya), the document lists the four new provinces of Egypt, Syria, Diyarbekir and Kurdistan (Imber 2002: 179). The Kurdish regions were reorganized more definitively after further conquests of Safavid territory in the 1530s by Sultan Süleyman (Selim's son), this time as the provinces of Diyarbakır, Ezurum, Van, Shahrizur (in today's Iraq) and Musul (also in Iraq). In the process 'Kurdistan' as an administrative entity seems to disappear. Özoğlu notes that in 1515 all territory south of Erzurum and Sivas fell under the authority of the Diyarbakır provincial governor (Özoğlu 1996: 14). He also tries to clarify the relationship between the provinces of Kurdistan and Diyarbakır as listed in the 1527 document: according to Özoğlu, there was in fact only one province (Diyarbakır), made up of tax-paying and non tax-paying regions. The document 'makes a clear distinction between the directly and indirectly governed parts of Diyarbakır. The former consisted of ten *sancaks*, whereas the latter, called *vilayet-i Kurdistan* (province of Kurdistan) included seven major and eleven minor emirates' (Özoğlu 1996: 21). Thus 'Kurdistan' appears to refer to the autonomous Kurdish principalities within the Diyarbakır province.[4]

4. The status and geographic extent of the province of Kurdistan is unclear however, as it is again listed as a province in a separate document in 1567. See Akgündüz (1992: 21).

Yet even in the classical period, and despite the predominance of and preference for a standardized model of territorial control and taxation, most commentators agree that the Ottoman government also cut its administrative cloth to suit local practices and conditions. Bureaucratic pragmatism (and a host of other factors, not all of them good or rational) resulted in various degrees of regional autonomy, land registration and absorption of members of deposed dynasties into the Ottoman ruling elite. Political arrangements in the Kurdish provinces demonstrated this same flexibility, as the legal formulae detailing their establishment and privileges show. Nevertheless Kurdish and Arab regions aside, by the sixteenth century autonomous status was exceptional: 'most of the sanjaks throughout the empire were under the rule of non-hereditary appointees, who had no permanent family of territorial connections with the area' (Imber 2002: 189). Why this difference in the Kurdish regions, and how has it been assessed?

Let us look first at just two of the most important documents detailing the 'treaty agreements'[5] in Ottoman Kurdistan. The first is a declaration in the Imperial Law Code, its precise date unknown but according to Akgündüz (1992: 22) certainly prepared during the reign of Süleyman (1520–66). The second is an imperial decree (*ferman*) issued by Sultan Süleyman in 1533. In the first document, the legal status of the autonomous Kurdish principalities is clarified:

> There are nine *hükümet*s [see explanation below], which were given under administration and property of their holders in return for their service and obedience. They govern (their districts) by way of free-holding. Moreover, their countries are set aside from the pen and cut off from the foot. All of their revenues were not included in the sultanic register. There is no one person from the Ottoman governors and servants of the Sultan within these areas. Everything belongs to them. And, in accordance with their charters (given by Ottoman sultans, regarding their rights and privileges) they are not subjected to dismissal and appointment. However, all of them are obedient to the orders of the Sultan. As other Ottoman district governors, they attend to campaigns together with the province-governors of whichever province they are subjected to. They own people and tribes as well as other soldiers. (cited in Öz 2003: 146–7)

According to Öz, the striking phrase 'set aside from the pen and cut off from the foot' refers to the *hükümet*s' (literally government) being independent from taxation surveys and exempt from military intervention.

The second document fills out some of the same details, but describes a second type of political-administrative arrangement, the *yurtluk* and *ocaklık*:

> [Kanuni Sultan Süleyman] gives to the Kurdish *beys* who, in his father Yavuz Sultan Selim's times, took position against the *Kızılbaş* and who are currently serving the

---

5. The phrase is taken from Aziz Efendi's 1632 advice to the Sultan.

State with faith ... both as a reward for their loyalty and courage, their applications and requests being taken into consideration, the provinces and fortresses that have been controlled by each of them as their *yurtluk* and *ocaklık* since past times ... under the condition of inheritance from father to son ... as their estate... In case of a *bey*'s death, his province shall be given, as a whole, to his son, if there is only one... If the *bey* has no heir or relative, then his province shall not be given to anybody from outside. As a result of consultation with the Kurdistan *bey*s, the region shall be given to either *bey*s or *beyzade*s suggested by the Kurdistan *bey*s. (cited in Özoğlu 1996: 18)

These same documents are cited by later Ottoman writers when discussing problems with the varied provincial administrations of the empire. Thus in 1609 for example the chancery clerk Ayn Ali Efendi repeats the distinction between the two systems, writing that

When their [*yurtluk* and *ocaklık*] governors die, these districts are given to their sons, not to outsiders. However, their revenues are registered like ordinary sanjaks; there are *timar* and *zeamet*s within them... But the *hükümet*s have not been surveyed, and there is no *zeamet* or *timar* in them. Their rulers keep and govern them through freeholding. They are 'set aside from the pen and cut off from the foot' and all their revenues, whatever they might be, belong to them. (cited in Öz 2003: 146)

Finally we might cite the 1632/3 treatise *Kanun-Name-ı Sultan li Aziz Efendi* (*Aziz Efendi's Book of Sultanic Laws and Regulations*) and its recommendations regarding the 'country of Kurdistan'. Repeating the legal formula 'cut off from the foot and set aside from the pen'[6] as encapsulating the treaty agreements between the Kurdish commanders and Sultans Selim and Süleyman, Aziz Efendi claims that abuse of the Kurdish princes' rights by the provincial governors has led to their inability or unwillingness to join Ottoman military campaigns. To remedy the perilous situation – Rhoads Murphey in a footnote to the text notes that it was written at the 'nadir of their [the Ottomans'] strength relative to the Safavids', after they had lost Baghdad – Aziz Efendi, a high-ranking bureaucrat and close adviser to Sultan Murat IV, drafted for the Sultan's official proclamation the following proposal:

I have decreed that, first of all in accordance with the treaty arrangements granted to each of you by my great forbears, you should inherit the jurisdiction of your governorships (*hükumet*) generation after generation as is right, and each be confirmed and maintained in your posts, and whenever one of you should, by the decree of God the Exalted die, the provincial governors shall not interfere in dismissal or assignment ... [then you] would also act as a firm barrier and a co-terminous boundary and obstacle between the territory of the Iranian 'redheads' and [my] well-protected realm, thereby ... bestowing the

6. The great Ottoman traveller Evliya Çelebi repeats the phrase too in his description of the independence of the Bitlis government. See Dankoff (1990: 61).

governors-general of Diyarbakır, Erzerum, and Van with the fortune and strength to be able to challenge the Shah of Iran and his redheaded soldiers. (Aziz Efendi 1632/1985: 17, 23) (my translation)

Clearly, the *hükümet* and *yurtluk ocaklık* arrangements elaborated in the imperial decrees and repeated thereafter in bureaucratic discourse meant that the Kurdish provinces were an exception to the much more typical and highly centralized administrative pattern described by Inalcık and Imber. Nevertheless, the *significance* of their particular difference needs to be interpreted and assessed, as does the potential dissonance between the imperial decree and the historical development of actual power and influence in the region. In this process the very questions addressed to the documents, indeed the way archival material in the first place is identified as relevant and then selectively quoted also reflects the concerns of their writers, and beyond them their imagined interlocutors. In other words, we need to establish more clearly what the discourse on Kurds has stressed as the vital issues emerging from this incorporation of the Kurdish regions into the Ottoman and Safavid spheres of influence.

To do so, and using Piterberg's idea of a 'historiographical corpus', what I want to do now is to quickly compare eight longer or shorter analyses of the integration of the Kurdish regions into the Ottoman empire.[7] By 'historiographical corpus' Piterberg means a group of texts representing or interpreting a series of events – in this case the constitution of Ottoman Kurdistan – that when read in relation to each other 'brings to the fore differences not only in narrative events but [also] in the minutest interpretive nuances' (Piterberg 2003: 53). Apart from their subject matter what makes the selected texts a corpus is their use of a number of common documents, including the *Şerefname* (Kurdish History) of Şeref Khan (1597), the travel epic of Evliya Çelebi (1655) and of course the legal documents cited above. Further, later texts cite earlier ones. What I hope to show is that the textual corpus under discussion, which admittedly is not a closed one, while also being characterized by significant shades of difference amongst its individual parts, is unified by a shared political imagination. In its exploration of the Ottoman Kurdish history of the sixteenth and seventeenth centuries, the theoretical obsession of the corpus centres on the meaning and extent of the Kurdish principalities' *political* autonomy. Why were the Kurdish princes offered – or able to negotiate – special privileges? How did these privileges change over time? In the granting or taking of this autonomy how important was the geopolitical position of Kurdistan as a buffer zone between the Ottoman and Safavid spheres of influence? Connected to the judgements made in answering these problems is a series of related questions generated by the centre/periphery distinction. Who truly exercised power in Kurdistan? Where did the determining

---

7. The articles under discussion are Zeki (1947/2005); Van Bruinessen (1988); Özoğlu (1996); Kılıç (1999); Özkan (2001); Sinclair (2003); Öz (2003) and Çem (2005).

agency reside, with the Ottoman state or with the regional actors? How and whom did actors resist? Finally, and often unstated, the findings of the individual texts are articulated with [interpretations of] the present situation in Kurdistan. Thus the corpus is also latently concerned with what the contemporary consequences of the perceived political dynamic should be.

Let us look at some of the answers of the corpus to this very limited range of questions. Öz's history is a cautious account that attempts to track the changing balance of political authority in the *hükümet* of Bitlis in the sixteenth and seventeenth centuries. Nevertheless, the article's express aim is to delimit the apparent autonomy of the *hükümet*s as described in the legal decrees, by arguing that the power of the central government or its provincial appointees was the dominant force unless otherwise obstructed or appropriated by Kurdish lords in 'temporary period[s] of decentralization' (Öz 2003: 153). On the other hand, Öz also draws attention to the resilience of the powerful pre-Ottoman families throughout the period. Kılıç too seeks to investigate the extent to which the formal features of the *ocaklık* category were applied in the regions denoted as such. His claim, much less cautious, is that if the bestowal of autonomy was not quite a dead letter, the Ottoman state only ever extended the privileges of formal autonomy to regional lords (he is careful never to mention the word *Kurdish*) for instrumental reasons. Similarly he is concerned to stress that the state's apparent devolving of authority to powerful local families should not be thought of as revealing administrative weakness but, on the contrary, as being merely a precaution to secure their obedience and strengthen central authority in areas where for various reasons it did not have total control. His conclusion should be quoted:

> The *ocaklık* and *hükümet sancak*s only had responsibility in times of war, and the *bey*s and their men were always in turn under the authority of the provincial governors. Apart from this they had no responsibilities and in contemporary terms did not possess autonomy... Because of certain political needs, the Ottoman state thought to benefit from the dominance of these local lords, and therefore initiated this form of administrative unity. However the lords were never allowed the scope to act without the central authority's supervision... In order to establish security, political stability and military order the local lords were officially authorized to perform the state's duties as part of their service to the state. Thus in these regions the tribes were generally prevented from creating internal strife, and like the classic authorized governors of the provinces, the majority of them performed faithful service to the state. (Kılıç 1999: 136–7) (my translation)

For Kılıç then, the sole actor with political agency was the Ottoman state, which delegated at its discretion and under close supervision some of its authority to local notables. In his account the power (and the Kurdishness) of the region's actors are eliminated, as is their autonomy. Local *bey*s faithfully obeyed the well-intentioned and all-powerful central authority. Kılıç makes no mention of the diplomacy of

Idris Bitlisi, or of the agency of Kurdish lords in switching their allegiance from Ottomans to Safavids or vice versa for money or titles. (Matthee 2003, for example, relates the career of a certain prince Taymur Khan, who in Iranian Kurdistan in 1578 transformed his support from the Safavids to the Ottomans in return for an annual sum of 100,000 *akçes*, contributing to the Persian stereotype of Kurdish unreliability.) Writing from the perspective of the centralized State, Kılıç's is a history of regional obedience that equates the political agency of local notables with treachery. Easy as it is to discern in his construction of the past clear if unspoken advice to 'Eastern Anatolians' in the present, the influence of the present in his narrative of the past is also apparent.

In fact, depending partly on the particular years of the sixteenth and seventeenth century under examination, most of the texts of the corpus (barring Kılıç and Özkan below) find evidence for both regional independence and the influence of Ottoman provincial appointees.

Sinclair (2003) and Özoğlu (1996) are more nuanced in their discussion of the relative autonomy of the Kurdish principalities. Sinclair's article discusses the Kurdish principalities of the Lake Van region (and after 1548, of the new Ottoman province of Van), in particular the *sancak* of Bitlis throughout the sixteenth century. He argues that apart from Bitlis, the land of the Kurdish principalities in Van were never surveyed, and hence despite the designation of some of the Van *sancaks* as *ocaklık*, they were in fact all *hükümet* in 'respect of rights granted and exercised' (Sinclair 2003: 138). Yet Sinclair also notes that in certain circumstances the power of the princes was undermined, most particularly by the interference of the *beylerbeyis* in the hereditary succession. His considered conclusion on the integration of the Kurdish regions is that 'the attempt to marry the *sancak* system with the tribal principalities and their hereditary institutions resulted in something unstable and difficult to control' (Sinclair 2003: 142).

Quite apart from the struggle over political hegemony however, Sinclair also finds that *kızılbaş* insurrections throughout the sixteenth century in Anatolia meant Kurdistan took on the nature of an ideological (doctrinal) barrier between the Safavids and non-Sunni elements further to the west. Accordingly the Ottomans tolerated the Shafii legal school of the Kurds, and the *mufti* (legal jurist) of Bitlis was not of the Ottoman Hanefi school of jurisprudence but of the Shafii rite, appointed by the Kurdish ruler (Van Bruinessen 1988: 27). Nevertheless, the Sunni sympathies of the Kurdish emirates were not the only reason for their choosing of the Ottoman 'yoke' over that of the Safavids. According to Van Bruinessen and Özkan, the Ottoman promise to restore lands and titles previously given by Safavid Shah Ismail to 'governors chosen from the Kizil-bash (sic) tribes' (Minorsky 1927: 457) was more important. By contrast, Çem's construction of the incorporation of the regions populated by Kurds into the Ottoman empire denies their buffer status, at least as regards the region of Dersim. Indeed, for the *Kızılbaş* Dersim Kurds, the Ottomans were a 'foreign, repressive and colonial power' (Çem 2005: 23). The autonomy sought by Dersim's Alevi Kurds occurred not because of a religious affinity but because of a religious antagonism: 'the language of the state was not their language; its religion was not their religion; [nor was] its culture and law theirs' (Çem 2005: 23) (my translation). For Çem the essentially oppressive and thus always resisted politics of the Ottomans towards Kurds in Dersim were continued after the 1923 institution of the Turkish republic, yet now extended moreover to all the Kurdish regions. Indeed, founded by Ottoman cadres and through Ottoman institutions, the Turkish republic was a continuation of the empire, not a new state. 'From that perspective, it is not wrong to call [them] the new Ottomans' (Çem 2005: 24) (my translation). Çem's historical narrative implies the opposite advice to that of Kılıc's (above): given this history, Alevi Kurds should disobey and resist the ongoing assimilation policies of the ill-intentioned republican Ottomans.

Özoğlu like Sinclair focuses on the question of the 'tribalness' of the Kurdish emirates, although he too does not examine the internal workings of the 'hereditary institutions'. More explicitly than Sinclair, Özoğlu argues that Idris Bitlisi's linking of selected Kurdish principalities to Ottoman rule not only contributed to the strengthening of those princes' positions vis-à-vis rivals and subjects, but was the determining factor in the very formation of the powerful Kurdish tribal confederacies. Describing the Ottomans' strategy as a 'unite-and-rule' policy, the centralized confederations of tribes were at least partially created by the state. Consequently, the authority of their Kurdish lords was reinforced through state patronage. Perhaps most significantly, Özoğlu's history gestures towards the 'Ottomanization' of the principalities (although he doesn't use the term), noting that their elaborated forms of stratification replicated the structure of the Ottoman state. Beyond this however, the internal and external dynamics constituting the confederations are left disconnected.

Van Bruinessen's long introduction to the English translation of Evliya Çelebi's visit to Diyarbakır in 1655, some 140 years or so after the city's Ottoman 'conquest', covers the greatest range of topics in the corpus, with sections on the ethnic composition and population of the city, its economic life, and its religious education. However, it too begins its discussion with an examination of the administrative arrangements of the province and of the degree of autonomy of the Kurdish rulers. Van Bruinessen's reading of Evliya's description of his visit to the five *hükümet*s of the Diyarbakır province is that, despite the century and longer incorporation of the emirates into the Ottoman administrative system, the autonomy of the hereditary Kurdish princely families was 'still quite considerable' (Van Bruinessen 1988: 27). By contrast, Özoğlu interprets Evliya Çelebi's account as showing that the *hükümet*s 'had lost a great degree of autonomy' (Özoğlu 1996: 13). For Van Bruinessen the longevity of the emirates is mainly due to ongoing Kurdish resistance to Ottoman interference, whereas for Kılıç delegation of authority was only ever a utilitarian Ottoman strategy. Interestingly Özoğlu, Van Bruinessen and Zeki (following the *Sherefname*) all draw attention to the role of Idris Bitlisi in 'winning the Kurdish rulers for the Ottomans' (Van Bruinessen 1988: 14), thus emphasizing accordingly their voluntary assent to the Ottoman project rather than their forced incorporation into it via military conquest. The agreement brokered by Bitlisi is seen as of mutual benefit to both the Sultan and the Kurdish princes. Özoğlu writes that Idris 'used his intermediary position productively for both the Ottoman state and the Kurdish chieftains. Kurdish *beys*, becoming part of a larger and stronger political structure, secured and consolidated their political power over their subjects' (Özoğlu 1996: 14). Zeki's reference to Idris Bitlisi is also worth repeating:

> Idris of Bitlis was the famous Kurd who engineered the internal administration of Kurdistan. This was also advantageous to the Ottoman state. He established a federation (the unified *hükümets* and the unified provinces) that prepared the foundations of Kurdish nationalism. In the process he also protected the regional Kurdish emirates. Despite this, he was unable to prevent these emirates from quarrelling and eventually from going to war with each other. If cooperation and an alliance between those emirates had occurred, a much more secure future for the Kurds would have ensued. (Zeki 1947/2005: 151) (my translation)

Finally, not all of the writings in the corpus that mention Idris Bitlisi's mediation are equally enamoured with his achievement.[8] In a long article in the newspaper *Özgür Politika* (see note 9, Chapter 1) written on the anniversary of the 1639 treaty (17 May) between the Safavids and Ottomans, Özkan argues that with its signing Kurdistan was split in two, as well as turned into a colony (colonized). The motivation for the 'incorporation' of Kurdish territory into the Ottoman empire was not only to produce a buffer zone limiting the ability of the Safavid state to incite *kızılbaş* rebellion in Anatolia but the occupation and exploitation of Kurdistan itself.[9] Logically therefore, Idris Bitlisi acted as an agent of the 'Ottoman-Turks' (sic), who also wished to use the Kurdish princes against the Safavids. In Özkan's words:

> Idris Bitlisi played a major role in creating and relaying propaganda favourable to the Ottomans [against the Safavids]. Sultan Selim needed someone who was both very familiar with Kurdish customs and traditions as well as with their internal social relations, and who was also well-respected by the Kurds. For this reason Idris Bitlisi was given the duty of and rewarded for constructing a Kurdish alliance against the Safavid state. (Özkan 2001: 2) (my translation)

As with a number of the texts, Özkan then goes on to summarize the main points of the legal treaty struck between the Kurdish emirs and the Ottoman empire. Unlike

8. Similarly see Vali who argues that the princes' partial autonomy obstructed independence from 'Persian and Ottoman overlords', initiating forms of clientistic ties with extra-regional states that continue to this day (Vali 1996).

9. Allouche by contrast stresses a broader geopolitical context for the Ottoman-Safavid conflict, 'including the relations of the [Ottomans and Safavids] with the other Muslim powers in the area on the one hand, and with Western Christendom on the other' (Allouche 1983: 148).

Öz, Kılıç and Özoğlu however, Özkan directly 'ethnicizes' the treaty: hence the promises that 'Kurds will help the Turks in their wars', and 'Turks will protect the Kurds from all outside attacks' (Özkan 2001: 3). He also argues that the centralizing policies of Sultan Süleyman continually sought to curtail the agreed autonomy of the emirates. Like Kılıç, but for the opposite reasons, Özkan too emphasizes state action, the Ottomans gaining despotic control over Kurdistan by deceitfully promising its princes not to interfere in their internal affairs. Like Kılıç, but again for different reasons, he minimizes Kurdish agency or self-interest. The feudal structure of the Kurdish emirates, their tribal loyalties, and the personal rivalries between their princes, combined with Ottoman oppression, resulted in minimal progress towards the founding of an independent Kurdish state.

It is clear, then, that the overwhelming concern of this somewhat arbitrarily collated textual corpus has been the *political* consequences of the Ottoman-Kurdish encounter. And yet in the process, and despite the importance of this issue, the corpus' constructing of the Kurdish Ottoman history of the sixteenth and seventeenth centuries has also obscured a number of other vital social processes. Indeed, even on the political level, the imaginative focus of the corpus is strikingly narrow. The political faultline of interest is that between the imperial centre and the peripheral elite, nearly always analysed as a zero-sum relation. There is therefore no consideration, say, of farmer resistance to fief holders or princes, or of peasant compliance with codified rights and obligations, or of revolts other than those of the emirates' princes.[10] Neither is there any use of provincial court records as an entrée into local forms of governance and political negotiation, or as a way into the construction and practice of 'gender' issues involved in the relations of power and affection that characterize marriage, divorce, sexuality, inheritance etc.[11] Indeed, none of the articles even mention the *kadi*, or take an interest in the workings and decisions of Islamic institutions in Kurdistan like the *sharia* court. Again, the corpus' narrow presentation of the local elites evinces little curiosity about whether or how Kurdish princes sought to become Ottoman, or about their interpretation and appropriation of Ottoman legitimacy. But why not also Kurdish Ottomans, or an Ottomanist provincial society?[12] The assumption of their polarity leads to

10. Amy Singer's (1994) analysis of the tax surveys (*tahrir*), imperial decrees (*ferman*) and court records (*sijill*) involving rural social relations in the province of Jerusalem in the very same period shows how the 'weapons of the weak', such as the peasants, might be studied.

11. Here I have in mind Judith Tucker's (2000) exemplary study *In the House of the Law: Gender and Islamic Law in Ottoman Syria and Palestine* as an example. But see also Gerber 1980 for a study of the Bursa kadi records in the 1600s in relation to women's economic status.

12. See Michael Meeker's (2004) research on the appropriation of Ottoman military and religious institutions, and equally importantly of the Ottoman political culture, by the eastern Black Sea local lords (*derebeys*) in the late seventeenth- and eighteenth-century period of decentralization. Meeker examines the 'migration of power' from provincial appointees to regional lords, describing them as 'usurpers' of the tactics of political power of the Ottoman centre.

a focus on *either* the power of the Ottoman Sultans *or* of the Kurdish princes, on Ottoman identity *or* Kurdish identity. Further, apart from Van Bruinessen, there is little interest in social relations or institutions that transcend the Kurdish regions or link them with other places, such as in the travels of Kurdish scholars or *ulema*, or more broadly in what Faroqhi calls the inhabitation of a common world, given the similarity of trade and petty commodity production all over the empire (Faroqhi 2004: 211). Finally, the perspective of the corpus is determinedly macro, pitched at a level where the understandings, practices and capacity for agency of individuals are of little account.

Why is this the case? Why is the imagining of Kurdish Ottoman history and identity reduced in the texts to an obsession with the extent of and reasons for the emirs' political autonomy? Clearly the writers fear that Kurdistan's historical status, whether independent of or loyal to 'outside' authority as the case may be, is paradigmatic for the present. Thus if the Kurdish rulers have always been fiercely independent, what of the Turkish and Iranian republic's claims to sovereignty over the region? On the other hand, if they have always been loyally obedient, what of Kurdish nationalism's claims for a separate status or state? There is thus a nationalist anxiety – Turkish, Kurdish and Persian – revealed in the corpus. That this anxiety reflects the post-Ottoman nation building that has violently re-structured the region is clear. Indeed the *significance* of the autonomy of the Kurdish emirates (however relative) derives from the linking of the concept to the wider vocabulary of nationalism as a political ideology. Yet the nationalist imaginary that informs the corpus also reduces the richness and suffering of the lives of Kurdish men and women merely to power relations organized through the state. In this narrowing down of the political imagination, other relations of domination and resistance are obscured. What all these insufficiencies suggest is that current perceptions of the Ottoman and Safavid history of the Kurdish provinces (most importantly Diyarbakır, Van, Mosul and Shahrizur) are refracted through a nationalist prism.

Curtailing Kurdish Autonomy: Deconstructing Ottoman 'Modernism'

As a generalization, the discourse on Kurdish history and identity agrees on the importance of a number of past occurrences or 'real' events. Nevertheless, if there is a standardized listing of key experiences, the narrative significance of each of them is constantly and bitterly debated. Although this 'gap' between an event and its multitude of interpretations is typical of historiography in general, the seeming standardization of key moments in the production of historical knowledge by and about Kurds makes this gap seem even more striking. Let me briefly trace the most commonly repeated landmarks of Kurdish historical experience, before examining more particularly how the discourse on Kurdishness imagines the 'second' critical incorporation and transformation of Kurdistan in the nineteenth century.

As we have seen with the monopolists in Chapter 1, writers often begin with a discussion, extensive or otherwise, of the origins of the Kurds. This discussion acknowledges its lack of documentary sources to varying degrees. History 'proper' is invariably said to begin with the Arab Muslim invasions of the region in the seventh century, when the term *ekrad* (Arabic plural of Kurd) is mentioned in the Arabic sources. Accounts of the associated process of the conversion of the majority of Kurds to Islam are bitterly contested.[13] Next often comes comment on the dissolution of a number of eleventh-century Kurdish dynasties (most importantly the Marwanids and the Shaddadids) and the devastation of Kurdish society by the invasions of the Mongols and Turkoman tribes in the thirteenth to sixteenth centuries is deplored. The treaty in the early sixteenth century with the Ottomans that consolidated an extended period of Kurdish rulers' autonomy in Kurdistan is accorded tremendous importance. As we have seen, the outcomes and significance of the agreement are disputed. Nevertheless and despite the treaty, Kurdistan is also presented as a battlefield in wars between the Ottomans and Safavids, implicated in contributing to its underdevelopment. Finally nearly all accounts then jump to the nineteenth century as the next locus of significant historical action, where the crushing of Kurdish rebellions by soldiers of the reconstituted Ottoman army brings to an end the autonomy of the Kurdish principalities. The destruction of the *hükümet*s is often seen as influential in paving the way for the increased presence of the Sufi brotherhoods (*tarikat*s) and their leaders (*Şeyh*s) in Kurdish society and political life. Accordingly the nationalism or otherwise of the rebellions of both the emirs (in the 1840s) and the *Şeyh*s (in the 1880s) is contested, as is their role in preparing the ground for a Kurdish nationalist identity to emerge.

How is the pre-history of these crucial nineteenth-century revolts imagined? In a brief footnote at the end of his article on Kurdish and Ottoman relations, Özoğlu (1996) notes that regardless of the case in the sixteenth century, by the eighteenth century the Kurdish emirates were virtually independent from Istanbul. The assumption of declining Ottoman power and political de-centralization after the glories of the mid fifteenth and sixteenth centuries is not his alone: many writings on the empire and on the Kurdish region assume both a collapse of imperial control and a re-assertion of provincial and Kurdish autonomy that continued until nearly the middle of the nineteenth century. In the weakening of a centralized state system, this independence of the seventeenth- and eighteenth-century Kurdish principalities is usually interpreted in the discourse on Kurds as a reassertion of feudal and/or tribal structures, whose structure in turn is commonly related to the ecological conditions of the region. Much less often is it treated as a consequence of the local

---

13. See for example the debate between Rohat (1991) and Malmisanij (1991) over the forced conversion of the Kurds to Islam via the sword, religion as an obstacle in the present to the national liberation struggle and most heatedly over the work of the Said-i Nursi, an influential Muslim thinker of Kurdish origins in republican Turkey.

ruling elite's increased participation in a less dynastic and much more decentralized Ottoman imperial system. Indeed, as a generalization we might say that discourse on pre-nineteenth-century Kurdish history consistently stresses the difference between the Kurdish regions and the Ottoman empire to be symptomatic of their *separation*, rather than as resulting from their continuing yet changing *relationship*. The assumption that Kurdistan's particularity in the seventeenth and eighteenth centuries derives from its disconnection from the imperial space might be sustainable – but it is usually stated with minimal comparative analysis of the experience of the Kurdish regions in the light of developments in the empire as a whole, or of changes and transformations in provinces like ilk.[14]

Beyond the issue of the Kurdish emirates' independence, however, the discourse on Kurdish identity shows a striking unified disinterest in late seventeenth-, eighteenth- and early nineteenth-century Ottoman Kurdistan, revealing again how the question of the princes' autonomy has dominated the historiography. Changes to Kurdish political autonomy aside, it is as if in these years nothing else of importance had occurred. Yet paradoxically this autonomy is often also represented as a millstone around the neck of an emerging Kurdish nation-state. Kutschera's introduction to his book *Kürt Ulusal Hareketi* (The Kurdish National Movement) is a good example:

> At the beginning of the 19th century when nationalism, a completely new phenomenon for Kurdistan, began to dominate the [political] agenda, Kurdish society had not developed beyond the form described by Şerefxan Bitlisi [in *Şerefname*] in 1596. The old and aristocratic lords, living in mansions that resembled the feudal mansions of the European Middle Ages, ruled over the Kurdish villagers, the Kurdified or Christian population, the soldiers, and the settled, half-settled or nomadic tribes. In this mountainous country, especially in the absence of [trafficable] transportation routes, state officials could only exceptionally overcome the hegemony of the lords. Even if the principalities were successful in maintaining their autonomy there was no available words for 'state' and 'nation' in the Kurdish language. (Kutschera 2001: 18) (my translation)

Further and ironically, given my comment above about Kurdistan's asserted exceptionalism, this narrative of the 'silence' (Yılmaz 1991: 39) or of the 'frozen

14. See Meeker (2002) for the appropriation of the functions of central government (taxing commerce, raising armies, requisitioning supplies, imposing labour, exacting punishment, etc.) by local elites in the seventeenth and eighteenth centuries for the province of Trabzon. His claim is that this is a widening of participation in imperial institutions leading to the generation of a new 'state society', and not an expression or reassertion of a local political system. Somewhat similarly, Hathaways' study of Ottoman Egypt in the seventeenth and eighteenth centuries revises the standard approach to the domination of the local lords (*beyler*) by denying that it is a throwback 'to the conditions prevailing at the end of the Mamluk sultanate, just before the Ottoman conquest' (Hathaway 1997: 15). Kurdistan is not Trabzon or Egypt of course: nevertheless, similarities between imperial provinces caught up in the same broader political and economic processes should be considered before Kurdistan is claimed to be an exception.

dynamism' (Kendal 1980: 25) of seventeenth- and eighteenth-century Kurdish society and history conforms in a clear way to an older and discredited account of the empire's disintegration and decline in the same period.[15] For Inalcık (1973) and Lewis (1961) most famously, with the corruption of the highly developed administrative system of the regime's 'classical age', the empire enters its long terminal phase, which, despite heroic attempts at renewal, is only put out of its misery by the Kemalist revolution, when 'the Turks [sic] finally abandoned this concept of state' (Inalcık 1973: 4). For 'while ... Europe was ridding itself of all forms of medievalism, the Ottoman Empire clung ever more zealously to the traditional forms of near-eastern civilization ... The Ottomans, convinced of their own religious and political superiority, closed their eyes to the outside world' (Inalcık 1973: 52). Compare this with Kendal's comment on why the Kurdish people were unable to seize the moment and create an independent state in seemingly propitious circumstances in 1919:

> They were unfortunately still at a stage of development in which the only leadership to emerge was far more susceptible to clerical and feudal influences than any other. Torn as it was by the conflict between traditionalists and modernists ... this leadership could not rise to the occasion. The task of building a national state was beyond its capacities: it lacked the necessary historical and political intelligence. Those whom one could consider as the 'radicals' of their time were in fact *Ottoman* intellectuals, products of Ottoman culture, with all that implies in terms of a philosophical and political conception of the world. (Kendal 1980: 39)

For Inalcık and Kendal respectively, these stagnant, localized and insular seventeenth and eighteenth century social orders could only be salvaged by the introjection of a new form of politics entirely, by a dose of Turkish and Kurdish nationalism. Universal history, when not artificially obstructed (as in the case of Kurdistan), evolves inevitably towards the formation of the modern nation-state. Most significantly, for both writers the empire and Kurdistan are positioned as '*pre-*' national in the seventeenth and eighteenth centuries and it is via this vision that their insufficiencies and specificities are imagined.

Nevertheless, despite his exaggerated disconnection of the Kurdish provinces from imperial developments and practices, Kutschera's identification of the early nineteenth century as harbinger of radical change in the Kurdish regions is shared by many. His hinting that these changes will be instrumental in the development of the words 'state' and 'nation' in the Kurdish language is also widely argued. In the rest of this section I want to explore how the discourse on Kurdishness imagines or represents a second vital process or series of events, the transformation of the Kurdish provinces throughout the nineteenth century in conjunction with Ottoman

---

15. For a contrasting argument see Abou-El-Haj (1991), and his analysis of the critical transformation – emphatically not decline – of the social formation of the Ottoman empire in the seventeenth century.

imperial 'Reordering' (*Tanzimat*), first announced as a coherent policy for the Ottoman territories in 1839.

Briefly, what were the Ottoman *Tanzimat* reforms, which are represented as triggering much of the chaos in the Kurdish provinces? Perhaps the best short summary is Deringil's, who writes that the institutions of the modern state – mass schooling, a postal service, railways, lighthouses, clock towers, lifeboats, museums, censuses and birth certificates, passports and parliaments – were all aspects of, or constituted after, the *Tanzimat* (Deringil 1998: 9). If none of these seem on the surface to be particularly threatening, their underlying logic was an attempt to increase the 'infrastructural power' of the Ottoman state. Citing Michael Mann, Rogan (1999: 3) defines infrastructural power as 'the capacity of the state to actually penetrate civil society, and to implement logistically political decisions throughout the realm'. In the wake of territorial losses in the Balkans, including the proclamation of an independent Greece in 1830, *Tanzimat* reformers placed a new importance on consolidating control over the eastern peripheries of the empire, including the extension of direct government rule over frontier provinces. In the same period the Qajar dynasty too was seeking to increase its infrastructural power over its non-Persian territories (see McDowall 2000).

Although in the first instance the consequences of the *Tanzimat* on the Kurdish regions was a series of Kurdish rebellions, the reasons for and the motivations of these revolts have been intensely debated. Let me quickly illustrate the period of the Kurdish uprisings with two examples.

One of the most famous of the Kurdish revolts against the Ottomans [in Kurdistan] in the nineteenth century is that of Bedir Khan, emir of the powerful Botan confederacy. Virtually all Kurdish histories discuss his rebellion, and the political activity of his sons and grandsons, who were afterwards influential figures in a number of Kurdish nationalist organizations, as well as founders of the first Kurdish newspaper. They were also important members of the nationalist movement Xoybun (Independence), established in Syria in 1927, and implicated in the rebellion in the Mt Ararat region of north-eastern Turkey between 1928–30 that proclaimed the 'Kurdish Republic of Ararat' (Fuccaro 2003: 199). Analysis of the key actors involved in Bedir Khan's revolt provides some idea of the complex political interactions contributing to its denouement, and are revealing of the eastern aspect of the 'Eastern Question' – the phrase given by the Great Powers to the 'problem' of the besieged Ottoman empire and its Christian minorities in the nineteenth century. According to McDowell, Bedir Khan became Emir of Botan in 1820, remaining loyal at first to Ottoman authority. In 1839 he was awarded official rank in the Ottoman army for a campaign against the rebellious governor of Eygpt. The subsequent rout of the Ottoman troops emboldened him and he began to enlarge his sphere of influence in Kurdistan by bringing under his authority the territory and tribes from former emirates (Baban and Rawanduz) already suppressed by Istanbul. He also took advantage of a schism in the emirate of Hakkari, which involved the large Nestorian Christian tribes in the area and their split alignment to different contenders to the leadership. The Nestorian Assyrians, too, were in schism, partly due to the influence of Protestant missionaries. On the pretext of Assyrian disloyalty Bedir Khan marched on the Nestorian region in 1843, massacring its inhabitants. He invaded again in 1844. Although the Ottoman governors had most likely encouraged the attack, they were happy to receive the expected sharp protests by Britain and France and to move against Bedir Khan in response. Following his defeat of the first Ottoman expedition against him, Bedir Khan announced himself independent of the empire, minting coins in his own name. A second and larger force besieged his fortress in Eruh for eight months in 1845, and upon his surrender he and his family were exiled to Crete.

Of equal importance to the literature on Kurdish history is the revolt of Sheihk (*Şeyh*) Ubeydullah some forty years later in 1880, son of an influential Nakşibendi leader who became in turn 'spiritual leader of Kurdistan' (Kendal 1980: 31). *Şeyh* Ubeydullah began his movement in the wake of the Russo-Turkish war of 1877–8, when the ravages of Ottoman regulars no longer paid by the government in Kurdish towns resulted in a severe famine in northern Kurdistan. The *Şeyh* both demanded compensation from Istanbul for damages and began to collect weapons for his campaign. He was also concerned by clauses in the Berlin Treaty, signed by the Ottomans in 1878 to end the war, that promised to take preventative measures to protect eastern Armenians and Nestorians (Özoğlu 2005: 97). Assembling 220 tribal leaders and their supporters together in Şemdinan, *Şeyh* Ubeydullah formed (according to the Armenian Patriarchate) the 'Kurdish Tribal League'. Under his command the combined force attacked Iran, declaring in the process an independent Kurdistan and taking control of much of the same areas in south-eastern Turkey and north-eastern Iran as Bedir Khan had forty years earlier (Olson 1996: 127). He also sent what has become the most famous letter in Kurdish history to the British Vice-Consul in Başkale:

> The Kurdish nation ... is a people apart. Their religion is different [from that of others], and their laws and customs are distinct... The chiefs and rulers of Kurdistan, whether Turkish or Persian subjects, and the inhabitants of Kurdistan, one and all are united and agreed that matters cannot be carried on this way with the two governments [Ottoman and Qajar] and that necessarily something must be done, so that European Governments having understood the matter, shall inquire into our state. We are a nation apart. We want our affairs to be in our hands. (cited in McDowell 2000: 53)

The revolt, however, soon became embroiled in the continuing politics of the four influential state powers in the region (Russia, Britain, the Ottomans and Qajar Iran), and with the withdrawal of British support and the threat of a joint military attack from both the Qajar and Ottoman armies at the same time, Ubeydullah surrendered to the Sublime Porte (Göktaş 1991: 19). He was exiled to Mecca in 1882.

Much more than the details of events, however, the motivations and objectives of these and other uprisings have been of constant concern. Were these Kurdish nationalistic movements or not? What did they seek to institute? What relationships were there between the 'feudal' economic and political structures of Kurdistan and these rebellions? Sometimes the debate proceeds by identifying as an ideal type the constituting components of nationalism, and then asking to what extent these revolts conformed to the model. Contrasting definitions of nationalism lead of course to different conclusions. Other writers bring different criteria to bear. For example, *Şeyh* Ubeydullah's revolt is argued by White (2000) and Olson (1996) to be the first *authentic* Kurdish nationalist movement, a position argued partly on the evidence of his letters, and partly on anthropological theories about his religious status allowing him to mediate between and transcend the 'narrow' tribal interests supposedly dominating previous rebellions.[16] By contrast Özoğlu (2005) and Strohmeier (2003) are inclined to see in his revolt more Ottomanist aims of political autonomy, based on Ubeydullah's apparent desire to be recognized by the central government as the paramount authority in Kurdistan, and because of his expressed loyalty to the Sultan. A third, more Marxist-influenced, perspective attempts to make a synthesis between an 'objective' stress on feudal relations in Kurdistan (between peasants/tribesmen, their princes and the Sultan) and a 'subjective' acknowledgement of nationalist sentiments. One particularly interesting treatment in such vein is that of Yılmaz (1991).

Perhaps equally importantly, we need to interrogate the obsession over the question of the revolts' nationalism: why this concern for classification? Obviously the debate over the Kurdish nationalist character or otherwise of the nineteenth-century uprisings is no mere 'academic' discussion. Indeed it is clear that one of the major reasons for the emphasis on their makers' nationalistic motivations and objectives is as response to explicit or implicit accusations (after the institution of the Turkish republic) about their retrogressive and fanatical character. In his study of the changing keywords of what he calls Turkish state discourse on the Kurds, Mesud Yeğen argues that throughout the first seventy years of the republican period, the one unvarying aspect of state discourse has been the categorical denial that Kurds constitute a separate ethnic element in Turkey. Accordingly the Kurdish rebellions in the first years of the republic, particularly the uprising of the Nakşibendi *Şeyh* Said in 1925, have been perceived and constructed by both the state and historians of the Turkish republic as reactionary religious revolts seeking both to overthrow the

---

16. Both Olson and White express a profound contempt for the *Seyh*'s followers however, assuming as a matter course their ignorance, passive obedience and fanaticism. For Olson, 'many of his [the Sheikh's] illiterate and intensely religious followers (*murids*) could readily see their sheikh as a *mahdi* (messiah), a saviour come to bring justice and hopefully a better life' (Olson 1996: 130). For White, 'in so far as they were tribesmen acting completely along traditional (that is, premodern) lines, they were acting as the blind instruments of political modernization' (White 2000: 84). See Yalçın-Heckmann (1991: 109) for a critique of the assumed irrationality of followers and an argument for how people 'construct their own ethnicity or Islamic community'.

young republic and to reinstitute the Caliph and Sultan. As he says, 'it is a supreme irony that this first rebellion in the republican period was coded as a revolt seeking to re-establish the Caliph and Sultan, when the last Kurdish uprising before the institution of the republic (Şeyh Ubeydullah's?) was repressed in the name of its opposition to the Caliph and Sultan by those who would go on to found the republic' (Yeğen 1999: 132, my translation). The claim made by many writers that there is a proto-nationalist continuity between the rebellions of the two Nakşibendi religious leaders (*Şeyh* Ubeydullah in 1880 and *Şeyh* Said in 1925) and also of the *Alevi* leader Şeyh Seyyid Riza in the Dersim rebellion of 1937, counters the discourse of the Turkish republic that retrospectively constructs their continuity as inhering in a reactionary endeavour.

Finally we should draw attention to one other continuity between the Bedir Khan and *Şeyh* Ubeydullah uprisings, namely the complicated matter of their violent engagement with groups of Christians in the region. Somewhat over-simplistically, Karpat writes that the *Tanzimat* reforms 'sought to change a basic arrangement that had endured for four hundred years ... by seeking to unify a religiously diverse population under one common identity of Ottoman citizenship (Ottomanism)' (Karpat 2003: 6). Karpat's comment is especially pertinent for the empire's non-Muslims, whose protected but inferior status under Islamic law was to be potentially upgraded by the reforms.[17] But Ottomanism was to take on different meanings for many Muslim Kurdish leaders, especially after the successful attempts at centralizing Istanbul's control over the Kurdish provinces in the 1830s and 1840s. According to Strohmeier, 'the reforms and intrusions of the central government and the mounting influence of the West were seen as different aspects of the same phenomenon, a victimization of Muslims' (Strohmeier 2003: 11). At the same time the nineteenth century was also a period of intense Christian missionary activity in the Ottoman empire and particularly in its eastern provinces, where large numbers of Armenian, Nestorian (Assyrian) and Syrian Christians lived.[18] The French, British and Russian

17. Finkel notes that equality was produced more by levelling the status of Muslims to that of Christians than by raising the status of Christians to resemble Muslims. Hence rather than abolish the discriminatory head tax or 'poll tax' levied on Christians as unbelievers in lieu of their exemption from military service, the tax was now applied to all: 'Muslims and non-Muslims alike were now required to pay a graduated tax, according to the value of their land holding' (Finkel 2005: 451). Conscription of Christians into the Ottoman Navy took place in 1845 and 1847 (Finkel 2005: 455).

18. See the book *Armenians in Turkey One Hundred Years Ago* (Köker 2005) both for the population figures for Armenians of the eastern provinces and for postcards depicting the massive new interventions in the built environment of Ottoman Armenian life, including churches, missions, schools, orphanages, hospitals, shops and factories. New Ottoman government buildings too dot the cityscapes as instruments of imperial policy. The book is organized in chapters according to Ottoman province, and gives two sources for the population estimates, the Ottoman census of 1914 and the demographic data published by one Maghakia Ormanian in 1912. The census figures are invariably lower than Ormanian's, indeed sometimes significantly so. For example, for the province of Bitlis the figures are

states' vociferous guardianship of the rights traditionally extended to non-Muslims made Kurdish Muslims anxious about the possible institution of new Christian states in the eastern imperial provinces, as *Şeyh* Ubeydullah's complaint to the Ottoman district governor shows. According to British sources, upon learning of the Berlin Treaty of 1878 Ubeydullah said: 'What is this that I hear – that the Armenians will establish an independent state in Van, and that the Assyrians will unfurl English flags and declare themselves English citizens?' (Özoğlu 2005: 98, my translation). Ottoman policy under Sultan Abdulhamid II (1876–1909) was to encourage these fears.

Alongside this, the hesitant beginnings of Turkification as an Ottoman practice post-*Tanzimat* made Muslims anxious. According to Deringil again, some time in the nineteenth century the Ottoman elite 'borrowed' Western colonialism. As part of its colonial project to penetrate and reform its eastern peripheries, Ottoman discourse produced its own stock phrase to inform its 'White Man's Burden wearing a fez': tribesmen 'live in a state of nomadism and savagery' (Deringil 2003: 312, 317). This civilizing colonial project involved new models of Ottoman education for the peripheral zones, including the setting up in Istanbul of the *Aşiret Mektebi* (tribal school) for the sons of Kurdish, Arabic and Albanian community elites and, more fatefully, of a tribal corps of irregular cavalry (the *Hamidiya* regiments) in the eastern provinces. Named after their founder, Sultan Abdulhamid, the *Hamidiye* cavalry units received arms and training from Istanbul. According to the Porte, these units were to be 'deployed against Armenian brigands' (Deringil 1996: 16). The Sunni Kurdish chiefs who chose to participate received various forms of exemption from taxes, and sometimes tax-collecting rights on local Armenian villages (McDowell 2000: 60). One consequence of this anti-Armenian policy of the Ottoman state was the intimate involvement of these regiments in both the massacres of Armenian in the 1890s and in their mass deportation in 1915 and after, which were to result in the deaths of up to a million Armenians (Bloxham 2005: 10).

In brief, what the *combination* of these political and cultural projects produced in the Kurdish regions post-*Tanzimat* was a transformation of alliances – both intended and unintended – and an escalation of violence and murder, which in turn impacted back upon the new ethnic, religious and national identities being forged in the region. Russian, European *and* Ottoman imperialists, Christian missionaries, and the nuanced reactions to and attempted appropriations of these imperial and cultural projects by local actors (in this case by Armenians and Kurds in particular) resulted in new interactions between groups and individuals, culminating not only in *Hamidiye*

114,132 Armenians in the Ottoman census and 165,000 in Ormanian (p. 348). For Van province the discrepancies are even more striking: 67,792 and 121,700 respectively (p. 352). The book also divides up the Armenian population according to Christian denomination (Orthodox, Catholic or Protestant), showing the varying impact of missionaries across the region.

Kurds' involvement in the Young Turk government's forced deportation and killing of Armenians but the involvement of other Kurdish tribesmen as well.[19]

Victims and Actors: Remembering Kurdish–Armenian Relations

Because of the participation of Kurdish regiments in the CUP's (Committee of Union and Progress) decision in 1915 to ethnically cleanse Armenians from the empire's critical eastern provinces, this final section of Chapter 2 needs to address one further crucial element in the discourse on Kurdish identity, the representation of Armenians in the imagining of Kurdistan. This is obviously a sensitive issue and deserves a comprehensive treatment in itself, as does the politics of Kurdish historiographies that choose to minimize Kurdistan's linguistic, religious and ethnic diversity. It also raises one critical question: what's in a name?

In short order, how are Armenians represented in the variable discourse on Kurdistan? Sometimes it is the absence of Armenians in presentations of Kurdish history that is most important, emblematic of the violent and intolerant processes of nation-building in the region that have repressed Kurds as well. Other texts imagining Kurdistan ignore the historic presence of Armenians in the 'Kurdish/ Ottoman' provinces, or mention the genocide of Armenians without acknowledging the role of Kurds in its realization.[20] Very often it is the Western imperialist powers that are made responsible for bringing local people (Kurds, Armenians, Assyrians) to enmity against each other. (This same narrative, but with a stress on the humanistic treatment of Armenians by justice-loving Turkish states, is adhered to by Turkish nationalists – see for example Şahin 1988.) Occasionally an eternal rivalry is posited between these groups (i.e. Yüksel 1993.) Yet at other times a discourse of the shared historical experience of suffering has envisioned a solidarity of the oppressed linking Kurds and Armenians. The varied emphases of these historical constructions testify in a banal way to the unfinished politics of assigning responsibility for the organized murder of Armenians, given the plurality of actors involved in a period now objectified and sanitized as *transitional* in the change from empire to Middle Eastern nation states. Further and not surprisingly, the imagining of Armenian history and the claims for a greater Armenia by Armenian nationalists has also involved in

---

19. See Bozarslan (2003a) for one of the frankest discussions of the complex development of Armenian-Kurdish, or Muslim/non-Muslim relations leading up to the 'massive Kurdish participation in the extermination of the Armenians'. The quote is from p.171. For an incisive dissection of the killings and an argument asserting the moral responsibility of the great powers but the legal responsibility of the CUP Ottoman government respectively for 'genocide' see Bloxham 2005. One might also note the constant attempt by Turkish nationalists and certain institutions of the Turkish state to reduce the debate to a political issue centred on a supposed historic dislike or envy of Turks.

20. Hassanpour writes for instance that 'After the genocide of the Armenian nation in 1915, the Ottoman government began a deportation program in Kurdistan' (Hassanpour 1992: 58).

turn a discourse on Kurds and on the territory constructed as 'Kurdistan'. The historiographical discourse of Kurdish nationalism sometimes indirectly addresses their arguments in response.

One initial way of concentrating our discussion is by very selectively sampling how the discourse on Kurds has interpreted two foundational texts for narrating Kurdish political history, the *Şerefname* of Şeref Han (1597) and the seventeenth-century 'travel-epic' or *Seyahatname* of Ottoman Evliya Çelebi (1655).[21] Şeref Han's *Şerefname* is a history of the various Kurdish emirates and notable Kurdish families and their contribution to general life in Kurdistan at the turn of the seventeenth century. Its introduction casts a more quizzical eye over various contradictory stories concerning the origins of the Kurds than many later texts.[22] For Şeref Han (who was also former Emir of Bitlis), the admirable Kurdish preference for independence (and the less admirable propensity for conflict) had prevented until then the emergence of a united Kurdish kingdom or state.

As an illustration let us look at just one important writer on Kurdish literature, Amir Hassanpour, and his use of the *Şerefname* and *Seyahatname*. Hassanpour (2003: 14) interprets the *Şerefname* as presenting Kurdistan 'as a geo-ethnic entity belonging to the Kurds', as well as voicing a Kurdish 'national feeling' (a nationalism) against foreign domination (Hassanpour 1992: 56). In keeping perhaps with the *Şerefname* itself that mentions the Christians of the region only in passing, Hassanpour presents what he calls the Kurdish 'national awakening' expressed in the book as produced in relation to the foreign domination of Ottoman Turks and Iranians.[23] But why not also

---

21. *Şerefname* was first translated by Emin Bozarslan into Turkish from an Arabic translation (it was written in Persian) and published in a popular edition in 1971. The author was arrested and tried as a result, accused of 'making propaganda aimed at destroying or endangering [Turkey's] national feeling on the basis of race' (Introduction to Şeref Han 1597/1990: 535).

22. For example, Şeref Han describes as 'bizarre' an account of the prophet Muhammed's cursing of the Kurds to internal conflict because of his dislike of the ugliness of a Kurdish envoy to him (Şeref Han 1597/1990: 24). Incredibly, Ankara University historian Aydın Taneri uses this very story to show that the Kurds were a Turkish tribe aligned to the first historic 'Turkish' state (the Oğuz Han), because the story (anachronistically) says that the envoy was from the court of Oğuz Han king Mete (200BC). Accordingly Taneri concludes that the origins of the Kurds lie in Turkistan. See Taneri 1983: 5ff. Note Taneri's date of publication, not long after the 1980 military coup and in a period of greater-than-usual state emphasis on the Turkish descent of Kurds and thus of the lack of ground for any special rights.

23. Hassanpour also ignores how Şeref Han's history of the distinguished rulers of Kurdistan is related to the huge increase in Ottoman historiography written in the very same period. According to Piterberg, by the end of the sixteenth century three subgenres of Ottoman historiography had emerged: 'The first comprised works confined to a single event or reign... The second was the *Tarih-i Al-i Osman* [Histories of the Ottman dynasty] in straightforward Ottoman Turkish. The third consisted of universal histories into which Ottoman history was woven; their language was high and suffused with Persian, and their authors were highly educated, usually in the more prestigious medreses' (Piterberg 2003: 38). *Şerefname* conforms most fully to this third genre. If Hassanpour omits to connect Seref Han's history with this broader historiographical movement, Piterberg in turn fails to consider how Seref Han's

in relation to the cultural difference of Christian Armenians? And did Armenians experience such an awakening in their relations with Kurdish overlords? Hassanpour also notes that the 'de-ethnicization' of geographic space engaged in by the modern nation states of Iraq and Turkey is targeted at eliminating the word 'Kurdistan' from maps and texts, but he does not remark upon the equally systematic erasure of Armenian names of villages and geographic landmarks from the region. He does write however that Armenians constituted 30 or 40 per cent of the population in 'northern Kurdistan' in the seventeenth century (Hassanpour 2003: 129).

In a more recent article Hesenpur's (sic) references to Evliya Çelebi's *Seyehat-name* are similarly made through an overwhelming interest in (or a bias towards) the historical experiences of the region's Kurdish inhabitants. Much more than the *Şerefname*, Evliya Çelebi's *Seyehatname* gives a wealth of clues as to the cosmopolitanism of the Kurdish provinces, even if the community of Christians too is not of direct concern. Reporting on his visits to Bitlis in 1655 and 1656, for example, he notes that Bitlis has seventeen Muslim and eleven Armenian Christian quarters (Çelebi in Dankoff 1990: 70, 71). His account gives a good sense of the multi-religious and multicultural population of Diyabakir as well. Despite this, in an article on the language murder or attempted 'langua-cide' (*dilkırım*) of Kurdish by contemporary nation states, Hesenpur fails to mention Armenian as being spoken in the emirate of Bitlis or as affected by the 1876 legal reform making Turkish the official Ottoman state language. The article compares the variety of languages (Kurdish, Turkish, Arabic and Persian) used by the literary class in Çelebi's Ottoman Bitlis with the treatment and endangered status of Kurdish in the 'modern period' (Hesenpur 2005). By contrast in his introduction to *Evliya Çelebi in Diyarbekir*, Van Bruinessen makes the point that Çelebi's references to Armenians – but not to Kurds – were omitted (censored) from the late Ottoman translation of the work (Van Bruinessen 1988: 7). If Hesenpur's reading of these two texts is typical (and I think it is) we must conclude that accounts drawing on them to defend the 'distinctiveness of the Kurds as a people with a claim to sovereign rule' (Hassanpour 2003: 137) do so at the cost of underplaying the Armenian presence in Kurdistan and by neglecting its social heterogeneity. (See too Özoğlu 2005 and his concentrated focus on *Kurdish* identity as portrayed in the *Şerefname* and *Seyahatname*).

If the Kurdish 'claim to sovereign rule' in Kurdistan appears to create a theoretical impasse with a discourse on Armenian-ness that similarly casts the Armenian nation as an autochthonic presence in the region, this is not to say that writers emphasizing Kurdish identity or history are necessarily unsympathetic towards the Armenian experience. Nevertheless, Bozarslan argues that the generation involved in the anti-Armenian alliance between Turks and Kurds during the First World War possessed

---

regional and ethnic history might revise or challenge texts produced in and about the centre. In other words, in this instance both fail to bring together the text(s) they consider with their proper historical interlocutors.

a collective memory of guilt about what had happened to the Armenians which 'traumatized' the 'Kurdish psyche'. This repressed memory was fearfully evoked in relations with the new post-war Kemalist regime instituted in Ankara. Thus a declaration prepared by the leaders of the 1925 *Şeyh* Said rebellion states that: 'They [Kemalists] have in mind [the project] of subjecting the Kurdish *müteneffizanin* [those who hold authority, the men of influence] to the same treatment as that which was meted out to the Armenians' (cited in Bozarslan 2003a: 182, 183).

Would it be too far-fetched to suggest that the (under)representation of Armenians in much of the discourse on Kurdistan continues to be haunted by the Kurdish role in the Ottoman 'treatment' of Armenians, especially given the constant endeavour of nationalism to manufacture a collective political identity and kinship between actors of different generations or periods? Marx expresses the same idea in somewhat similar language, declaring that 'the traditions of all the dead generations weighs like a nightmare on the brains of the living' (Marx 1977: 300). If the 'memory of massacres creates history, identity and the focus for future mobilization' (Humphrey cited in Bozarslan 2003b: 36), the memories of massacres carried out by 'forbears' need to be forgotten, repressed and deflected for such mobilization to occur. We see all these modes of remembering in the imagining of Kurdistan.

So, for example, in a chapter titled '*Emperyalist Egemenliğin Oyunlari Altında Iki Ulus: Ermeniler ve Kürtler*' ('Armenians and Kurds: Two Nations under the Hegemonic Games of Imperialists'), Yılmaz argues that because the economic and social structures of Armenia acted as an obstacle to a modern national war of liberation, Armenian uprisings took the form of a religious struggle directed against Kurds. Accordingly an armed struggle broke out between the Kurdish *Hamidiye* regiments, created by the Ottomans, and the Russians and Armenians. Not receiving the support that they had envisioned from Russia, the Armenians then approached the other imperialist powers (France and England), who used the Armenian problem to strengthen their own regional hegemony. With the beginning of the First World War, Armenians attacked Muslim villages, supported by the Russian army. Using the excuse of the war, the Unionists decided in response to seek a permanent solution to the Armenian problem. With the release of local notables from formal control, the situation turned to genocide. Despite their promises, the imperialist powers failed to support the Armenian nationalist movement (Yılmaz 1991: 64ff, my summary and translation). Informed by Marxist theoretical categories, Yılmaz's construction of the past both extends and denies agency to the Armenian actors: although represented as actively pursuing a nationalist course, structural forces condition that struggle to take a religious form. Similarly imperialist powers disappoint but they do not create Armenian nationalists. By contrast, the agency of the Kurdish actors is represented in a rather passive manner – the Hamidiye regiments are *formed* by the Ottomans, Kurdish villages are *attacked* by the Armenians, local leaders are *released* by the State. Genocide *happens*... Memory of *active* or willing participation in a massacre is repressed.

A second Marxian political analysis is that of Faik Bulut in his book *Dar Üçgende Üç Isyan: Kürdistan'da Etnik Çatişmalar* (*Three Rebellions in the Narrow Triangle: Ethnic Conflicts in Kurdistan*). As with Yılmaz, the analytic categories of historical materialism (feudalism, tribal structures, bourgeois revolution, ruling or hegemonic class, imperialism etc.) produce a complex historical description of politico-economic developments and conflicts in the region. More strongly than Yılmaz, Bulut presents both the Ottoman and imperialist states as primarily responsible for ethnic massacre in the region: the Ottomans, in cooperation with backward feudal Kurdish elements, incited their Kurdish villagers to oppress the religious minorities, while the British and Russians used Armenian and Syrian Christian minorities to further their own influence in the disintegrating Ottoman domains. But Bulut's project is not merely analytical: the historical construction is intended to forewarn and inform revolutionary movements in the present. Summarizing the characteristics of the three rebellions under examination, he concludes with their meaning for today:

> These rebellions were distant from international developments; they signify the dead end of thinking only in relation to Kurds, or Armenians or Nestorians, and of trusting England or Iran. Especially in places and times when a national liberation war cannot be total, collaborative, unified and united, this politics is controlled by its opponents (colonialists and imperialists). They cause the common people to destroy each other. For this reason and above everything else, whoever wants to resist oppression and be liberated should in their own home and place practise equality and freedom, and should not oppress the minorities among them or neglect the rights of ethnic communities. The reason for this is clear: the Nestorians, Armenians, Turks, Kurds, Circassians, Syrian Christians, Muslims, Sunni, Shiites, and Christians who are struggling for power [against the ruling class] shouldn't make distinctions [between themselves]. Those who do that are generally the ruling class with the imperialists. The moment you do this it means you are unwittingly playing the game of your enemies and the external powers. The meaning of the narrow triangle is this. (Bulut 1992: 166) (my translation)

Those who would take Bulut's advice must walk a political tightrope. According to him, a revolutionary struggle, while recognizing and protecting the national identities of different peoples, cannot allow those identities to become the basis for political action. A distinctive national history should not become the basis for a nationalist politics or for a politics of cultural rights. In the revolutionary struggle there is no legitimate interest or agency other than that of class. Any political action fracturing the unity of the masses (*halk*), particularly identity politics (ethnic or religious), is necessarily inspired by the ruling class and imperialists, and works against the true interests of those involved. For Bulut, revolutionary struggle requires the freezing of the production of ethnic identities and a return to their pre-political state before their oppression by hegemonic forces or manipulation and incitement by imperialist powers. Logically, *memories* of massacres that targeted victims on the very grounds of their ethnicity, or memories of continuing forced ethnic assimilation should not become a basis for political mobilization in response. Similarly, *memories of participating in massacre* should be deflected onto the real perpetrators, in the first instance European imperialists and in the second instance the Ottoman government. Here we see how the posited omnipotence of imperialism – what Bloxham (2005) condemns as an 'abuse of context' – translates as a theory of lack of local agency explaining away Kurdish involvement.[24]

Nevertheless, we need to remember that most Kurds – and in particular Kurdish women – were not involved in the killing of Armenians. We need to add this because of the way that analyses of politics in the Kurdish regions have nearly always focused on relationships between men and not on relations between men and women. McDowell notes further that some Alevi Kurds gave sanctuary to Armenian refugees (McDowell 2000: 104). And even if an exception, one famous cooperation between exiled and refugee Armenians and Kurds in Syria resulted in a united nationalist struggle against the Turkish republic. This was the alliance between the Kurdish *Xoybun* and the Armenian *Taşnak* organizations that produced a 19-article declaration in 1927 envisioning a principled sharing of territory in the outcome of an independent Kurdistan and a united Armenia. The declaration also pledged cooperation in military and propaganda operations. In the jointly signed Memorandum of Understanding the articles most revealing of how the organizations were imagining Kurdistan and Armenia included:

Article 1. Each side recognizes the right to establish an independent Kurdistan and a united Armenia and agree to support each other to defend these rights to whatever extent is possible.

Article 2. Each side agrees to continue the war to liberate their two countries against their mutual enemy without looking at which land belongs to Armenia and which to Kurdistan. The border between the two nations will be determined according to the following principles:

A- The local populations of Kurds and Armenians before the war (1914) will be used as a baseline.

B- While the ethnic and legal principles agreed to in the Sevres Agreement stand, article 89 of the Agreement that leaves to Armenia the provinces of Van, Bitlis and Erzurum is null and void. This being said, each side undertakes to respect the claims of the other vis-à-vis these provinces.

24. Logically Bulut also reduces missionaries to agents of imperialism, and hence is uninterested in how and why local people respond to, appropriate or resist their work. The dismissal is in accordance with his assumptions concerning the ethical agency of local people. For a more considered account of the politics of Protestant mission work in Dersim and its impact in the nineteenth century see Danık 2005.

C- In establishing the boundaries each side is obliged to take into account the legitimate defensive, economic and political interests of the other. (cited in Alakom 1998b: 133, 134) (my translation)

Despite their cooperation, it is immediately apparent that neither the *Xoybun* nor the *Taşnak* organizations imagined Kurdistan or Armenia as a multicultural entity. Accordingly the status of the three provinces with historically heavy concentrations of Armenians is left unresolved. Similarly the declaration makes no mention of the killings of Armenians by Kurds (or vice-versa), nor of the possibility of compensation. It is the common enemy that allows the nationalism of the two organizations to coexist.

Given, then, that at least in this agreement the same place might end up either in Armenia or in Kurdistan, what's in a name? More than one writer notes that although there was never a state named Kurdistan, until the institution of the nation-states of Turkey and Iraq, there was also never a taboo about calling that place where Kurds made up the majority of the population, Kurdistan. Yet clearly many people speaking languages other than a Kurdish dialect as their mother tongue also lived there. Today their numbers are miniscule. Inevitably *naming* that place Kurdistan in the post-massacre period is a political act as much as a geographical one. It entails a claim to the sovereignty of Kurds over that area. It assures Kurds of their indigeneity. It imagines a country or region that is not the land of the Turks or the Arabs, despite the renaming of its mountains and settlements in Turkish and Arabic. But it also constitutes the territory thus denoted as ethnic space, homeland of the Kurds despite the historic presence of other groups.

Would Kurdistan smell as sweet (in spring) by any other name? It would not, at least for many of the authors selectively sampled here. In much of the discourse on Kurdishness, Kurdistan is a place of hope, reassuring Kurds of a rooted identity. But as we have seen, it is also imagined through a selective forgetting of its complex histories. On that level at least, for many Kurdish nationalists, their imagining of Kurdistan resembles the Turkifying of the Ottomans by Turkish nationalists, as we have seen in Chapter 1.

–3–

Representing Kurds: A Brief History of Kurds and Kurdistan in Ethnography

In Chapter 3 I seek to switch perspective from historical discourses on Kurds and their relations with imperial powers to anthropological analyses of Kurdish societies and their internal relationships. The switch is as much rhetorical as substantial, as ethnographic representations of social relations in Kurdistan also present, if often only implicitly, those relations as supported or subverted by the actions of 'external' forces. Further, as a generalization we can argue that one theoretical trend in the discipline of anthropology since the 1960s has been towards a more explicit acknowledgment and theorization of the history of colonialism and nation-state building, or a shift away from assumptions that posit the self-generating qualities and functional integration of distinct societies.[1]

In this chapter we will examine a number of ethnographies, some of which, if not particularly influential in producing a dominant knowledge for or about Kurds – Edmund Leach's (1940) and Fredrik Barth's (1953) monographs were only translated into Turkish by Kurdish publishing houses in 2001 – were written by scholars of unusual theoretical acumen. The works under consideration will be Sykes' (1908) article 'The Kurdish Tribes of the Ottoman Empire'; the sections on Kurds in the first and second editions of the Leiden *Encyclopaedia of Islam* (1927 and 1981 respectively); Leach's *The Social and Economic Organization of the Rawandaz Kurds* (1940); Barth's *Principles of Social Organization in Southern Kurdistan* (1953); Ismail Beşikçi's *Doğu Anadolu'nun Düzeni* (1969) – 'the only Turkish anthropologist to have published a full study of Kurdish groups [and] who was imprisoned for his pains' (Andrews 1989: 43)] – and Van Bruinessen's *Agha, Sheikh and State: The Social and Political Structures of Kurdistan* (1978/92). But before examining the selected ethnographies, it would be appropriate to say something about this book's organization of chapters, as well as how the ethnographies under investigation might be related to developments in general anthropological theory.

---

1. In *Minima Ethnographica* Michael Jackson discerns a second movement in the history of anthropological analysis in the twentieth century, what he terms the successive deconstruction of the subject as actor.

Anthropology, Colonialism, Nationalism

It is clear that the bulk of anthropological writings on Kurds are based on research conducted beyond the institution of the nation states of Turkey, Iraq and Iran. The tremendous influence of these states' military, cultural and spatial policies on the lives of their inhabitants and the targeting of their Kurdish regions for special treatment suggest that, logically, an analysis of these political projects should precede and inform the examination (in this chapter) of more locally oriented studies. Nevertheless I intend to explore Turkish, Persian and Arab Kemalisms in Chapter 4. One reason for this arrangement derives in part from the nature of ethnography. Ethnographies of Kurdish society partake of a complex admixture of power and knowledge, their production and findings influenced, as we have also seen for historical works, by the power of nationalism and nation-states. But their representations are further connected directly or indirectly to international cross-disciplinary trends in intellectual paradigms, to the histories and conflicts of the ethnographer's own country and finally to the personal political commitments and subjectivity of the ethnographer. All of these factors apply to the gleanings of their readers as well. Being a science that takes as one of its research tools the researcher's experience of cultural dislocation, ethnographic knowledge is inevitably partial, its texts like doors that open out onto, if one knows how to use them, more than one reality.[2] Ethnographic representations exhibit their own complex politics that give them in turn a somewhat different relationship to nation-state building than histories examining the founding and development of national institutions. One of their potential virtues is their fine-grained analysis of the local. One of their potential faults, as we will explore in some of our chosen ethnographies, has been their tendency to focus on the regional scene without properly incorporating into their studies the role of nation-states in enforcing frameworks of meaning and practice for citizens. Ironically, the accusation (made in the late 1960s) that classical anthropological monographs obscured the presence of colonial power in their analyses has been compensated for, especially by those anthropologists influenced by cultural studies and postcolonial theory, by a new emphasis on the discourse and impact of Western imperialism, minimizing once again the mediating institutions between local and global politics.

Readers will note that the ethnographic studies selected for examination, starting with Leach's, were written roughly in successive decades. This spacing of texts is more than coincidental: if Kurdish society as the changing object of these studies conditions the changing analyses, theoretical shifts in the discipline are equally responsible for how ethnographers listen to and discern the words and actions of

---

2. See for example Henrika Kuklick's essay on Evans-Pritchard's *The Nuer* and her reading of it in terms of the bitter conflict between two opposing views of political history in Britain (Kuklick 1984).

their subjects. Michael Meeker describes how, in the period of his first fieldwork in the eastern Black Sea region in 1965, the dominant anthropological assumptions about local social systems and their separate logic from the emerging orders of new states precluded certain other possible interpretations, making them literally 'unthinkable' (Meeker 2002). But this insight was arrived at only years later when he was able to come to an alternative analysis. Although writers may not draw attention to them, disciplinary arguments always condition writers' choice of subject and interpretations of political dynamics.

Very briefly then, how might we relate societal and theoretical change as reflected in these texts? One of the most enlightening studies of the development of anthropology is Joan Vincent's *Anthropology and Politics: Visions and Trends*, which divides anthropological theorizing into three different periods, each marked by clear shifts in the dominant paradigm. As with other historians of anthropology, Vincent argues that the post-First World War years heralded both the institutionalization of anthropology as a distinct discipline in the Anglo universities, and the elaboration of variants of 'structural-functionalism' as its enabling theory. Slightly changing the focus, Patrick Wolfe also writes a concise account of the *eclipse* of evolutionary theories after the war by what he calls synchronic relativism (i.e. Vincent's structural functionalism), indexing it to two other crucial developments. The first was the transition from direct to indirect rule by colonial governance and the second was advances in physics whereby the discovery of the atom's autonomous generation of energy via interaction of its subatomic particles served as a new metaphor for society (Wolfe 1999).

Wolfe also notes a second defeated theoretical pretender to the anthropological throne in the post-war years, the theory of diffusionism, or the view that 'the key issues in ethnography were embodied in the task of reconstructing a global culture history of human migrations and cultural borrowings' (Barth 2005: 16). Less sympathetic than Wolfe to the analytic power of diffusionism, Fredrik Barth stresses the 'dark side' of diffusionist theories, their propensity to racist claims about the genius of certain peoples in the spreading of cultural enlightenment, and the biological incapacity of others to create their own social institutions.[3] Feuchtwang too argues for a correspondence between the post-war discipline, with its typical fictive unit of analysis – tribes or 'stateless' societies – and broader imperial economic and political power. For Feuchtwang, sponsorship of research by the British Colonial Office between the wars exercised a negative influence over the discipline, obstructing the development of a more properly historical and comparative anthropology

3. Turkish anthropology in the 1920s and 1930s adopted certain diffusionist positions. See Maksudyan's MA thesis at Boğazici University analysing the journal *Turkish Review of Anthropology* ('Gauging Turkishness: Anthropology as Science-Fiction in Legitimizing Racist Nationalism', 1925–39).

(Feuchtwang 1973). These three parallel paradigm shifts in anthropology, science and colonial governance – as we have seen, Ottoman rule throughout the nineteenth century undergoes a similar transformation, although rarely commented on by the historians of anthropology – provide the *conditions of possibility* for much of the early ethnographic representations of Kurds.

Wolfe and Feuchtwang then, along with many others, have pointed out the problematic relationship between early post-war anthropology and colonialism. Their critique also centred on the extent to which anthropological knowledge was appropriated by imperial power, making anthropologists complicit with the exploitation of the colonized population. Yet if some anthropologists were dismissive of anti-colonialist movements (most famously Malinowski), others were expelled from their posts for supporting 'national liberation' struggles. For this reason we need also to be reminded of the equally ambiguous relationship between anthropology and nationalism in the very same period. Fascinatingly, nationalism and classical anthropology can be analysed as having similar visions and vocabularies of society, imagining them through categories such as authenticity and indigeneity, social boundedness and autochthonic cultural production. The influence of the outside world upon the integrity of the local cultural situation is a cause of anxiety for both, minimizing as they do inter-societal cultural creation. According to Joel Kahn, these similarities indicate a shared modernist intellectual heritage, what he describes as 'social expressivism' (Kahn 1995). And even while in the present a post-classical critical anthropology stresses the constructed nature of the discourse on nationalist origins by the nation-state, it often takes (as I do in this study) a more sympathetic approach to the identity claims of subaltern or 'stateless-nations', despite the formal resemblance of their approach to the work performed by intellectuals of the nation-state. Similarly, anthropological studies of *indigenous* 'systems of thought' or 'local knowledge' do not appear to take the same critical or even mocking perspective to their subject as studies, say, that examine the claims of Muslims to the validity of an Islamic science. What these inconsistencies indicate is that a more coherent research project in the present would be the study of the historical *production of knowledge* about Islam or Kurds or Turks etc., endeavouring in the process to encompass some of the many different disciplines, institutions, associations and individuals creating or appropriating such knowledge.

Lastly then – and this should be kept in mind while examining our selected ethnographic studies – we should emphasize that analysing the production, dissemination and consumption of this anthropological knowledge about Kurds involves consideration of a complex web of power relations. In the first instance we might talk about a diversity of overlapping 'circuits of knowledge' about Kurds – diverse because particular types of knowledge flow between people who make up the different circuits. Thus for example, one circuit of knowledge is that represented by *Kırkbudak* (a 'journal of Anatolian folk beliefs'); another by *Munzur* (the 'Dersim ethnographic journal')[4] and a third by *Milli Folklor* (an international and quarterly journal of folklore). If the circuits are not sealed – in fact they leak constantly and often orient their discourse towards an imagined impartial reader – their knowledge production is mainly closed to outsiders. Thus knowledge-disseminating institutions such as political parties, social movements, newspapers, journals, publishing companies, mass media and Web sites (some private, some state controlled) write and broadcast for a known if imagined audience, using a familiar and limited range of writers. Circuits exclude and are exclusive. Yet writers keep a close eye on the knowledge produced in other circuits, which allows them to revise and reorient their own production of new and recycled knowledge.

A second form of power enabling and controlling the dissemination of knowledge about Kurds relates to the languages of its production and the unequal ability of consumers in various circuits to translate and appropriate that knowledge. The present global dominance of English means that producers of knowledge unable to read or write competently in that language are also unable to dispute with or profit from English-medium circuits. Yet exclusion from the disputatious circuits producing knowledge about Kurds in English or other European languages does not necessarily mean exclusion from the most *influential* – in terms of an applied political practice impacting upon Kurdish actors – knowledge-producing circuits about Kurds.[5] The inability of Kurdish nationalism to reconfigure the production of knowledge about Kurds by education systems in Turkey or Iran, or to hinder its dissemination for consumption by Kurdish children, is a case in point. Further the production of varied anthropological knowledge about Kurds in Western universities receives a mixed reception in the nation-states of Turkey, Iran and Iraq (if and when translated), depending upon its palatability to different circuits of knowledge about Kurds in those countries. Circuits of knowledge antagonistic towards or critical of state discourse are potentially subject to censorship (see note 7). Finally the production of knowledge about Kurds by Kurds themselves – especially but not only if written in one of the Kurdish dialects – is sometimes transmitted to Western circuits via academics and students at Western universities, with their own biases and limitations. This book itself is a part of that process.

'The Kurdish Tribes of the Ottoman Empire'

Lt.-Col. Mark Sykes' article 'The Kurdish Tribes of the Ottoman Empire' was first published in the *Journal of the Anthropological Institute of Great Britain* in

4. Its interests are signalled by its subtitle: Dersim was the name of the province before its forced change to Tunceli by the Republic after a violently repressed Alevi Kurdish uprising in the late 1930s.

5. I am puzzled by Edward Said's (1978) argument, in his book *Orientalism,* that the discourse of Western scholars (orientalists) is more important in the present in representing or constituting the Orient (here Kurds) than in this case the discourse of the Turkish or Iraqi nation-states.

1908 and reprinted thereafter in his book *The Caliphs' Last Heritage* in 1915. The book itself is a crafted mixture of history and travel diary, its history ending with the vast enlargement of the Ottoman empire (with Sultan Selim adding its 'Asiatic territories') in 1517, its diary concluding with an eyewitness account of the unraveling of 'Turkey-in-Asia' due to the policies of a corrupt post-Ottoman constitutional regime in 1913. Yet whose testimony are we reading? Sykes was no neutral or powerless observer, but a British diplomat influential in constructing the 'eastern' policy of the British government. Indeed he was its chief negotiator in the secret Sykes–Picot Agreement (1916) between Britain and France, which divided up the Arab Ottoman territories into respective spheres of direct and indirect British and French rule.[6] He was also particularly well travelled in the region.

Nevertheless, the book does not discuss the role of the British in eastern affairs, nor does it give any reasons for his being there. Rather it is addressed to those who wish to understand the present state of the realm, for 'to understand the composition and problems of the Ottoman Empire in Asia, it is necessary to make an impartial and general study of its past history' (Sykes 1915: 2). Yet, as we have acknowledged, ethnographic knowledge is also a personal, experiential knowledge: thus while Sykes hopes that his article on the Kurdish tribes will 'simplify the work of future students', he also reveals that the study brings the 'results of about 7,500 miles of riding and innumerable conversations with policeman, muleteers, chieftains, sheep drovers, horse dealers, carriers and other people capable of giving one first-hand information' (Sykes 1915: 553). If it is too simplistic to talk about a fusing of ethnographic and imperial knowledge in Sykes' work, it is vital to consider how in it these two endeavours of ethnographic knowledge and political control relate.

Sykes' study of the Ottoman Kurdish tribes is not a history or an analysis of local social relations. It instead comprises a detailed map, a list of the names of Kurdish tribes and their approximate distribution, and information about those tribes in the form of 'such particulars as I can supply' (Sykes 1915: 554). The devil is in the particulars. Sykes divides up the region inhabited by Kurds into six zones (A to F) and then again into classes within each zone. He remarks that the zones are not ethnological but merely a convenient form of grouping. His classification of internal classes within each zone, however, is based on his identification of either their geographical, moral, religious or racial characteristics. It is in these 'particulars' that Sykes' anthropological theory is expounded, for it is here that he comments on the features of each tribe (their moral character, their appearance, the beauty of their women and so forth) and speculates as to their causes or origins.

Thus the non-tribal *Zazas* of Zone B, for example, are deemed a class unto themselves:

6. The boundary between Iraq and Syria (although obviously not their governments) is still derived from this agreement, which gave south-eastern Turkey, Syria, northern Iraq (Mosul) and Lebanon to France and Jordan, Iraq and Haifa to Britain.

Their state is almost anarchical, and they seem, although not naturally cruel or vicious, to have hardly any regard for human life; they frankly say they are of beasts of the field, and hardly have any religion… The Zazas are small impish people with shrill voices, and are extremely shy before strangers. I should imagine that they are the remains of a primitive mountain race. (Sykes 1915: 570)

By contrast the Kurds in Class 1, Zone E are

completely sedentary, build fine villages, are industrious and intelligent, peaceful, but extremely treacherous, and on occasion ruthless and cruel. Fair hair and blue eyes are not uncommon among them; the men are generally short but handsome and very submissive in their demeanour. To each of these tribes are attached certain families of nomads, all extremely poor, dark skinned, and repulsively ugly, who claim common origin with the village dwellers. (Sykes 1915: 583)

Similarly, the tribes of Class 1, Zone D 'are of a distinct and distinguishable race of tall, heavily built men, of surpassing ugliness of face and peculiar uncouthness of behaviour. Many travelers have generalized from them and imagine all Kurds to resemble them' (Sykes 1915: 580). But the Hamawand tribe of Class 1, Zone A (1,200 families) are the

most valiant, courageous and intelligent of the Baban Kurd tribes. Splendid horsemen, crack shots, capable smiths, bold robbers, good agriculturalists; such as enter the government service prove capable officials … the men are famous for their prowess and intelligence, and the women for their beauty. The Hamawand intermarry freely with the Arabs, and reckon themselves of Arab origins. Most of the Hamawand speak Arabic, their language is, however, Kurdish. (Sykes 1915: 558–9)

Examples could be multiplied. It is clear that the anthropological imagination at work is diffusionist in inspiration, the apparent heterogeneity of Kurdish people resulting from the waves of conquest or migration of different groups into the region and their mixing with the 'original mountain race'. Social class distinctions between landlords and commoners reflect most typically the conquest of autochthonous populations by more warlike tribes. Although not sketched out in the article, anthropological knowledge of the Kurds would presumably consist in a proper tracing of the origins and links between these groups, which would also partially explain the inferior and superior qualities to be found distributed amongst them. Would such knowledge, if it could be worked out, be useful for colonial rulers? Only indirectly, one would think: it might indicate from which tribes of Kurds recruits should be trained for devolution of local duties for example, or which groups might be essentially less trustworthy. But its more direct relationship to imperial knowledge lies in its general conformity to assumptions pertinent in constructing an evolutionary racial schema, which justified of course European rule over different races of diverse origin and 'particulars'.

Kurds and Kurdistan

In the famous Leiden *Encyclopaedia of Islam* (first edition 1913–36) Victor Minorsky begins his entry on Kurds, probably written in 1927, with a section headed 'Origins', concluding in the process that the Kurdish traditions themselves 'do not help us to solve the puzzle of the origins of the Kurds' (Minorsky 1927: 1134). But neither does the article help us resolve why Minorsky thinks knowing those origins are so important. (On the other hand and as we have just seen, Sykes' study, often cited by Minorsky, casts light on exactly this theme.) Both the organization of the entry and the cited bibliography suggest that the dominant anthropological approaches of the nineteenth century (evolutionism and diffusionism) had produced a scattered wealth of material about Kurds, which Minorsky sought to synthesize. His opening paragraph is revealing:

> The classification of the Kurds among the Iranian nations is based mainly on linguistic and historical data and does not prejudice the fact that there is a complexity of ethnical elements incorporated in them. The type of the latter varies visibly from place to place. It is probable that the expansion of the Kurd element took place from east (western Persia) to west (central Kurdistan) but there is nothing to have prevented the existence in central Kurdistan, before the coming of the Kurds, of a nationality of different origin but bearing a similar name (Kardu) which later amalgamated with the Iranian Kurds (Minorsky 1927: 1132).

'Origins' is followed by a much longer section titled 'History', which begins with the Arab conquest of Kurdistan and takes the reader up to the allocation of the Ottoman Kurdish province of Mosul to Iraq in 1925 and the Şeyh Said rebellion in Turkey of the same year. (These two sections are reprinted *verbatim* in the Encyclopedia's second edition (1981), with a new third part added by Bois 'from 1920 to the present day'.) Minorsky's third section 'Anthropology, Sociology and Ethnography' returns to issues left unanswered in 'Origins'. His conviction that contemporary Kurds are an amalgamation (Arab type; Mukri type; Biblical Jew type; Nestorian and Hakkari types) means that 'any idea of finding a general formula for the "Kurd type" is quite illusory' (Minorsky 1927: 1150). If disentanglement of 'ethnical elements' is impossible – or more precisely, if the knowledge about Kurds that disentanglement of their varied ethnic origins would bring is inaccessible – how might we know about them in the present? Minorsky isn't sure. The problem is that 'scientific measurements [of all the Kurdish tribes] have rarely been taken' (Minorsky 1927: 1150), which would presumably enable the mapping/matching of racial distributions with cultural characteristics in Kurdistan. In the absence of such a survey he is left to posit three general features 'of the mode of life of the Kurds' (Minorsky 1927: 1150). These are:

The historical tendency ... to group themselves on territorial fiefs around strongholds occupied by the chiefs, who often are of origin foreign to the local tribes; the existence of a warrior caste which supports the chief and conserves the ethnic agglomeration formed; the presence among the Kurds of shepherds (nomads and semi-nomads) as well as of agriculturists (settled or semi-settled). (Minorsky 1927: 1150)[7]

What is striking (and shocking) in the greatly expanded entry on 'Kurds, Kurdistan' in the second edition of the *Encyclopedia of Islam* (1981) is the continuity of certain key themes and language. The consecutive entries 'Kurdistan' and 'Kurds' in the first edition have been collapsed into one, although the description of the physical landscape, climate and geography of Kurdistan that precedes the discussion of Kurds and their history suggests the same division is adhered to. In the vital short section 'An anthropological profile of Kurdistan' the author, concerned still to identify the origins of the Kurds, begins by asking whether 'the Kurdish people possess characteristics such that it may be distinguished very clearly from the others?' (Bois 1981: 446). Like Minorsky he concludes that the fragmentary and 'relatively restricted numbers of ... really scientific measures obtained' (Bois 1981: 446) means that the search for origins needs to be combined in philological fashion with the study of language. Yet this does not prevent Bois from reintroducing various physical classifications of Kurds, including repeating Minorsky's point that the Sykes' photographs reveal the 'Arab, Jew, Biblical, Nestorian and Turkoman' types among Kurds, or claiming that Field's confirmation of these 'in a more scientific fashion' allowed him to discover 'Armenoid, Balkan, Modified Mediterranean, Eur-Anatolian, pure or mixed Iranian, Alphinoid, Mongoloid and Negroid' types (Bois 1981: 446). Finally he cites approvingly Field's portrait of Iraqi Kurds:

The Kurd is of medium height with a relatively long body and short limbs. The forehead is wide and the head wide and round. The brachycephalics predominate... The Kurd is more hirsute than the Arab. His hair, rather wavy and pliant, is normally dark brown and the eyes black. But blond hair and blue eyes are also to be encountered, especially in the western regions. The colour of the skin is more clear than that of the Assyrians. The teeth are normal and well-placed. The musculature is good, as is the health, in general, of those who have been observed. (Bois 1981: 446)

Bois's representation of previously published sources, as if they were merely objective descriptions of existing reality, confirms Said's argument about the

---

7. The translation into Turkish of the *Encyclopaedia of Islam* demonstrates the intersection and clashing of different circuits of knowledge: the Turkish translation (1955?) of Minorsky's article cut out its two long concluding paragraphs, in which the writer gives information on Kurdish nationalist newspapers. Where it ends abruptly the Turkish translation writes simply: *Bu makale aslından tadilen alınmıştır* ('This article has been modified from the original').

constant repetition of earlier ideas (that is to say, the self-referential quality) in orientalist discourse. (And of course the archetypal Iraqi Kurd is male.) What is more noteworthy perhaps is how this search for origins is reproduced in much recent nationalist discourses of Kurdish identity, including the use as evidence of many of the nineteenth- and early twentieth-century sources (including Minorsky). Rather than accept the disaggregating and potentially racist tendencies of the anthropological quest for origins or types however, the discourse on origins by the Kurdish monopolists (see Chapter 1) seeks to identify a continuing Kurdish essence amongst this cultural and linguistic variety. Kurdish nationalism's discourse on the origins of Kurds is also understandable in relation to a similar search on the part of Turkish nationalists, pursued however to prove the *Turkish* roots of Kurds. Animated by diffusionist assumptions too, this project appears to extend back to the 1930s and earlier but is periodically upgraded and re-seminated via engagement with other circuits of knowledge. Thus Kırzıoğlu Fahrettin's 1963 book *Kürtlerin Kökü* (Origins of the Kurds) attacks Minorsky's article on the Kurds in the *Encyclopaedia of Islam*, drawing attention to his Russianness and the 'propaganda' intent of Soviet Kurdology, as well as explaining how the article unfortunately made its way into the Turkish translation in 1955 without proper 'correcting'. Fahrettin argues by contrast that the 'Kurds' are Turkish, descending from the Bogduz and Becen sections of the Oğuz tribe.[8] Stepping back somewhat, it is interesting how the discourse on origins of Kurds can be connected in different ways to not one but three circuits of nationalism: English, Kurdish and Turkish.

But it would be unfair to suggest that Bois's article is merely repetitious. What *is* different in the second edition, after the updated history on Kurdish politics in Turkey, Iran, Iraq and Syria, is a new section on 'Kurdish Society', which includes subsections titled 'The Fundamental Structures of Kurdish Society', 'The Religious Aspect' and 'Customs and Social Traditions'. In these pages we see a shift in perspective from origins to social systems, or a change from bemoaning the lack of scientific research able to produce a conjectural history to a consideration of functioning if evolving social relations and institutions. The bias is now towards rural transformation, with discussion of nomads and sedentarization; peasants, land ownership and reform; changing tribal organization and chiefly duties. Even if Kurdish urban life is not yet on the horizon, the spectre of origins has been partially exorcised.

The Social and Economic Organization of the Rawandaz Kurds

In the 50 years (1927/1981) between the two editions, despite some disturbing continuities, the aims and theoretical assumptions of anthropological research had

---

8. The cumulative impact of such publications on a portion of the educated Turkish public is significant and would be of some importance to study.

obviously shifted. Our examination of first Leach's and then Barth's studies of Iraqi Kurdish society will illuminate these changes more fully. There are also strong theoretical continuities between these two works: indeed, Barth's study might be seen as completing Leach's abandoned project. Leach's shortish monograph (83 pages including photographs) is the result of just five weeks' fieldwork in rural areas of southern Kurdistan, cut short because of the war in Europe. The author justifies its publication by citing the paucity of serious ethnographic material concerning the 'Muhammedan' peoples of the mountainous areas of western Asia. By contrast, there is a wealth of romanticized travel stories about time spent amongst the Kurds: publication is also intended therefore to correct the 'fabulous distortions' (Leach 1940: 24) of lay and official accounts of Kurdish life, most particularly a stress on their inveterate banditry. In like vein Leach describes as 'fantasy' the view of earlier travellers that tribal leaders or landlords are descendants of conquering overlords – and as an 'absurdity' that they are of finer stock than the peasants (Leach 1940: 23).[9]

If the existing literature on Kurds was so unsatisfactory for Leach, on what theoretical principles does his revision or new knowledge stand? Rather than attempt to make a historical record of the ethnographic 'facts' of a group, anthropologists should 'study [a] particular group as a society in functioning existence at the present time' (Leach 1940: 1). Again, rather than merely describing the patterns of cultural norms, they should show their 'social significance [or demonstrate] the fundamental interrelationship between them' (Leach 1940: 1). Most simply, anthropological study should give us a 'picture of the functioning of any single society' or an 'indication of [its] practical organization' (Leach 1940: 2). Thus Leach's intention is to take a snapshot view of the interdependence of kinship, political and economic arrangements in the Kurdish villages under investigation, and thereafter generalize the analysis to the whole region. In this model an understanding of history is not considered important for observation of local society's interconnecting parts.

Yet what effects do such recommendations have on analysis of the political system? And is Leach's monograph really the result of observing a functioning society? In order to proceed according to these theoretical tenets, Leach has to perform a sort of dual manoeuvre. What Leach actually observes in his fieldwork is 'a society undergoing extremely rapid and at times violent social change' (Leach 1940: 9). To make sense of this Leach seeks to create a portrait of a functioning and hypothetical Kurdish tribal society as an 'idealized norm', of which the observed present is then to be understood as a variation. The reconstruction of an ahistorical (ideal type) tribal form balanced in equilibrium, as well as the assumption of its

9. For these reasons perhaps the introduction to the 2001 translation into Turkish argues that the text is best appreciated in relation to the historical yet still influential politics of representations of Kurds, presenting it as an antidote to Western stereotypes about their wildness, violence and primitiveness (*vahsi Kürtler*).

functioning local autonomy is the key to the procedure. To do so the 'political structure' of the present is severely and arbitrarily shrunken to encompass only local relations, which becomes the object of the ethnographic description. Then the impact of the 'external administrative authority' (Leach 1940: 9) is admitted as 'perverting' the local tribal system and his ideal model – but Leach does not call the motor of such 'perversion' colonialism, imperialism or nation building.

Given Leach's severe circumscribing of the relevant field of political relations, where does the political unit under discussion begin and end? In the first instance Leach pinpoints the system of land tenure, noting that all cultivated land and each village is the inherited property of a landlord (*agha*), even if actual ownership is vested in the state. Tenants pay rental in the form of a large proportion of their yields, and work the fields at the theoretical discretion of the landlord. On the other hand the right of tenancy is inherited, and eviction by the landlord rarely occurs. However, this focus on productive relations is misleading: 'the real nature of the relationship between the various *aghas* and their followers can only be understood in terms of kinship' (Leach 1940: 19). Thus Leach's concern is to explore 'the essentially conditional nature of the *aghas'* authority' (Leach 1940: 19). (A later, more Marxist-inspired generation would reconceptualize this as the question of domination and exploitation, particularly of women, in lineage society. See Kahn 1981.) Leach argues for the limited authority of the *agha* over his tenants because the norm of endogamy and orthodox cousin marriage means the *agha* of the village and nearly all his tenants are members of the same lineage. Further, because only the *agha* has more than one wife (often twice as many as given permission by the Koran) and thus a disproportionate amount of children, many 'tenants' are near kinsman. Thus kinship obligations and an established system of tenancy rights ameliorate the power of the *agha* over his tribesmen. Leach's focus on the *ordinarily constrained* authority of the chief and landlord (before the British colonial administration's policy of buying the loyalty of the *aghas*) is highlighted by his treatment of the village guesthouse, always managed and provided for by the *agha*. Leach seeks to understand the institution in terms of its economic *profitability*, calculating outputs in terms of hospitality and inputs in terms of gifts from guests but not as later writers would do as a site accumulating symbolic capital for its host.[10]

Leach's emphasis on the more consensual aspects of the local tribal system is reminiscent of an extremely influential book edited by Evans-Pritchard and Fortes in the very same year, *African Political Systems* (1940). In its introduction Evans-Pritchard and Fortes also argue for the structurally produced 'balanced' nature of political arrangements in Africa, particularly those societies character-ized by segmentary lineage systems (see Barth below). Some thirty years after

---

10. The reference is to the anthropology of Pierre Bourdieu, but Barth too in a later book (*Political Leadership among Swat Pathans*, published in 1959) interprets the guest or men's house as a key site of political power.

its publication, however, Talal Asad (1973), in an influential revisionist critique, charged that the representation and description of the political types identified in that study (centralized state and stateless political structures) elided real colonial control in the ethnographic present, and thus in fact give us not an account of existing African politics at all but the ideologically loaded study of 'pre-colonial African history'. Does Leach's methodological procedure of constructing an idealized and autonomous Kurdish society prior to 'external administration', as well as his stressing of the chiefs' 'conditional authority' over followers, echo *African Political Systems*? And if so, would Asad's point apply that the key political fact obscured by such writings is that they were written after colonial pacification, in this case both Ottoman and British?

Although Evans-Pritchard and Fortes' book and Asad's critique of it pertain to the modern history of Africa, I think it clear that Asad's argument can be extended to Kurdistan and Leach's monograph. As befits a functionalist study of Kurdish tribal social organization in the present, Leach provides the reader with almost no historical material. Leaving aside vital developments in Ottoman Kurdish history discussed in previous chapters (i.e. Ottoman post-*tanzimat* colonialism in the Kurdish and Arab regions), what does Leach's monograph exclude? There is no mention of the form of the British or French mandate or continuing British colonial power in Iraq nor of the monopoly granted the Iraq Petroleum Company over the country's oil fields; nothing on the British bombing of Kurds in Mosul province in 1924; nothing of the British appointing of an Arab King of Iraq; nothing (amazingly) on the formal independence of the state of Iraq in 1932 nor on Kurdish responses to the new constitution and treaty; nothing on the League of Nations' conditions about the rights of the Kurdish minority that the new state was supposed to honour; no mention of Arab or Kurdish nationalism, nor of the nation-building strategies of the new Iraqi state; no mention of the various coups in the latter half of the 1930s or the changes of Iraqi Prime Ministers nor the policies of the new governments towards the Kurdish regions. The only clue that any of these historical developments are of relevance to the region under investigation by Leach is his mention in passing of the closing of the secondary school in Rowanduz because of a 'nationalist strike by the students who demanded to be taught in the Kurdish language instead of Arabic' (Leach 1940: 10). But as this is made in the context of a cursory discussion of the education system in the region, he does not consider what the strike signified. He also mentions a feud between *aghas* that has politicized the whole region and 'become entangled with all sorts of wider issues – Kurdish nationalism in particular' (Leach 1940: 57). Again he makes no more of it than this. In other words, the insufficiency of earlier evolutionist writing about Kurds that Leach's study of their present social organization is designed to overcome brings with it its own set of very real limitations.

One clear problem involves the *covert* historical construction of a 'past' social organization presented as still functioning underneath the messy political realities of the present. But given the present is not properly theorized (other than as a debased form of an essential typological past), how this past connects to it is unclear. Ironically both the search for origins (Sykes) and the rejection of the search for origins (Leach) of the Kurds appear unable to grapple with the history of the Kurds or the politics at work in the *traditionalization* of what are clearly newly emergent social forms and practices. By bracketing out 'history' in the name of its speculative character and by concentrating in its place on the systematic interrelationships of social, economic and political factors in the ethnographer's presence, the *historical* production of the continuity of the social system is obscured. True, understanding a society's 'functioning existence at the present time' (Leach 1940: 1) requires consideration of how historical narratives (as ideologies) contribute to that functioning. But this requires, in turn, study of the historical creation and development of those narratives and their discourse on origins. To cite Piterberg again, and somewhat out of place: we need to make the 'occasion of history writing itself a historical topic' (Piterberg 2003: 31). In brief, examining how the past 'functions' in the present – both how it is made, what is imagined and what it does – is a historical task.

Nevertheless, perhaps we should not be too harsh on the study, given the unavoidably short duration of the fieldwork. Leach concludes by hoping that his analysis will be put out of date by further research. And in his last two paragraphs he proposes some possible resolutions to the dilemmas that the theoretical perspective of the monograph produces. Aware of the difficulties that functionalism gives rise to in terms of mediating continuity and change, structural principles and action, and normative positions and conflict, Leach's conclusion points towards the negation of these polarities via an anti-structural stress on the individual. Thus

> [if] it is true that the structural pattern of a society does impose upon individuals some standardization of behaviour ... this structural pattern affects the interests of different individuals in widely different ways and their resulting reactions differ accordingly. There can never be absolute conformity to the cultural norm, indeed the norm itself exists only as a stress of conflicting interests and divergent attitudes. All cultural groups, no matter how stable they appear in the light of history, are within themselves at any given time in a constant state of flux and potential change, the balance is always precarious.
>
> Thus the changes, often violent and disintegrative, that arise under conditions of Culture Contact differ only in degree and not in kind from smaller incipient changes that take place all the time even when the group is functioning under 'natural' conditions, however these may be defined. The mechanism of culture change is to be found in the reaction of individuals to their differential economic and political interests. (Leach 1940: 62)

Regardless of how satisfactory these conclusions are – and imagine calling colonialism and nation-building 'Culture Contact' – Leach's gesturing towards the importance of the strategizing individual [male] is picked up and extended in Barth's study as well.

Principles of Social Organization in Southern Kurdistan

Fredrik Barth was a student of Leach's, who also supervised his study *Principles of Social Organization in Southern Kurdistan* at the London School of Economics. Barth's focus in the study is the villages of the tribal and freeholding Hamawand farmers (remember Sykes' 'the most valiant, courageous and intelligent of the Baban Kurd tribes'?) and of the non-tribal and share-cropping tenant farmers in the valley around the Iraqi city of Suleimaniye. As with Leach, Barth's ethnography is determinedly local, a study of the surprising variation of Kurdish village political organizations and land tenure arrangements in the region where in 1951 he stayed for some six months. Rather than attribute such variety to any diversity of origins, Barth attributes it to the geographical positioning of Kurdistan on the 'shatter zone' between Arab, Turkish and Persian cultures. Picking up from Leach's conclusion, Barth notes how this gives competing factions in the region the opportunity to observe and manipulate social forms and principles from all three societies in pursuit of their own interests.

On the other hand, however, Barth identifies one type of basic organization as autonomously Kurdish amongst all this variety: 'this is usually called *tribal*, and is based on the *lineage principle*' (Barth 1953: 10). Although the towns of Suleimaniye, Halabja and Chemchemal lie close to the villages under examination, Barth deliberately excludes them from his study because of their 'numerous "Western" influences' (Barth 1953: 15). The object of study, then – the Kurdish countryside, its inter-village relations and those villages' tribal (lineage) or non-tribal (feudal) political relations – is brought under magnified view by stripping it of its relationship with the towns. Barth retells a popular story to justify his claim about the villagers' intense localism: a donkey escapes from a farmer, and not wishing to lose it the man pursues it high up into the mountains, never looking back. He catches it on the mountain top and turning to go home gasps. 'I never knew the world was so vast', he says, looking at the plain below. But the story can be given an opposite meaning to Barth's gloss on it: we might interpret it as a tale revealing the Kurds' worldly knowledge of their own parochialism. Despite the importance of the adjacent towns as nodes of wider political, administrative and economic networks encompassing all of Iraqi Kurdistan, Barth's ethnography has little to say about the localized workings or the political history of the Iraqi state. Rather than one interconnected but variegated national territory and society, the study assumes two separate social orders, the local Kurdish (tribal or feudal) system amenable to analysis using the theoretical categories from the broader anthropological literature (i.e. segmentary lineage organization) and the 'external administrative' system. In fact, Barth does not attempt to analyse the incorporation of the 'indigenous social organization' (Barth 1953: 139) into wider processes of nation building, capitalistic property relations, world markets and bureaucratizing state systems. But this disinterest is connected I think to his representation of the determining deficiency of the Kurdish political system, whose lineage organization, close family endogamy and plethora of small corporate groups is seen as impeding the development of any natural larger units. Thus his book's concluding paragraph: 'This problem of integration the local non-tribal political institutions were unable to solve satisfactorily; and the secondary role played by the quite large Kurdish population in the history of the middle east may be to a considerable extent related to this failure' (Barth 1953: 140).

Despite Barth's identification of the structurally produced separatism of the Kurdish countryside and villages, he is also concerned to explore the 'de facto' gaining and exercise of power by particular individuals. Thus he traces the modification and convergence of the two formal Kurdish political organizations (the lineage type headed by a tribal *agha* and the feudal type dominated by the landlord) according to 'one basic principle, the universal application of status difference, and the resulting lack of conceptualization of "the office", as apart from the person occupying it at any one moment' (Barth 1953: 49). Adopting the Weberian distinction between the authority of an office and the status position of an individual, Barth argues that tribal leaders are not followed by virtue of their formal position but because of their total higher status position and personal charisma. Nevertheless, superordinated and subordinated status are not fixed: indeed, given Kurdistan's geographical promiscuity the traditional prescriptions governing the legitimate exercise of authority connected to positions in the religious, political and economic hierarchies are constantly disputed by holders, rivals and subordinates. In Barth's memorable phrase, 'the theme of power attains an overwhelming importance, following the line of reasoning that if you can get away with something, it can't be very wrong' (Barth 1953: 52).[11] Here Islam appears as an idiom organizing the scale of prestige in the religious field, convertible into influence and power.[12] But Barth's discussion about the ability of the individual to manipulate status categories is more historically contextualized than Leach's, in that Barth situates the emergence of a new class of landlords over a new class of detribalized (tenant) farmers as connected to the opportunities afforded

11. Speculatively one wonders whether this stress on the importance of personal attributes (skill and charisma) in the exercise of real power in 1950s and 1960s anthropology is written in contradistinction (explicitly or implicitly) to contemporary accounts of political life in the West stressing its mass organization and bureaucratization? The use of Weber's work to exaggerate the distance between the West and the Rest might also be seen as a form of Occidentalism, where the rationality and impersonality of bureaucratic power in the West is maintained though downplaying the importance of informal relations and personal influence in bureaucratic work. (By contrast, the efficacy of the 'work to rule' strike depends upon the importance of informal relations and personal *nous* in actual work organization.) See Frank Capra's 1946 film *It's a Wonderful Life* for a different representation of the social efficacy of a single life lived well.

12. Barth's (1953: 81) discussion of status positions or hierarchy within the religious field ('Derwish, Shaikh, Sayyid, Mullah, and Hadji') is both very interesting and very reductive, interested in utility rather than meaning, as the metaphor 'convert' shows.

by the break-up of the centralized and feudal Kurdish Baban principality by the Ottomans in 1851.

Perhaps unfairly, let me finish this discussion by using Barth's own recent account of the history of anthropology in Britain in order to reflect upon his ethnography. I say unfairly because whereas Barth deliberately refrains from commenting upon his own work and its influence(s) in this critical narrative, it is tempting (and instructive) to read it in the light of his particular historical reconstruction. Even a cursory examination of *Principles of Social Organization in Southern Kurdistan* shows that one of its chief intellectual inspirations is the abstract descriptions of social structure found in Evans-Pritchard's work on the Nuer (Fortes and Evans Pritchard 1940), a work described by Barth as defining the 'direction for anthropological research in Britain – [and] indeed … probably the most influential monograph ever published in anthropology' (Barth 2005: 33). Barth's analysis must be seen as an attempt to compare and conform Kurdish political organization to a typological class of society ('segmented lineage systems as the prototypical stateless polity' – Barth 2005: 30) made famous through the African ethnographic material.

Yet despite the surprising number of partial similarities Barth is able to make with this African material, the comparison essentially does not fit. As we have seen, it is sustainable only by Barth's radical delimiting of the political field that acknowledges the existence of, but brackets out, the social influence of both the Kurdish cities and the Iraqi state. But even within the narrow confines of his description of Kurdish tribal social organization, Barth is forced invariably to explain how the African model is insufficient for illuminating social relations in Kurdistan. Thus after outlining the institutionalized blood feud as 'described in numerous African societies' (Barth 2005: 73) he then goes on to say: 'In this form, the blood feud is not found in Southern Kurdistan. In fact, the basic principle underlying the institution, namely the collective responsibility of the members of the descent group, seems to be lacking' (Barth 2005: 73, 74). Elsewhere he notes how the rigidity of the Kurdish tribal system in comparison to that of the Nuer leads to a host of very different consequences ('Among the Kurds, on the other hand, the general practice of FaBrDa marriage and other close family endogamy makes any initial *rapprochement* impossible between conqueror and conquered, and encourages caste separation. Furthermore, kinship through female links is given no political recognition. The principle of 'sociological' kinship is unfamiliar and would be in conflict with Islamic doctrine' (Barth 2005: 59)). More basically, he admits that most Kurds are not grouped in lineages, while the rate of detribalization means that 'it is only a matter of time, probably less than a generation, till the segmentary lineage type of tribal organization is completely replaced by the non-tribal type in Southern Kurdistan' (Barth 2005: 135). Again the Kurdish lineage system's lack of flexibility (when compared to the Nuer system) is to blame for its demise.

What happened? How did this misapplication occur? Barth's history gives us the clue:

Evans-Pritchard made salient to readers and disciples the powerful structural abstractions of status and corporate group, disentangling the form of social structure from the confusing complexity of local life. It was this operation that dazzled younger anthropologists at the time and led to a spate of studies of 'lineage societies'... Perhaps the appeal of these modes of analysis, particularly among young anthropologists writing up their first data, lay in the way unwieldy field materials could be cut down to size and given a tidy analytical framework by such drastic focusing operations. (Barth 2005: 33, 34)

He then goes on to ask a number of critical questions about the status of these abstract models, especially regarding their operation in relation to locals' own much less consistent practices and understandings. As we will see in relation to a different set of theoretical models below, this problem is never easily sidestepped. Nevertheless in the light of the wisdom attained during a long and brilliant career, Barth's diagnosis of *lineage theory's* bewitching of young anthropologists just back from the field is an autobiographical revelation and a nameless self-criticism.

The Order of Eastern Anatolia: Social-Economic and Ethnic Foundations

Ismail Beşikçi's book *Doğu Anadolu'nun Düzeni: Sosyo-Ekonomik ve Etnik Temeller* (*The Order of Eastern Anatolia: Social-Economic and Ethnic Foundations*), first published in 1969, takes the reader into another world entirely. Here the question over the functioning of the Kurdish variety of segmented lineages is unimportant: what is vital is knowledge about class struggle and feudal order, capitalism and the hegemonic local classes, imperialism and underdevelopment, religion and ideology. Here we are back in the realm of history and historiography in which the oppressive social relations of the present are clarified by their insertion in a longer historical sequence. Here the analytic problem is not the isolated village or even region but the *East's* under-development – economic, social and cultural – as produced by Turkey's 'fundamental social structural dynamics' (Beşikçi 1992: 31). Africa is not an imagined comparison. Whereas Barth cites Weber, and conceives of economic classes in Kurdistan as one manipulable status category amongst others, Beşikçi cites Marx and conceives of economic classes as determining structures of historical development, influenceable nevertheless by political action. Whereas Barth's study earned him his doctorate, Beşikçi's had him first sacked from his university post, and then taken to court, charged with communist and Kurdish propaganda (Beşikçi 1992: 24). The result was a 13-year gaol sentence. One apparent puzzle is the discrepancy between the decision of the court and Beşikçi's foreword to the 1992 third edition, where he describes his conversion *in gaol* (i.e. after the writing of the book in 1969) to an anti-Kemalist understanding of the Kurdish problem, free from the influence of the 'official ideology.' Why was he gaoled then? In fact, the puzzle is solved simply enough: in the early 1970s, especially after the 1971 military intervention, any discourse on the 'East' that asserted (as Beşikçi's did) the influence of ethnic discrimination as a partial factor in Ankara's policies, was considered potentially subversive of Turkey's national unity, regardless of its conformity to other tenets of Kemalism.

Before looking at the text proper we need to dwell a little more on Beşikçi's (1992) self-criticism in the foreword to the third edition, as it is revealing in outlining his revised understanding of the book's flawed representation of the 'eastern' region. But perhaps equally important, his radical reassessment is revealing also of the emergence in the 1970s of an alternative and competing socialist discourse in Turkey, whose elaboration of an ethnic dimension to the politics of eastern Anatolia *irreducible* to class oppression redefined it as the 'Kurdish' problem. In the process, according to one's perspective, it also cast into relief the propagation of Turkish nationalism in the discourse and practice of apparently more orthodox Marxist groups, who, in its light, might further be seen as elaborating a form of *Marxist-Kemalism*. The author's rereading of his book is addressed to this continuing and bitter cleavage amongst the Left in Turkey.

Published in 1969 and 1970 respectively, the forewords to the first two editions make clear the political intent and theoretical premises of the research. In both Beşikçi makes a similar series of related arguments. In the first place Turkey is presented as living through a period of fundamental social change, paralleled and informed by a struggle for rights and a growing class consciousness of the mass of people (*halk yığınları*). At the same time, the classical sociology adapted from the West has lagged behind these real social developments, leading to the need for a new mode of sociological analysis. This new science has to built on two foundations: '1) No understanding can be gained and no problems solved without a social class analysis' and '2) Any study of the economic and social discrepancies between regions [in Turkey] and the related ethnic factors, until now a taboo subject, is inadequate and incomplete without this class analysis' (Beşikçi 1992: 11, foreword to the first, 1969, edition) (my translation). The book is also an attempt 'to reveal in its full dimensions and details the "Eastern Problem" [Doğu Sorunu], which is one of the important problems of the collapsing present order and which the ruling classes and political powers have portrayed to the people in a different way' (Beşikçi 1992: 12, foreword to the second, 1970, edition) (my translation). Note that although the 'Doğu Sorunu' is put in inverted comments, Beşikçi does not yet conceptualize it as the 'Kurdish problem.'

By the 1992 re-edition however, and in fact way before then, Beşikçi has changed his mind. In the third edition, along with a new foreword Beşikçi also reprints two other pieces of writing: the foreword to his 1976 book *Bilim Yontemi* (*Scientific Method*), and an article titled '*Doğu Anadolu'nun Düzeni*'nin Başina Gelenler' (The Things that Happened to the *Order of Eastern Anatolia*). All three pieces articulate the author's retrospective sense of the book's deficiencies.[13] His major critique, in short, relates to what he calls the book's 'Kemalist approach' (Beşikçi 1992: 26). The major reason for this approach was the inability of the author at the time of writing to step outside the bounds of the official ideology. In Beşikçi's own words:

> When I [re]read these sections and others like them, I am shocked and amazed. The hypothesis posited and the documents thought to prove these arguments all lean upon official documents.[14] Because there is not the slightest doubt felt about these documents, because they are accepted as they stand, because there was no felt necessity to evaluate the truth or falsity of them [these sections] have no relation to a scientific methodology... There is not the slightest criticism of Kemalism. In the name of its revolutionary spirit, in the name of its left-wing politics Kemalist principles are defended and an effort is made to apply them to life and persuade of their truth... When we examine carefully the leftist publications, the Turkish media and the studies from Turkish universities of the sixties this same characteristic is apparent in all of them. (Beşikçi 1992: 15) (my translation)

Nevertheless, putting aside for the moment Beşikçi's own critical distance on his study, what knowledge about Kurdish society does it produce? Because it is such a large and complex book (734 pages, two volumes) and organized in a somewhat complicated way, we can only indicate some of the building blocks contributing to its argument. One key concern of the introduction, titled 'What is the Fundamental Problem?' (*'Ana Sorunu Nedir?'*) is to emphasize first the urgent dependency between research topic and social problem and, secondly, between a scientific analysis of those problems and the making of changes that seek to solve them. Mis-identification of the fundamental determining factors that shape the continuing superstructural institutions of *feudalism* in eastern Anatolia, which include the economic, social and cultural politics of the central authority, results in only superficial solutions to those problems. Permanent solutions require social structural transformation of those factors. In brief, because the problems originate mainly in the class relations of the mode of production, their alleviation requires

13. Why publish it again, given these faults? Beşikçi explains how the second edition (1970), which involved an extensive rewriting and lengthening of the text, was deliberately sabotaged (under political pressure) by the publisher, with numerous mistakes and omissions. The third printing is a corrected version of this second edition.

14. The official documents referred to by Beşikçi here include his citing as unquestioned truth the interpretations of the independence struggle and the new republic's politics made by Mustafa Kemal and other important Turkish nationalist leaders. By contrast, his change of mind also involves his questioning of these documents' factual quality, or their status as 'information' about military or political events. Instead these documents too become *historiography*, self-interested, political and politicized constructions of history.

establishment of a more equal mode of production (or socialism).[15] Yet because
the eastern problem also has an ethnic dimension, its solution demands, minimally,
an end to the policies suppressing expression of the East's ethnic difference. Most
succinctly:

> it should not be overlooked that the Eastern problem is an ethnic problem. At the same
> time, this problem has to be examined together with the mode of production in Turkey
> and its determination by the forces and relations of production and especially the process
> of the evolution from feudalism to capitalism. (Beşikçi 1992: 34) (my translation)

Beşikçi's analytic imagining of Eastern Anatolia as half-feudal/half-capitalist
then is both influenced by and contributor to a broader Marxian circuit of knowledge
globally influential in the social sciences and anthropology in the same period. He
begins by sketching out a large-scale historical model asserting a deterministic relation between modes of production and the political/social institutions characterizing
them. Each mode of production creates super-structural institutions (including
the form of state) whose main function is to prevent the evolving contradictions
characterizing its productive relations – in the feudal context, the relation between
landlord and peasant – from transforming that mode of production into another.
Representing Eastern Anatolia as critically poised in the transition from feudalism
to capitalism provides a powerful analytic vision, giving both an overall direction to
historical change but also a handle on the uneven and often contradictory array of
social relations in the present. It also engages with a widespread debate in Turkey
and elsewhere at the time concerning the historical development of an Islamic
feudalism or the 'Asiatic mode of production', which sought to differentiate between
European and Ottoman forms of agrarian power relations.

15. Beşikçi's desire to revolutionize the order of Eastern Anatolia highlights the quite different
intellectual and political aims motivating the studies of Leach and Barth. Most importantly, for Barth
and Leach there is no 'eastern problem', in both terms of that phrase. (That is, there is no east and
there is no problem.) The integrity of their object of study (Kurdish society) is guaranteed by their
quarantining it from broader class and ethnic relations in Iraq, on the assumption of Kurdish society's
political autonomy. Not for nothing does Barth entitle his study *Principles of Social Organization
in Southern Kurdistan*, rather than *Principles of Social Organization in Northern Iraq*. For Beşikçi,
Marxism is a social theory that seeks to understand the flow and development of history as key to
the social relations of the present and the future. But it is also a theory and practice of political action
that seeks to influence that development or act as midwife to its unfolding. Glibly, if class analysis is
the theory, class struggle is the practice. But these two activities are better seen as different aspects
of the same thing. If debate – say in anthropology – between intellectuals of Marxist persuasion is a
form of class struggle, it is because these debates are seen as vital in identifying the class ideology of
official history. But neither are they divorceable nor inextricable from the political programmes and
actions of Marxist groupings and their political struggles, given intellectuals were often aligned with or
themselves active in different groups.

Very briefly, what characterizes the feudal economic and political order in Eastern Anatolia? In the first place, feudalism implies a set of legal and social obligations between landowners and villagers. Religion is presented as the most important institution ensuring the smooth reproduction of unequal relations between the ruling classes and the population. Yet the legitimacy of this superstructural legal order in Eastern Anatolia rests less on a functional reciprocity of duties between classes and more on the despotic power of the landlord. Given their interest in land tenure arrangements and despite the different analytic language they use, Barth and Leach might partially agree. But Beşikçi's evolutionary schema makes it clear that feudalism is not a closed system. Further, its continued existence as a mode of production in Eastern Anatolia is assured by the policies of the government, as well as by a related alliance between the hegemonic classes of eastern and western Turkey. So for example, despite the state thrice sending the Eastern Anatolian land-lords (*ağha*), tribal chiefs (*aşiret reisi*) and religious leaders (*şeyhler*) into exile (in 1926, 1937, 1960), the lack of accompanying action to produce new institutions there meant both a social crisis in their absence and an increase in their influence upon their return (Beşikçi 1992: 53).

Nevertheless, feudal property and productive relations are not uniform throughout the region, as Beşikçi's case studies of varying structural arrangements in different areas show. Indeed capitalist relations of wage labour are presented as typically dissolving feudal productive relations in many places, resulting in overlapping feudal, semi-feudal and capitalist modes of production. As we have seen, the weakening or displacing of feudal relations and forces of production occurs in tandem with parallel developments in political institutions, in this case the collapse of divisions between once self-sufficient tribes and the transformation of the dominance of the religious or landed classes. Similarly, the revolution wrought by capitalism on feudal structures leads to a new form of 'legitimate' political institution, the national state with its distinctive ideology, nationalism (*ulusçuluk*). Analysis of the Eastern Anatolian political economy then gives on to an analysis of the national problem, or the problem of ethnic differentiation and discrimination in the region. In a nutshell, it consists of the refusal of the Turkish state and central authority to recognize as equally legitimate the next stage of development, the economically conditioned rising national consciousness of many Kurds.

Finally for the curious, according to Beşikçi, what was 'Kemalist' about this set of arguments? In his foreword to the third edition he writes that readers of his later books would notice immediately the contradictions between them and *Doğu Anadolu'nun Düzeni*. And the title of the book he cites as evidence – *Devletlerarası Sömürge Kürdistan* (*Kurdistan: A Colony between States*) – certainly shows no mincing with synonyms. Interestingly, what makes *Doğu Anadolu'nun Düzeni* 'Kemalist' is its conformity to Kemalist *historiography*, particularly its acceptance of a certain version of the independence struggle in Turkey in the 1920s and its related construction of the Kurdish rebellions in Eastern Anatolia after the founding of the Republic. As Beşikçi says himself, 'the events and their factual relations are the same. What has changed is the way I look at those events' (Beşikçi 1992: 26).[16] In brief, Beşikçi has drastically tempered his initial enthusiasm for Kemalism's war against feudal elements in Kurdistan:

> From the perspective of Kurds and Turks, the Lausanne Treaty carries completely different meanings. For the Turks, the Lausanne Treaty founds an independent state. It brings the independent Turkish state an international guarantee. For the Kurds by contrast it founds captivity, slavery and colonialism... To look at history always from the perspective of class struggle, and to ignore the desires and will of ethnic groups, is not always to understands events (Beşikçi 1992: 21, my translation).

Agha, Shaikh and State: The Social and Political Structures of Kurdistan

Our last ethnography is probably also the most widely-cited study of Kurdish society, Martin van Bruinessen's *Agha, Shaikh and State: The Social and Political Structures of Kurdistan*. Published first in German in 1989 and in English in 1992 (but submitted as a doctoral thesis in 1978), Van Bruinessen says in his introduction that under the influence of 'the political and intellectual climate of the late 1960s' he (like Beşikçi) became strongly interested in theories concerning 'peasant revolts, messianic movements, nationalism and class consciousness' (Van Bruinessen 1992: 1). Kurdish history and politics appeared an ideal case to test such theories. He also talks about the political constraints upon his fieldwork caused by the (in)securities of the three nation-states within which the majority of Kurds live and the impact of these constraints upon his representation of society. It is this discussion that illuminates his choice of subtitle: refused a research permit and thus forced to travel around as a tourist in Iran, Iraq and Turkey, he chose to focus on trans-national Kurdish social institutions as conditioned or modified by those nation-states. Van Bruinessen puts it somewhat differently: 'Because of ... the difficulties in obtaining permission, I decided to continue my research by visiting a number of other parts of Kurdistan and surveying a variety of forms of social organization and processes of social change' (Van Bruinessen 1992: 5).

If the survey of varieties of forms of social organization is reminiscent of Barth's enterprise but on a grander scale (and with an un-Barthian concern for their creation by surrounding states), the methodology is uncannily reminiscent of Sykes. (His study is the 'result of about 7,500 miles of riding and innumerable conversations with policemen, muleteers, chieftains, sheep drovers, horse dealers, carriers and

---

16. For an enlightening contextualization of Ismail Beşikçi's work in the context of the broader Turkish left and the founding in 1961 and evolution of the Turkish Workers Party (TIP), see Tanil Bora's 2002 article 'Türkiye'de Siyasal Ideolojilerde ABD/Amerika Imgesi' ('The Image of the US/America in Political Ideologies in Turkey').

other people capable of giving one first hand information.') A different name for transnational Kurdish social institutions and Van Bruinessen's preferred term, is 'primordial loyalties'. These include loyalties to family, tribe and to tribal chieftain or *ağha*, as well as religious loyalties to sheikhs, popular mystics or leaders of dervish orders. The study's subject is the question of the continuing relevance of these so-called primordial loyalties amongst rural and village Kurds. As with Beşikçi, Van Bruinessen assumes that these primordial loyalties act against peasants' or tribesmens' 'objective interests' or to negate their own rights vis-à-vis tribal chieftains and landlords, even if he does not pursue this critique with an equivalent missionary zeal.[17] Unlike Beşikçi, however, he does not assume that their presence stands as an obstacle in the passage from feudalism to socialism.

Van Bruinessen's study then has a much greater geographical scope and historical depth than those of Leach and Barth, covering in principle both the whole of Kurdistan as well as its changing social formations since incorporation into the Ottoman empire and Middle Eastern nationstates. Indeed, it makes a virtue out of necessity, in the extensive use of historical documents (including Ottoman texts, and accounts of travellers and colonial officials) to clarify and reconstruct the varying messy social arrangements encountered in the fieldwork. Kurdish society in that case is somewhat awkwardly imagined as a synthesis produced by contingent historical events (often connected to wider 'incorporation in military and/or administrative hierarchies' (Van Bruinessen 1992: 62)), and more enduring structural patterns, understood as basic to the wide variety of Kurdish social and political organization. 'The first of these general patterns is a structural one: the *segmentary tribe*, consisting of patrilineages with a preference for endogamy' (Van Bruinessen 1992: 50, emphasis in original). The specific forms of organization are *historically determined variations* of this tribal structure. With its emphasis on the contribution of the preference for endogamous marriage to the isolation of segments from each other and to their often conflicted relations, the resemblance to Barth's work is clear. But his articulating of these lineage solidarities and rivalries with the 'external world' extends the analysis to consider how both imperial and national states, political parties and even pan-tribal nationalist fronts manipulated segmentary oppositions for control and influence, as well as how lineage leaders manipulate these processes in turn in order to gain an advantage over local rivals. On the other hand, like Barth and Leach, Van Bruinessen decides to exclude the social dynamics of the Kurdish cities from his study.

In brief, Van Bruinessen's study is a historical anthropology, although not tied systematically into the dialectics of historical materialism and its evolutionary sequences.[18] It is historical because of the author's concern to trace via various

17. We should note that this is also the ideological assumption of the modernizing Kemalist states in the region.

18. Van Bruinessen very occasionally uses the vocabulary of Marxist analysis, noting for example (as does Beşikçi) the impact of new forces of production (the mechanization of agriculture) on local relations of production, as landlords were freed from the need for villagers' labour.

texts and fieldwork both the changing social stratification of Kurdish society – its very complex mixture of tribal and non-tribal groups, nomads, peasants, gypsies, as well as numerous different religious and ethnic identities – and the real 'trajectories of social mobility' (Van Bruinessen 1992: 122) of these groups *over time*. These trajectories of mobility lead him to stress the fluidity of membership of ethnic and caste groups against diffusionist theories of an original non-tribal peasantry and their conquest by tribal overlords of different ethnic origin (see Sykes). Social mobility is always also conditioned by the pervasive influence of regional states, as shown by Van Bruinessen's long sketch of the political history of Kurdistan over the last five centuries. His conclusion is of interest, especially given its reversal of Beşikçi's more orthodox Marxist categories:

> Kurdish society has thus, during the past five centuries, passed through what are generally recognized as crucial stages in social evolution: tribe, chiefdom and (proto-)state, but in *descending* order. This devolution of Kurdish political institutions is an immediate consequence of the development of the political institutions of the states into which Kurdistan was incorporated. (Van Bruinessen 1992: 195, emphasis in original)[19]

In the process, Leach's brief structuralist explanation for the apparently 'conditional nature of the *aghas'* authority' in Rowanduz in 1940 (Leach 1940: 19) is corrected – it was the result of increasing state control over Kurdish society, or better of *decreasing* delegation of power by central authorities to Kurdish political units.[20] In short, Van Bruinessen's ethnography seeks to establish the defining relevance of specific historical events (i.e. the Ottoman Land Code of 1858) on processes of Kurdish social and political organization in the present.

Nevertheless there is also a certain ambiguity embedded in the analysis, exemplified in Van Bruinessen's comment that 'I was looking for materials that would allow me to compare a present *state of affairs* with that in the past' (Van Bruinessen 1992: 6, my emphasis), or 'I describe tribes and dervish orders as I found them functioning in Kurdistan, or as I reconstructed them in the past from interviews and literature' (Van Bruinessen 1992: 7). Which past will Van Bruinessen choose for his explication of the difference of the present? Which present state of affairs is to be compared? (Obviously not the urban one.) Are primordial loyalties to be understood as *historical* 'states of affairs' too? And despite their apparent competition with more 'modern'

---

19. Richard Tapper describes the more general historical and anthropological enterprise somewhat similarly: 'A focus on the role of tribes in state formation in the Middle East needs to be complemented by awareness of the role of states in 'tribe formation' – and deformation' (Tapper 1990: 52).

20. There is, then, a similarity between Van Bruinessen's historicization of the relative contemporary powerlessness of tribal chieftains in 1940s Iraq and Nugent's 1982 revision of Leach's study of *Political Systems of Highland Burma* (1954), in which changes in political structure are attributed not to internal systemics of marriage exchange and kinship arrangements but to external developments related to control of the region's opium trade and the political profits accruing from it.

forms of consciousness such as class or nation, are these loyalties best described as primordial? Finally what of the status of the abstract 'general patterns' of Kurdish society that Van Bruinessen identifies? Are they historically produced, or are they its essential structural features, Kurdish society at its repetitive moment of origin, environmentally calibrated, from which the distance of the transformed present can be measured? Marx's famous comment from the *Grundrisse* – 'everything social that has a fixed form merely is a vanishing moment in the movement of society' (cited in Starr 1992: 175) – hints at how potentially circular it is to simultaneously reconstruct the past via an interpretation of social relations in the present, while identifying the present based upon an interpretation of the past's difference.

Of course, Van Bruinessen grounds the power of the Kurdish notable families (and tribal chiefs or landlords) on more than their connections with external states. Hence the second major theme explored in his study, the analysis of the role of religion in the politics of Kurdistan and in the legitimizing of the influence and esteem of its local leaders. Similarly to Barth, van Bruinessen too begins this investigation by briefly summarizing the various positions (*Sayyid*, *Mulla*, Prophet, Shaikh) through which people have historically 'derived political and economic leverage from association with the Divine' (Van Bruinessen 1992: 205). (Like Barth, Van Bruinessen confines his discussion to the Islam of men.) The most important of these and the role on which he concentrates is the position of shaikh or what van Bruinessen defines as the leader-instructor in mystical brotherhoods, or the dervish and Sufi orders.[21] Unlike Barth, however, Van Bruinessen is particularly interested in the relationship between the Naqshbandi order and Shaikh Said's revolt against the new Turkish republic in 1925 and more generally in the influence of the shaikhs in the historical development of Kurdish nationalism. Barth, we might remember, dated the rise of a new class of landlord in southern Kurdistan to the nineteenth-century destruction of the Baban principality by the Ottoman state. Van Bruinessen, too, historicizes the rise of the shaikhs and their influence to the same disruptive post-*Tanzimat* Ottoman policy, and more particularly to the shaikhs' sudden filling of a power vacuum in mediating between warring tribes no longer welded together in larger tribal confederations. Shaikhly families also consolidated their spiritual power by taking advantage of the 1850s Ottoman land registration to become some of the biggest landowners in the region. As 'the most influential indigenous leaders in Kurdistan [they became thereafter] the obvious focal points for nationalist sentiment' (Van Bruinessen 1992: 234).

Like Beşikçi, then, Van Bruinessen weaves together the shaikhs' religious authority, class exploitation and leadership in rebellion against the Turkish and Iraqi nation-states' domination over the Kurdish regions. Beşikçi's emphasis is on religion as a mode of exploitation over peasants; the feudal shaikhs' leadership

---

21. Van Bruinessen says that the two main dervish orders present in Kurdistan are the Qadiri and the Naqshbandi.

of rebellions is attributed primarily to their defence of their class interests and the unthinking obedience of their followers. But Van Bruinessen's concentrating on the political power of the shaikhs (as Kurdish nationalists, as landlords and over their disciples) does not completely detract from his interest in the shaikhs' more humble followers (*sufis*) and their experience of the brotherhoods. His descriptions of meetings reveal the orders as sites of intense conviviality and personal relationship. In his introduction he writes that 'because of my own fascination with them, I describe more than only those aspects that have political relevance: philosophy and ritual receive much attention' (Van Bruinessen 1992: 8). In another place he writes that he personally 'shares the conviction [of the Naqshbandi] that the Naqshbandi meditations … have greater spiritual value than the gross techniques of inducing ecstatic states as practiced in the Qadiri order' (Van Bruinessen 1992: 225). What Van Bruinessen's study opens out towards – if not explicitly theorized in these terms – is the perspective of the followers and an understanding of why the disciples of shaikhs might agree to their submission, or why the economically exploitative relations between a shaikh and local peasants or tribesmen continue. Here there is a gesturing to the affective dimensions of such brotherhoods and to the forms of pleasure and meaning their members create. On the other hand, Van Bruinessen never gives much ground to the agency of the dominated to produce 'undercurrent[s] that run counter to the dominant system of values' (Van Bruinessen 1992: 249).[22]

Van Bruinessen's final chapter is devoted to the 1925 Shaikh Said rebellion in Turkey. After an orthodox sketch of its historical antecedents – nationalist currents in the late Ottoman empire, the Turkish nationalism of the Committee of Union and Progress, the partition of the Empire and the Treaty of Sevres, the Turkish war of independence and the new Lausanne Treaty, the republic's nascent policy of forced assimilation of the Kurds – Van Bruinessen follows closely the fortunes of its principal actors, using a combination of archival material, published works and oral testimonies. His reconstruction and analysis is extremely valuable, as is his assessment of the role of the Naqshbandi brotherhood and nationalist and religious motivations in the revolt's unfolding. His concluding remarks return us to the question of the continuing influence of the primordial loyalties of many Kurds to an *agha* or a shaikh, set against the spread of nationalism and socialism. Unlike for Beşikçi, whose concern is coercion from above and not loyalty from below, such ties are not necessarily seen as retarded elements in the transition to capitalism: 'nationalism and socialism, rather, came to be used to lend additional legitimacy to traditional authority' (Van Bruinessen 1992: 316). Similarly 'economic change – notably intensified exploitation – may put loyalties under a heavier strain but will not

22. Beşikçi gives even less ground. For him religion and its ethics simply reflect the political economy and accordingly serve the hegemonic classes: disciples' own meanings and experiences of religious practices are literally of no account. To be sure, in the socialist future with its alternative institutions there would be no need for the 'comfort' of religion.

necessarily lead to their breakdown. In any given situation, economic factors alone cannot explain which loyalties will prevail – primordial, class or national ones' (Van Bruinessen 1992: 317). The tenor of this concluding quote demonstrates the virtue of Van Bruinessen's study, with its historical reconstruction of the way in which tribes came into existence and its complex empirical comparisons. On the other hand, for a major ethnography the material is remarkably under-theorized, particularly in its exploration of peasant consciousness and local meanings, or in its attempted discussion of simultaneously affective and exploitative relations. This applies even more so to kinship and gender relations, which are not even mentioned. And for a book so indebted to historical construction, it is also surprisingly uninterested in the politics of historical imagination in the lives of its informants or in the ideologies of the Iranian, Iraqi and Turkish nation-states.

Representing Kurdish Society: The Kurdistan of Anthropology

Let me conclude this chapter by reviewing in summary form some of the most important issues that this survey of ethnographic representations of social relations in Kurdistan reveals:

- Identifying the integrity of the appropriate political, economic or social unit of Kurdish society is always problematical and the anthropologist's imagined field of social relations needs to be argued for rather than assumed.
- As early as 1940 Radcliffe-Brown claimed that 'what is happening in a Transkeian tribe, for example, can only be described by recognizing that the tribe has been incorporated into a wide political and social structural system' (cited in Barth 2005: 30). The same applies to the Kurdish tribes too: yet what is the nature of the wider system into which Kurdistan has been incorporated? Is it modernity, or capitalism, or the colonial, or the nation-state? Naming and analysing its key dimensions are also always intellectual and political decisions. In the earlier ethnographies there is a lack of theorizing of nationalism, and Leach and Barth's ignoring of Iraqi 'nation-building' shows some similarities with much Kurdish historiography in its reluctance to imagine a conjoined 'Ottoman-Kurdish' past (see Chapter 2). Indeed for both there is an ongoing difficulty, in theory and in fact, in conceptualizing and then mediating Kurdish 'indigenous social organization' (Barth 1953: 139) with supra-regional networks.
- The ethnographies reveal a clear preference for either functional or historical analysis of social relations in Kurdistan. Barth's recent appreciation of the virtues of the new post-war anthropology can be cited to clarify the difference: wary of the search for origins as historical explanations, a better research project by contrast 'required the anthropologist search for understanding and explanation *within* the very object of study' (Barth 2005: 22, author's emphasis).

- The ethnographies engage in a recurring debate over the extent of the domination and exploitation of tribesmen and peasants by *aghas* and sheikhs. Both Leach and Barth emphasize aspects of tribal solidarity and kinship that minimize the ability of *aghas* to assert their authority. By contrast the unreformed Beşikçi appreciates the initial Kemalist assault on the east's feudal hegemonic classes, even if this programme was later abandoned. Many differences come into play here: certainly the varying political commitments of the anthropologists, but also the anthropological ideal of a sympathetic and nuanced understanding of social relationships. Kemalism preferred to stress the exploitative character (grounded in ignorance) of Eastern society and the need for external state enlightenment to transform it. In both cases local actors are seen as passive. Somewhat related to these differences is Beşikçi's application of a European-based and evolutionary Marxist model of history (feudalism, capitalism, socialism) to Kurdistan. This periodization is qualified by Barth and even Van Bruinessen, with their identification of a 'tribal structure [that] is, as it were, superimposed upon quasi-feudal dominance relations' (Van Bruinessen 1992: 50).

- There is a vital interest in the role and nature of religion in Kurdistan. Nearly all authors approach religion via consideration of its political intent, although this ranges from analysis of Islam as a resource for utilitarian self-interest to its function in shoring up class hegemony. Whereas Van Bruinessen (1992: 8) claims to describe 'more than only those aspects [of brotherhoods] that have political significance', Beşikçi's militant stance produces religion as something not to be elucidated but to be opposed. For Beşikçi the miscomprehension of their own situation by the masses is facilitated by religious institutions and understandings of the world, which need to be demystified so as to reveal their true role in the process of domination.

- Accordingly the texts are characterized in the first instance by a concern for socio-economic exploitation and secondly for ethnic/nationalist oppression, and remain uninterested in women's lives and the question of gender oppression or in gender as a system of inequality. The exploitation that matters is a male prerogative. Despite this there is still confusion over the primary characteristics of the oppressed and hence of the true emancipatory actor in Kurdistan: is it a class or the nation or both? It is definitely not women.

- With the partial exception of Barth there is little discussion overall on the question of individual agency and constraint or of the knowledge of actors themselves, nor on the question of the relationship between the 'activist' structures (feudal or lineage) and subjects' own experience and organization of living arrangements and relationships. Far from a 'successive deconstruction of the subject as actor' in anthropological texts over the century (see note 1), there have rarely been any individual subjects in Kurdish ethnography.

- Significantly, there is nothing on the city, or on the transformation of 'enduring structural patterns' like segmentary lineages in urban contexts. The focus of all the ethnographies is the social relations of rural Kurdistan.

What final conclusions might we draw from these ethnographic imaginings of Kurdish society? On first reflection there appears a distinct lack of continuity in anthropological knowledge about Kurds. Authors certainly make use of certain items of information from the work of predecessors, especially in matters such as the names of Kurdish tribes or in their territorial spread: but there seems no unified knowledge about social relations in Kurdistan or acceptance of a common theoretical paradigm. Indeed it is clear that the state of anthropological research in general is influential in determining which aspect of the Kurdish 'reality' is to be emphasized in the ethnographies. On the other hand, we have seen a focus on certain topics (say land tenure arrangements or tribal structure) that cut across the ethnographic texts and seem to indicate certain continuities of analysis.

Yet when we return to the notion of circuits of knowledge about Kurds, this apparent lack of continuity becomes less noticeable. Indeed from a perspective outside of the discipline of anthropology, the ethnographic analyses make up a recognizable textual corpus, despite their differences of approach and conclusion. Other circuits of knowledge production about Kurds – say Turkish or Iraqi state discourse – lend themselves less to comparison and more immediately to juxtaposition. But it is when we make (to adapt Piterberg) the occasion of anthropological writing about Kurds itself an anthropological topic that a range of other important issues arise: the conditions of possibility for ethnographic representations in the first place for example, or the question of anthropological knowledge and political control. As we have already seen, anthropology as a discipline has been accused of duplicity with colonialism in varied ways. Nevertheless we also noted how the cultural relativism of the classical anthropological imagination possessed a shared vocabulary or vision of society with nationalism. Further, in the post-colonial era the nationalism of nation-states manifests itself as both a civilizing regime and as a project of identity formation and assimilation which shares many of the authoritarian attributes of colonial governance.

These general links between anthropology, colonialism and nationalism take on a particular complexion then in the case of the production of ethnographic knowledge about Kurds. Post-colonial theory and its critique of that knowledge known as orientalism has long identified the way much Western writing about the Orient has served both to denigrate it and generate a Western self through this representation of the 'other'. Thus one relatively recent book begins its investigation by stating: 'This book explores the discursive dynamics that secure a sovereign subject status for the West. It is about the cultural representation of the West to *itself* by way of a detour through the other' (Yeğenoğlu 1998: 1).[23] But the overly focused nature of

---

23. Although it is plausible that Minorsky, Leach, van Bruinessen etc. construct for themselves and for their Western readers a superior self-distinction through their representation of Kurds, this still needs to be critically established rather than pre-emptively assumed. But it is also important to stress

this and similar analyses neglects to consider a range of other circuits of knowledge about Kurds that likewise secure sovereign subjects through their textual or visual representations. Indeed I would argue that the production of anthropological knowledge about Kurds should *not* be assimilated to this general orientalist critique, mainly because a more politically efficacious discourse (originating in Turkish, Persian and Arab nationalisms) on cultural difference in those countries has denied Kurdish self-description of their otherness.[24] It is in this context that we can understand the decision of Kurdish publishing houses in Istanbul or northern Iraq to translate and reprint these accounts of Western observers. This is also to say that the meaning of these texts lies in the eyes of the beholder. In other words, it is arguable that at least since the institution of Middle Eastern nation-states (and even before them with the modernization of the Ottoman Empire) the centres of power primarily responsible for violent mastery (ideological and political) over the Kurdish regions are Turkey, Iraq and Iran. Further, it is precisely the nationalisms of these nation-states that have constituted sovereign ethnic citizens through their wilful representations of Kurdish history and society. The prime censorships in operation vis-à-vis anthropological circuits of knowledge are revealing: it was these states that denied Van Bruinessen permission to do research, or gaoled Beşikçi and banned his work. Beşikçi's analysis is important, not because he is a 'native informant' (Spivak 1999) but because his change of mind is just one more indication of the multitude of circuits of knowledge production in 'indigenous contexts' themselves.

To sum up, in comparison to the analysis of selected constructions of historical developments in Kurdistan presented in Chapters 1 and 2, Chapter 3 has sought more consciously to imagine Kurdish society from the inside, as a 'cultural-social unit with [its] own identity and internal dynamics' (Karpat 2003: 1). This is useful if only because it provides a contrast with much historical material that positions Kurdistan or the Kurds as 'unruly' or anarchic, at least from the perspective of the

---

that this difference is only one aspect of the complexity of those readers' lives. This issue comes out poignantly in one of Philip Larkin's poems (*The Importance of Elsewhere*). True, Larkin is glad of the separateness that his experience of Ireland (its look, its smell, its sounds) allows. But what this detour to Ireland's cultural otherness secures for Larkin is a legitimate strangeness not granted to his difference in his own home.

24. To give just one example, see the work *Türk Milli Bütünlüğü İçerisinde Doğu Anadolu* (*Eastern Anatolia Within the Turkish National Whole*), prepared by six academics aligned to Ankara University and published by the Institute for Research into Turkish Culture. In it they claim that Kurds are Turkish tribes from Eastern Anatolia, and then draw the logical conclusions:

> Right up to the present, those people and groups who are involved in Kurdish movements do so to profit from whatever fortune or position separatism might bring. As for revolts in the past, and no differently to other places in Anatolia, they occurred as reactions against the new changes and the spoiling of vested interests. Fanatics from inside Turkey and self-interested outside circles work to give these uprisings an ideological meaning. (Ögel *et al.* 1985: 162) (my translation)

centre. It is instructive to reverse the lens and review the literature that presents imperial 'centres' as peripheral to the Kurds.

Nevertheless, as our analysis of the ethnographies has shown, 'peripheral' obviously does not mean 'unimportant': by contrast it describes a certain type of vital relationship. Indeed, this conforms to one concern of this book as a whole: to understand how people (Kurds in particular) imagine Kurdistan in relation to others' claims and actions upon it. Perhaps neither the historical nor the ethnographic accounts are preferable. Both face the problem of writing about cultural and political differences constructed and maintained through people's connections with, not isolation from, each other. Indeed it is through this long history of encounter, both violent and peaceful, that Kurds and their others have co-constituted themselves as both the same and different.

–4–

Kemalism and the Crafting of National Selves in Kurdistan

The ethnographic accounts interpreted in Chapter 3 began with an assumption of the local political autonomy of Kurdish society and ended with an investigation of the impact of regional nation-states upon Kurdistan. Yet in nearly all the ethnographic representations (excepting Beşikçi's) these states are rather undefined presences, responsible in part for the transformation of social relations in the Kurdish regions but never made a proper object of analysis in their own right. What characterizes these emerging new centres of power? This chapter shifts its focus from discourse on Kurds in order to identify a *transnational* state political practice within which that discourse must be contextualized. The interlocutor of this discourse is Kemalism. As with disputes concerning the defining features of the Ottoman empire, so too have the political projects of these nation-states, particularly in reference to their Kurdish provinces, been interpreted and evaluated in radically different ways.

Chapter 4 examines some of these interpretations as they assess the ambitious projects of nation-building emanating from the modernizing capitals of Baghdad, Tehran and Ankara and accompanied by varying degrees of intolerance towards regional autonomy, minority ethnic languages and social identities. My focus zeroes in on the formative years of these new nation-states. Following Sayyid (1997) I label as Kemalist the ideology and social programmes of *all* the secularizing, modernizing and nationalizing Ottoman successor states that mediated independence in Muslim-majority areas following decolonization in the Middle East. Nevertheless, I will argue that Sayyid's definition of Kemalism is inadequate: most significantly because in prioritizing its disenfranchising of Islam as it core component he overlooks its equally important homogenizing nationalist project and its constructing of new sovereign ethnic identities. I begin by clarifying various ways in which the Kemalist project has been understood, before presenting my own modified definition. As we have seen in previous chapters, any selection and assessment of foundational events is simultaneously an expression of agency and an act of political intervention, most importantly for the social group with whom the writer identifies and whom the historical narrative privileges.

The second, third and fourth sections of the chapter examine in greater detail various of the governmental strategies of the Kemalist states of Iraq, Iran and Turkey, discussing in particular their attempts at constituting and mobilizing a Kemalist civil society. In this endeavour the Turkish republicans were probably the most radical in the sweep of their state activism, not merely with their reforms in what Kandiyoti calls the 'juridico-political and institutional realms' (Kandiyoti 1997: 13) but just as influentially in their making of a cultural revolution. Nevertheless, a cultural politics was likewise intrinsic to Kemalist rule in Iran and Iraq. Thus we will examine the Kemalists' creation and formalization of a range of practices, including new words or alphabets, musical forms, programmes of women's education, festivals and folklore, theatrical performance (including radio theatre), maternal training and sciences of household management. All of these can also be usefully reframed as state initiatives to sponsor new forms of embodied skills and knowledge. A final brief reflection on the efficacy or otherwise of these strategies in infiltrating people's practices and binding citizens to the principles of these Kemalist states will conclude the chapter.

Defining Kemalism

The makers of Kemalist regimes were polemicists and polemics still surrounds discussion of both the basic intentions and ideological character of Kemalism, let alone any critical evaluation of the continuing influence of Kemalism over the politics of Turkey and other Middle Eastern societies. In Turkey Kemalism is reinforced by a number of juridical and coercive measures, and according to the 1980 constitution is the official doctrine of the state. Political parties must show allegiance to its defining characteristics or face closure by the Constitutional Court. Nevertheless, there is controversy over the extent to which the Kemalism of the single party period (1923–50) still structures the field of Turkish politics: the debate often comes down to more-or-less literal readings of Kemalism's key features, as encapsulated for example in its six principles (or arrows). What is clear is that many political actors themselves – Laicists, Islamists and Kurds – root their defining convictions or grievances in the politics of the republic's first two decades, as these politics are made to live on for profit or loss in the present.

Let me give just three examples of these antithetical assessments of the Kemalist legacy in Turkey, which also reveal the way these analyses are intimately connected to intensely politicized and now globalized polemics around Islam, modernity, democracy and development. In an article on nationalism in Turkey, Seufert (2000) compares the work on civil society of two prominent Turkish scholars, Binnaz Toprak and Nilufer Göle, each of whom published an article in a book on that topic covering the broader Middle East. According to Seufert, in her essay:

> Toprak unqualifiedly welcomes the secularizing policies of the early Republic, and considers these as the only means of establishing firm ground in the wake of the overthrow of an ancient and authoritarian policy. She draws most attention to the universal, and inclusionary aspect of modern and secular values. Turkish secularization, she argues

was the only way to mediate between the competing beliefs, interests and identities of a people called upon for the first time to participate in decision making. (Seufert 2000: 26)

By contrast, Seufert notes how:

Göle questions the placement of secularizing efforts on the same level as efforts to generate liberty and civil society... On a political level, she refers to the fact that in many Middle Eastern societies, laicism was introduced by authoritarian means, and did not develop as the secularization of worldview in time ... Göle disagrees with the notion that the elite's secularizing politics be considered as a means of generating political participation and self-government, pointing out that along with Islamism, Turkey's modernizing politics similarly suppressed other trends such as liberalism, leftist ideology and kinds of local self-organization. (Seufert 2000: 27)

For Toprak, who models her claims on the historical experience of Europe, secularism in good Enlightenment fashion is a prerequisite for democracy. For Göle the proper question is how to democratize secularism itself, given its institution by post-colonial state elites as an integral aspect of a broader project of social engineering.

My second example is drawn from Resat Kasaba's and from Taha Parla/Andrew Davison's wildly discordant accounts of the single-party period. According to Kasaba:

When we examine this crucial interval [the 1930s], we are not dealing with an overtly planned and systematically imposed coherent body of policies that aimed to create a new, powerful, and centralized state. What we have, instead, is a state in the making, a state that was dealing with a set of difficult conditions that it had inherited from its predecessor – conditions that were exacerbated by the international conjuncture of the interwar years. The Turkish state tried to deal with these hard times by using policies that were not always coherent or consistent. (Kasaba 2000: 4)

Again by contrast compare Parla and Davison:

[There is a] widespread impression, described earlier, that Mustafa Kemal and the leading political organs of Kemalism lacked an ideology at all during the 1920s, at least until the arrows were announced in the RPP's [Republican People's Party] 1931 program... From our perspective, the early years constitute the formative years of Kemalist solidaristic corporatism, and the early statements – statements that illustrate a clear continuity with those found well into the 1930s and 1940s – comprise the foundational, ideological texts of the regime. They illustrate clear solidaristic corporatist ideological dimensions of Kemalist 'pragmatic' politics from its inception, and they are the texts that have set the basic ideological contours for Turkish political thought and practice since its founding. (Parla and Davison 2004: 59–60)

Whereas, for Kasaba, Turkish state policies even in the 1930s were pragmatically contingent on a range of other actors and historical contexts, for Parla and Davison republican governance over the whole of the single-party period demonstrated clear continuities of commitment and policy with the early 1920s.[1]

In brief, the inevitability, motivation, consequences and desirability of the Kemalist revolution are all disputed. The same extremities of assessment can be seen in more culturally oriented research. To give another example, in his article entitled 'Cleansing Islam from the Public Sphere', Hakan Yavuz presents the 1997 February 28 military-engineered suppression of the Islamist social movement in Turkey – described afterwards on national TV as a 'post-modern coup' by one of the generals involved – as an inflammation of the bitter cultural cleavage created in Turkey with the establishment of the republic. This cleavage divides what Yavuz calls the black and white Turks, for whom allegiance is signified by their authorized or unauthorized expression of Islam. White Turks are Turkey's Kemalist establishment, a 'pseudo-Westernized' elite symbolized by their 'display [of] Western roles, attire and habits' and their 'ability to imitate external European appearances' (Yavuz 2000: 22). Kemalism here is defined as an authoritarian project of Westernization, spearheaded by a military-bureaucratic enclave. By contrast, black Turks are Turkey's Muslim masses, the 'poor and marginalized sectors of society', inspired by the 'underlying Islamic vernacular of Turkish society' (Yavuz 2000: 23). Black Turks include Kurds within their ambit, shared religious traditions leading equally to their exclusion in this state-driven cultural transformation. In a striking simile, Yavuz (2000: 23) concludes that Turkey is like a transgendered body, where 'white Turks regard themselves as Western souls in the body of a foreign sociopolitical landscape'.

Yavuz is not the only writer to use the logic of a pervasive cultural difference between black and white Turkey to explain the fear and loathing that characterizes their interaction. In an equally arresting turn of phrase, Nilufer Göle describes the difference as resembling a caste system, where the infiltration of the Islamic 'untouchables' into the public spaces claimed as their own by secularists (the university, the professions, the municipal offices) necessitates a purifying counter-offensive by *beyaz* (white) Turkey (2000). She cites Islamist writer Emine Şenlikoğlu, who claims that Muslims are 'Turkey's Negroes'. In like vein Kevin Robins (1996: 72) explains such fear and loathing as incited by the 'return of the repressed', 'the real Turkey reasserting itself against official and state culture'. For Yavuz, Göle and Robins the major ongoing drama of Turkish politics resides in this cultural struggle and its mobilization of society's warring moieties. For each of them, then, Toprak included, Kemalism is understood as an exemplary case of paternalistic and authoritarian modernization from above and lauded or condemned for that reason. Represented in these terms certain binaries are also activated, both for

---

1. In his history of the Turkish republic, Zürcher (1995) pushes this continuity back to 1908 and the politics of the Committee of Union and Progress (The Young Turks).

analytic and political purposes: state versus society; worldview versus life-world; universality versus particularity; fakeness versus authenticity; homogeneity versus heterogeneity.

Yet as I will also argue below in reference to Sayyid, this narrative construction of a binary opposition between white state and black society ushers in at least four unhelpful generalizations. Firstly, the self-creation of subjects as different shades of 'grey' is obscured, positioning the cultural cleavage as existing primarily between state and society rather than within a heterogeneous, civil society itself. A second consequence of the opposition is that black society is homogenized, and given a Muslim character. Thirdly, the opposition means society is portrayed as a passive target of the state's modernizing zeal while Islamism, as product of black society, becomes by definition anti-modern rather than a producer of modernity, however understood, in its own right. And fourthly there is also a tendency to interpret the pristine republicanism of the single-party period as being in passive crisis vis-à-vis the threat of an activist Islamism, its once-and-for-all reforms as being rapidly wound back, its original energies as atrophying over time. An anthropological interest in the equally compelling drama of the continual fostering of the population's republican sentiments is too often absent.

As noted below, Sayyid's presentation of Kemalism shares some of these problems. But where his argument is compelling is in his recommendation that we view the work of Mustafa Kemal in Turkey as generative of a new political paradigm for the wider Muslim world. What is the defining characteristic of the paradigm? Sayyid categorizes the post-colonial regimes that came to power in Muslim majority areas in the following way:

> I am aware that by describing these regimes through the metaphor of Kemalism I am generalizing about many different kinds of political systems, geopolitical situation etc. In my defence, I would say that Kemalism is certainly more specific than terms such as 'nationalist' or 'secularist', which are habitually used to describe these regimes. Furthermore, there is a certain family resemblance between all these regimes in their policies towards the political role of Islam... [A]ll of them are unified in that they reject the use of Islam as the master signifier of their political discourse... In other words, Kemalism describes a hegemonic political discourse in the Muslim world, within which Islam was no longer a master signifier of the political order. (Sayyid 1997: 70)

Here Kemalism is understood as a political ideal type that denotes the mimetic project of *both* the new Turkish nationalist elite *and* their admiring counterparts in other Muslim states to forcibly Westernize their citizens, on the assumption of the progressive quality and universality of European civilization. For Sayyid, the key to the process is the inscription of Islam as a negative and antagonistic other in relation to this mission. Accordingly, one clear gain in analysing Kemalism in this fashion – and then generalizing it beyond its immediate context in the collapse of the Ottoman empire and the birth of the Turkish republic – is that it illuminates the motivation and constitution of Islamist actors. Islamism, then, in countries that have been exposed to a Kemalist project, becomes a social movement for 'the formation of the Muslim subject and agency which has been excluded from modernist [Western] definitions of civilization and history-making' (Göle 1996: 26).

Although Sayyid at times stresses Kemalism's *exclusion* of Islam from the new modernist public spaces (the university, the concert hall, the palace of justice, the stadium, the clinic and so forth) he notes, too, its simultaneous 'reinscription of Islam within Kemalism' (Sayyid 1997: 63). More simply, we might describe this as its intention to produce regime-friendly Muslims. Rather than benign indifference, strict separation or implacable hostility, Kemalism politicizes and instrumentalizes Islam in a *Hobbesian* fashion: that is, the state arrogates to itself the right or duty to tell the religious institution what doctrine to preach.[2] In Turkey itself the key legislation was decreed on 3 March, 1924, when the new regime abolished the institution of the Caliphate, closed down the *medreses*, made all religious educational institutions subject to direct state control in the form of the Ministry of Education and constituted the Department of the Affairs of Piety (Religious Affairs) (*Diyanet Isleri Bakanliği*). The first article of the law instituting the *Diyanet* stated that 'the administration of all matters concerning the beliefs and rituals of Islam will belong to the Department of the Affairs of Piety' (Berkes 1964: 485).[3]

Despite the usefulness of Sayyid's suggestion, his identification of Kemalism as the disestablishment and reinscription of Islam is a half-truth at best and the problems relate to more than his overextension of the term to cover even the religious policies of the Saudi Arabian regime *vis-à-vis* Islam. In that instance the canvas becomes too stretched, and the metaphor loses its precision. Much more significantly and rather ironically, his distillation of a model Kemalism defined by its attempt to remove Islam from the centre of political order and discourse runs into contradictions with the development of historic Kemalism in Turkey. Firstly, Sayyid posits as background to the recent global rise of Islamism an assumed 'failure' of Kemalism. His claim is that in large parts of the Muslim world political choices have become polarized between either Kemalism *or* Islamism. Yet rather than crisis,

2. This right is taken literally in Turkey: the military via the Department of Religious Affairs (Diyanet Isleri Baskanlığı) occasionally distribute the Friday sermon with orders that it be preached in every mosque in the land. Interestingly, Islamist journalist Hüsnü Aktaş has labelled the unceasing effort to produce a 'governmental interpretation of religion as "Byzantinism"' (not Hobbesian) (cited in Seufert 1999: 354).

3. On that very same day (3 March 1924) 'all Kurdish schools, associations and publications were banned by decree' (Seal 1995: 238). It is striking that many appreciative analyses of Turkish secularization fail to incorporate this detail into their accounts, thereby disconnecting the nationalistic Turkish chauvinism of the reforms from praise of their modernization. See for example Niyazi Berkes 1964/1998; 479ff; and Şerif Mardin 1993: 364ff.

my estimation of Kemalism in Turkey is that it is now more dominant than at any time since the politicization of Muslims after the 1980 military intervention. At least since the 1997 'post-modern' coup in Turkey, the armed forces controlled National Security Council has ruthlessly suppressed Islamist civil society (religious orders, communities, associations, foundations, educational groups and businesses). But this disbanding of 'Islamist groups' has also coincided with a far-reaching Islamist self-critique of their own earlier practices and concerns.[4] The two processes have resulted in a transformed political landscape. This self-reform is reflected most clearly in the split from Milli Görüş (National View) of many of its younger members to form the ruling AKParti (Justice and Development Party). The situation is very complex, with the issue of membership of the European Union complicating previous alignments. But it is striking that it is now the reformed 'Islamist' AKParti who are pushing for European integration, and the Kemalist centre that is obstructing it.

Secondly, Sayyid's polarization of Muslim societies as conflicted between the alternatives of Kemalism or Islamism seriously simplifies Turkey's political history. Contrary to Sayyid's claim, Islamism in Turkey has never been the only other game in town, as the fracturing of Islamist politics on ethnic *and* 'credal' grounds by the very formalization of the Sunni 'Turkish-Islamic' synthesis after the 1980 coup shows (see Houston 2001a). Indeed, as the most radical anti-religious aspects of Kemalist practice were disavowed in the wake of the generals' intervention, the military regime's decision to legitimize themselves through a new emphasis on the synthesis alienated both Sunni and Alevi Kurds and non-Sunni Turks. Öncü's pithy summary of the social fragmentation after 1980 illustrates the partial failure of the synthesis: 'The Turkish elite have discovered that their long pursuit of secularization and universalism in the name of enlightenment and modernity has been re-defined, almost overnight, as the oppression and internal colonialism of Islam and of the Kurdish people' (Öncü 1993: 261). Thirdly, if Kemalism as derived historically from Turkey is the word used to describe authoritarian laicism in all Muslim countries, why is not the *pluralization* of the Islamist opposition, also seen most clearly in Turkey, similarly exemplary for the Muslim world? That is to say, in Turkey Islamists are simply not homogeneous ('black') enough to constitute 'the only emergent counter-hegemonic discourse' (Sayyid 1996: 87) to Kemalism.[5]

But most importantly, Kemalism as political project is founded on more than its exclusion of Islam from the public sphere via a constructed synonymy between the West and true civilization. Although Sayyid identifies the multiple strands

4. See Kenan Çayır's (2007) illuminating tracing of this process in Islamic fiction in Turkey.

5. Despite this, it is all too common to read accounts positing Kemalism or Islamism as the only choices for the Muslim world. For the claim about either Atatürk or Khomeini for Islamic countries see for example Inalcık (1996: 28). For the best critique of the 'tutelary democracy' accounts of Kemalism see the work of Parla and Davison, *Corporatist Ideology in Kemalist Turkey* (2004).

of the Turkish Jacobins' legal and social revolution (secularization, nationalism, Westernization, modernization), analytically he reduces Kemalism to just one of these components, its 'rejection of Islam as a master signifier of political order' (Sayyid 1996: 70). There is thus a refusal to accord equal status to nationalism as constitutive of Kemalism: Sayyid subordinates the assimilating (Turkifying) project of the Kemalist nation state to its civilizing (Westernizing) mission. Yet Turkist-Republican discourse as modernizing practice simultaneously politicizes both Kurdish and Islamist identities in its formalization of the new national culture. The continual revolts in the Kurdish regions and the corresponding crisis of solidarity between Turkish and Kurdish Islamists testify to the fragmentation of Islamist subjects on ethnic lines. In like manner, the plurality of Kurdish opposition (Islamist and secularist) to Kemalism testifies to the fragmentation of ethnic subjects on religious lines. Kemalism understood in this more expanded sense illuminates then the motivation and constitution of Kurdish actors too, as well as Islamist. To modify Göle, in the countries that have been exposed to a Kemalist project, Kurdish nationalism becomes a social movement for the formation of a Kurdish subject and agency that has been excluded from official definitions of national identity. By generalizing only one aspect of the Kemalist reforms in Turkey as constitutive of the post-colonial polities of all Muslim-majority Middle Eastern nation states, Sayyid misidentifies and simplifies the *raison d'être* of the Kemalist project.

Last, we might note one final consequence of Sayyid's misinterpretation. Not only does his binary opposition between Kemalism and Islamism ignore serious differences amongst Islamists; it also obscures serious similarities between Kemalism and Khomeinism, Sayyid's paradigmatic example of Islamism. Nearly all writers on post-Ottoman history have stressed the efforts of the new successor states to consolidate their authority through the formation of national communities (Turkish, Arab or Persian). Yet Abbas Vali argues that not only did the emergent Kemalist states manufacture their sovereign nation through the forging of the collective identity of their populations: more specifically in Turkey, Iran and Iraq the violent denial of Kurdish identity was the necessary condition for this construction (Vali 1998: 82). Most strikingly, Vali extends this denial to Islamic Iran, in the process undermining Sayyid's conviction that Khomeinism presents a contrary and counter-hegemonic discourse to Kemalism. At least regarding the ethnic identity of political power, Vali sees no difference between Kemalist (Pahlavi) and Islamist Iran:

> In the present circumstances in Kurdistan ... it seem highly unlikely that the four sovereign states ruling the divided Kurdistan would ever want or dare to detach Kurdish identity from the conditions of political sovereignty, at least not in so far as their prevailing official nationalist/statist discourses and the requisite 'national' institutions remain in force. This is because Kemalism, Khomeinism and Ba'athism, despite their fundamental *differences*, all insist on the denial of Kurdish national identity as a prerequisite of their national sovereignty. (Vali 1998: 91)

If Kemalism and Khomeinism then share at least these common features, we have to wonder at the mutual investment of their supporters to repudiate such resemblances. Rather than emphasize only what distinguishes Kemalism and Islamism, we need equally to seek out their affinities. In the first place and against Kemalist stereotypes of the medieval backwardness of Islamism or its anti-modern character, Sayyid argues that Islamism is best seen as a species of modernization, a project that attempts to 'articulate a modernity that is not structured around Eurocentrism' (Sayyid 1996: 105). In the second place both these two political projects are violently assimilationist towards non-sovereign ethnic minorities, in the name of their claim to different forms of universalism (Western republican or Islamic).[6] These two shared characteristics lead to a vital and more theoretical question: what precisely is it that Kemalism and Islamism possess in common that makes each of them alternatively modern? My short answer is that both are radical projects of self-institution or autonomy. Their identical political extravagance, characterized by gratuitous invention of new social practices, florid polemics, rejection or rehabilitation of 'tradition' and the self-constituting re-narration of history demonstrate their politics to be inspired by an ideal of the triumph of the will.[7] The modernity shared by Kemalism and Islamism inheres in their creation of 'self-instituting' individual or collective subjects.[8] In his novel *The Black Book,* Orhan Pamuk (1994: 373) writes that Istanbul (after 1923) was changing 'in imitation of an imaginary city in a non-existent foreign country'. The phrase alludes to the occidentalism inspiring the republicans in the single-party period but it can be extended to the more recent imaginative reordering of Istanbul's built environment by Islamists as well (see Çınar 2001, Houston 2001b). It can also be extended to the Islamizing of urban space in post-revolutionary Iran. Far from an exercise in self-eclipse, mimesis – that is, the transformative imagining of oneself in and through the appropriation of selected 'significations' of other societies, whether Europe or the *Asrı-Saadet* (the period of the four 'rightly-guided'

6. The most polemical document I know that accuses Kurds in Iran of betraying the Islamic revolution by pursuing self-determination or regional autonomy is by Mustafa Camran, translated into Turkish in 1996. The book is titled *Kürdistan Hainleri (Kurdistan Traitors)*. Camran clearly subordinates ethnic identities to loyalty to the new Islamic government, while seeing the assertion of such identities as fostered by antagonistic powers.

7. By extravagance I mean sheer volume and variety of activity as well as the cultural creativity involved in imagining, interpreting and re-working in new contexts already existing idioms, social conventions and practices. That this Islamist extravagance has a long history – and indeed should be understood as emerging simultaneously with Turkist-Republicanism – is seen most clearly in Yusuf Akcura's 1912 formalization of and comparison between 'pan-Islamism', Ottomanism and Turkism, each seen by him as new political projects potentially capable of restructuring Ottoman State and society. See also Houston (2006).

8. The genealogy of this conception of modernity can be identified most starkly in Nietzsche but the presupposition of an intrinsic relationship between modernity and *autonomy* – literally the giving of one's law to oneself – stretches back to Kant and forward most recently to the work of Cornelius Castoriadis. See for further discussion the brilliant work of Ambrose (2003).

Caliphs, successors to the prophet Muhammad) – is an act of agency and self-constitution. The self re-creation at issue here is irreducible to historical antecedence or legacy: the examination of context, historical social institutions and collective cultural orientations can elucidate the actions of subjects but they do not account for them.[9] Significantly, this attraction to gratuitous self-creation is felt by the Kurdish movements of Kemalist nation-states as well, as we have seen most clearly in the case of the Kurdish monopolists (see Chapter 1).

Given this argument for the *resemblance* between Islamist and secularist projects of self-institution (but not necessarily their form), what are some of the consequences of disavowing Kemalists' and Islamists' identical desire for autonomy? In April 2005 the Dutch parliament published a report, recommending that 'the country's Muslims should henceforth effectively "become Dutch"' (BBC News, 28 April 2005). In like fashion, Olivier Roy (2005: 7) notes that if Muslims wish to stay in Holland they must now follow 'enculturation courses'. In that same article, however, he argues that the Islamist murderers of Dutch film maker Theo van Gogh in November 2004 – one of the acts that inspired the report's conclusions – were not 'traditional Muslims, barely able to speak Dutch' but Dutch citizens fluent in that language. Rather than expressing a clash of cultures or civilizational divide, Roy claims that such Islamists typically have very antagonistic relations with 'traditional Islam'. Indeed, theirs 'is an endeavour to reconstruct a "pure" religion outside traditional or Western cultures, outside the very concept of culture itself'. Further, their 'quest for authenticity is no longer a quest to maintain a pristine identity, but to go back to and beyond this pristine identity through a non-historical, abstract, and imagined model of Islam' (Roy 2005: 6–7). In other words and in the terms of my argument, Roy's Islamist actors are engaged in a project of arbitrary self-institution. Yet his sociological analysis of the factors associated with such 'uprooted' Islamism is not convincingly extended to the contemporary re-creation of Dutchness, European-ness or Western-ness pursued by secular nation states, as witnessed in the very programmes of assimilation referenced above. What will the enculturation courses on becoming Dutch entail, an appreciation of Rembrandt perhaps or a crash curriculum on the solid virtues guiding Dutch history?[10] In short, what is significant is how secular nationalism's (or Kemalism's) resemblance to Islamism is so often disavowed.[11]

9. The formulation is Castoriadis', who gives as his example the emergence of Christianity as a new society from the Roman Empire (Castoriadis 1997).

10. The Australian Government is in the process of constructing a new test of allegiance for future migrants to Australia, in which they will be asked to learn about 'Australian' values such as mateship (militarism?), equality between men and women, and acceptance of cultural differences. The explicit target of such re-education is Muslims, stereotyped and surveilled by the government as potential terrorists, and with a broader agenda of renationalizing the citizenry.

11. Clearly the processes and forces that suppress recognition of their essential commonality or their mutual mimicry need to be unearthed. One prime factor is the current phase of imperialist politics, and the attempts by both the US and certain Islamists to manufacture through violence the claimed exceptional status of either the West or Islam.

Iraqi Kemalism

I have argued, then, that Kemalism as a trans-national dominant discourse is a useful way of identifying a generic governing project characterizing state politics in many Muslim-majority countries.[12] Yet Sayyid's definition of Kemalism requires refashioning, to include as its *second constituting feature* its varied nationalisms and its suppression and attempted assimilation of non-sovereign ethnicities – for example Berbers in Algeria; Arabs, Azeri Turks and Kurds in the Iran of both the Pahlavi Shahs and the Islamists; Arabs and Kurds in Turkey; and Kurds in Iraq. In this next section I want to put some flesh on this skeletal framework, to explore how Kemalist projects in Iraq, Iran and Turkey in particular sought to produce new civil subjects and citizens from populations of diverse ethnic and religious intent. At least in this section, rather than dwelling on the dictatorial character of Kemalist nationalism vis-à-vis Kurds, it would be more illuminating to examine the attempts made by these varied Kemalisms to craft a new embodied-consciousness or a changed political identity of citizens through their campaigns and initiatives in the fields of culture and education. One vital strategy through which this was done includes a commitment to the emancipation of women, pursued most importantly through education and reform or (in the Turkish case) abolition of Islamic jurisprudence. A second strategy involved the fabrication and celebrating of pre-Islamic Arabic, Persian and Turkish identities via the attributing to them of values such as gender equality, rationality and discipline. In the process and by definition, other minority national groups (if acknowledged), were inscribed as lacking the legitimacy of the abiding but occulted modern. Finally, we will need to consider how successful these cultural politics have been in cultivating in citizens a new embodied knowledge and subjectivity.

In the three countries under discussion Kemalism as political practice obviously did not begin in the same year. Although it is plausible to date Kemalist governance in Iraq as commencing in 1932 with the end of the British mandate and the establishment of a formally independent Iraq under the control of an oligarchic monarchy, a rival date might also be the revolutionary coup of 1958 and its declaration of the People's Republic of Iraq. Kemalism in Iran should be dated from a different year again, beginning with the coronation in 1926 of the first Pahlavi monarch, Reza Shah. Reflecting the intensity of state supervised cultural production in Turkey, the richest and best theorized historical material appears to deal with the civilizing

---

12. In a recent article on Jordan, Antoun discerns a similar politics there. According to him, during the last fifty years in the Middle East 'three religious processes have grown together. One, the growth of fundamentalism, has received worldwide attention... The others, the bureaucratization of religion and the state co-optation of religion, of equal duration but no less important, have received much less attention' (Antoun 2006: 369). I find his use of the term *fundamentalism* fundamentally unhelpful: as argued above, a much better explanatory theory tying together these three processes is to explore their shared commitment to the 'imaginary signification' of autonomy and radical self-institution.

processes developed there by the Turkish Republicans after 1923. Nevertheless, in this section we will first look at Kemalism in Iraq and Iran before examining the Turkish experience.

Despite the domination of Britain over Iraq until at least the Second World War, the 'proto-Kemalism' of monarchical Iraq was most marked in two key areas of state policy and nation formation, namely in the institution and growth of a national education system and in universal military conscription.[13] Both sought to embody, in young men in particular, tenets of an Arab nationalist ideology complete with an Arab or Semitic version of the Kemalist myth of a primeval ancestor that transmits civilization to the rest of the world.[14] Simon (1986) and Zubaida (2002) note the combative influence of Sati al-Husri, Director-General of the Ministry of Education from 1921–41, over the development of an Iraqi education system dedicated to the inculcation of an Arab nationalist culture in its students.[15] The mainstay of al-Husri's primary and secondary curriculum was 'history, followed by instruction in civics, physical education in the form of military drill, and singing (select songs that have a nationalist content, which instil "zealousness and happiness" in people)' (Simon 1986: 40).[16] The primacy al-Husri gave to the role of educational indoctrination in awakening subjects to their true national identity can be gleaned from his account of a debate below, which should also be read as having autobiographical reference:

> ...so I said, 'I would like to know what our attitude would be toward someone who, having previously disowned his Arabism, says 'I am an Arab.' Should we say, 'He was not an Arab but then became one' or should we not rather say, 'He was not conscious of his Arabism, but when he discovered his true Arab identity, he recognized this fact?' ... Last year, I read an article by Salah 'Abd al-Sabur in which he eloquently and candidly described the development of his inner self and the change that came upon his views and emotions and restored him to Arabism... Should we say about [him] that [he was] not Arab but then became Arab at the moment when [he] published his confession and explained the change that had come over [him]? It is obvious that this would be absurd.

13. For an account of the revolt in the Yazidi Kurdish areas brought about by attempts to apply the National Service Law there in 1935, see Fuccaro (1997).

14. Readers might remember in Chapter 3 Leach's brief mention of a strike by Kurdish students in Rowanduz in 1940 over the Arab language content of the high school curriculum.

15. According to Karpat, al-Husri has been the 'most influential writer on Arab nationalism' (Karpat 1968: 55). He had also been a 'renowned Ottoman pedagogue' (Simon 1997: 93) before his conversion to Arab nationalism, a friend of Turkish nationalist Ziya Gökalp, and strongly impressed by the Turkish nationalism he observed in his years of training in Istanbul before and during the First World War.

16. Simon's accounts are less enlightening over a second major battle waged for the constitution of the Iraqi nation through the education system: this was between Sunni 'pan-Arabists' and Shi'i 'Iraqists'. See Zubaida for discussion of Sunni/Shi'a rivalries and coalitions in the Protectorate and monarchical periods and of a pan-Arab Sunni discourse in the 1920s and 30s that accused Iraqi Shi'a of being traitors to the Iraqi cause in favour of Iran (Zubaida 2002).

> Faced with the circumstances, we are, logically speaking, obliged to say that the fellow was unconscious of his Arabism but then came to discover his Arab identity. (al-Sabri 1961, as cited in Karpat 1968: 58)

Husri al-Sabri goes on to say that 'Abd al-Sabur's article expresses not just a single writer's feelings but mirrors 'the feelings and sentiments of a whole [Arab] generation' (al-Sabri 1961, as cited in Karpat 1968: 58). Even more importantly, this conversion to Kemalism of key segments of the 'last' Ottoman generation was a broader phenomenon, experienced not only by al-Sabri but also by Ziya Gökalp and, as we have seen in Chapter 1, by Muhammad Amin Zaki, writer of the first modern history of the Kurds (*The Brief History of the Kurds*). What is equally striking about al-Husri's conversion to Arabism is its blithe indifference to any equivalent 'restoration' of feelings or sentiments of national identity experienced by many Iraqi Kurds. It was al-Husri who resisted the Mandate's guarantee of education in Kurdish for northern Iraq. As Simon notes in passing about the Arabism of his schooling system, 'How the Kurds could become Arabs was an issue that did not seem to be of concern' (Simon 1997: 90).

Did the institution of an Arabized primary and secondary education system up until the 1940s also have as one of its main aims the schooling of girls? Neither Simon nor Zubaida mention the issue or the composition of the new student body, leaving one to suspect that a Kemalist discourse on the priority of female education emerged only after the declaration of the republic. Joseph's analysis of the Ba'ath Party's campaign after 1968 to resocialize females into 'new Iraqi women' draws attention to the constitutional clause from that period that made primary and secondary education compulsory and free for all citizens. Figures dating from before and after the Ba'ath Party's control of state power are striking. Citing the 1965 census, Joseph notes that 'of the almost 4 million females in the population only 23,000 had achieved secondary certificates or their equivalents' (Joseph 1991: 181). By contrast, a report from the General Federation of Iraqi Women, the female arm of the Ba'ath party, claimed that in 1980 females constituted 43 per cent of the children in primary schools and 45 per cent of university students (Joseph 1991: 181). Joseph's cautious conclusions about the intention and impact of the Ba'ath Party's programme for women has some similarities (as we will see) with analyses of Kemalist policies toward females in Turkey and Iran: she maintains that the reforms were intended to redirect female loyalty towards the party and state and away from what she calls 'primordial' kin/tribal or ethnic group allegiances. But why she doesn't describe women's identification with the Arab nationalism of the party or state as a newly constructed primordial tie is unclear.

A more fully developed Kemalist politics then can be seen as commencing with the overthrow of the monarchy in Iraq in 1958. Although the revolution was achieved by a broad national alliance that included the Iraqi Communist Party and Kurdish forces, the inclusive political structure of the new national state did not last long.

By 1963 the government had disintegrated and was deposed in a military coup, led by officers of pronounced 'pan-Arab' political persuasion. But even before this the coalition had broken with the Communists, the pan-Arab Ba'athists and the newly legalized Kurdish political party, leading to a new war in 1961 between the national government and Kurds in the north.[17]

The attitude of the opposition 'pan-Arabist' Ba'athists towards Kurds was non-conciliatory: in 1959 the party published a policy statement saying that

> The generous Arab nation has taken all these minorities under its protection ... to leave them the choice of either remaining within the homeland or else emigrate to their own countries, as is the case of the Armenians ... Arab nationalism supports the struggle of the Kurds for a Kurdish state. What are the frontiers of that state? The framework that contains Kurdish nationalism is Kurdistan as included by Turkey and Iran. (Cited in Haj 1997: 119)

Given the claim of Kurds to indigeneity in southern Kurdistan (northern Iraq), the communiqué's paternalistic assertion that the Arab homeland has provided sanctuary for Kurds was a declaration of Kurdish territorial dispossession and of Arab ownership. It signalled, too, an intention that the Kurdish regions would be subject to a politics of forced binding to the 'Arab world'. That this was not an isolated sentiment but shared by other pan-Arabists at the time can be seen in the book *Crisis of the Arab Left*, published in 1960 by the Lebanese Clovis Maqsud, described by Karpat as another well known 'ideologue of Arab nationalism' (Karpat 1968: 59). In the context of a discussion distinguishing between settlers to and occupiers of the Arab homeland, Maqsud suddenly raises the issue of Kurds who refuse to be *absorbed*:

> In Iraq, for example, certain elements (i.e. among the Kurds) encourage secessionist sentiments and call for independent nationalism. Since the international situation does not permit this, those elements exert pressure on the Communist Party in order to keep

---

17. The details above are taken from Haj (1997). Haj's study of the formation of Iraq is an incisive account of the political economy and internal class differences that she argues have determined political developments in Iraq. But the focus of her research on land ownership and class relations in central and southern Iraq means she is uninterested in tracing out the importance of ethnic and sectarian issues on the uneven processes of national integration and state building since 1921. Simon (1986) notes for example that even during the British protectorate, Iraqi Sunni Arabs were always in control of the national Education Department. Given her focus on the land-owning oligarchy and its influence over political and economic policy, one reads with surprise then, in her discussion of the dissolution of the 1958 revolution and the national alliance that fostered it, a footnote that begins: 'Since the formation of the Iraqi nation, the Iraqi Kurds were in perpetual revolt, calling for their right to autonomy and independence' (Haj 1997: 193). If this was the case, why isn't it theorized earlier in the study, along with an investigation of the Arab nationalism of the monarchical state and its impact on the Kurdish regions?

Iraq away from healthy interaction with the rest of the Arab world. But the noise that they succeed in making does not mean that they represent the group in whose name they claim to speak and whose aspirations they pretend to express. Even if, for the sake of argument, we admit that they do represent the majority opinion of those groups, this can only last for a certain time but cannot continue indefinitely. (Maqsud 1960, cited in Karpat 1968: 61)

Maqsud's hypothetical admission that spokesmen for 'secessionist sentiments' might express the feelings of a sizeable constituency amongst minorities is thereafter ignored. Predictably, he goes on to accuse the minorities of being tools in the hands of imperialist powers. Equally predictably, spokesmen for such opinions must not be tolerated. The reason is because the basis of their sentiment is 'racialist', unlike the sentiments informing Arab nationalism. Yet tolerated or not, time is on the side of the majority, given – and this is unspoken – their control of the state. Arabs' generous readiness to absorb minorities 'must be accompanied by a basic guarantee – namely, that such absorption will not mean the dissipation of the nationalist character of the nation to which the majority belongs' (Maqsud 1960: 62). What, then, does Maqsud's Kemalism offer indigenous 'minorities' except subordination to the Arab world, the making of which itself was a fraught contemporary political project?

In 1968 another military coup brought a rival group of Ba'ath leaders to power, including as one of its influential figures Saddam Hussein. In keeping with its political inheritance the new regime expressed an extreme pan-Arab ideology. Nevertheless, Baram's (1983a) analysis of its pan-Arabism shows how by the early 1970s any serious inclination for territorial and political unity with Syria and Egypt in proposals such as the United Arab Republic had long since dissipated.[18] More

18. This practical reluctance to pursue unification, or the determined politics of separate sovereignty pursued by the elites of Middle-Eastern Arab states is another reason why Kemalism, despite its Turkish origin, is a useful term to use in the analysis of such political projects. In his recent review of Adeed Dawisha's 2002 book *Arab Nationalism in the Twentieth Century: From Triumph to Despair,* Morrison (2006: 475) notes that 'the proponents of state-centric nationalism may (and in fact did) espouse Arabism but they were not Arab nationalists – they were Jordanian, Iraqi, Egyptian, etc, nationalists. The common parlance referring to these nationalisms as "Arab nationalism" obfuscates this distinction' (Morrison 2006: 475). Turkish Kemalism too famously rejected pan-Turkist visions. The assessment of Arab pan-nationalists that this pursuit of distinct independent States has been a failure or a tragedy – see Morrison again on Dawisha – is made on the assumption of some historic and cross-regional Arab political or cultural community. More generally their melancholic analysis is related to the acceptance of the legitimizing logic of nation-states: to the extent that such institutions justify their sovereignty on the basis of their representing a pre-existing nation, the scandalous existence of multiple nation states constituted on this identical ground is source for both irredentist discourse and a search for reasons explaining the fracturing of the essential national whole. Pan-Kurdism as political ideology is concerned to analyse a somewhat similar fragmentation, although the problem is not of course multiple Kurdish states but the division of Kurds among multiple nation-states.

interestingly for our purposes, Baram reveals how even in the first few months of its reign the Ba'th Party initiated a massive yet invisible – in terms of official party statements and doctrine – new cultural campaign, one that sought to create, in uneasy tension with its Arabism, a unique Iraqi identity based on pre-Islamic and potentially even pre-Arab sources. The fabrication of a 'Mesopotamian' heritage, internal to Iraq, which was posited as the historic basis of an 'Iraqi personality', had the virtue of inviting Kurds and other minorities to identify with an Iraq that potentially transcended the Arab nation. But the increased public awareness of Iraqi culture's direct links with the ancient past that the campaign was designed to disseminate was aimed also at the 'international community', as the global touring of Mesopotamian-Iraqi art and craft exhibitions demonstrates.

Using the work of Baram (1983a, 1983b, 1990), it is clear that the campaign was oriented towards cultural production in at least six different fields. The first was government-sponsored research in the field of Iraqi folklore, involving the recovery or invention of music, folk tales and poetry in local dialects, folk dances and regional arts and crafts. The second has been in the area of archaeology and an extensive series of excavations as well as the related building of new museums, culminating in the reconstruction of the ancient city of Babylon at a cost of some 100 million US dollars (Baram 1990: 425). The campaign also resulted in the 'resurrection of ancient, long-vanished cities, Hatra, Assur and Nineveh' (Baram 1983b: 428). The third was in the state's institution of a round of festivals for mass consumption, most famously in the introduction in the northern city of Mosul of 'a modern version of the ancient Mesopotamian spring rite' (Baram 1990: 425), and more spectacularly in the form of the annual Babylon International Music Festival. Related to this has been state encouragement to artists, sculptors, poets, novelists, playwrights and film makers to 'derive their inspiration from the civilizations and cultures that flourished in Mesopotamia-Iraq from remote antiquity to the modern age' (Baram 1990: 425–6). Baram notes the production throughout the 1970s of tens of plays and films set in ancient Sumer or Babylon, as well as the positioning of sculptures revealing 'Mesopotamian influences' in prominent places in the capital during the same period, including opposite the National Assembly building (Baram 1983b: 434). Fifth, there has been a drive to name and rename places, so that in a decade 'long-vanished pre-Islamic and mediaeval names like Babylon, Nineveh, Tammuz, Ishtar, Gilgamesh, Qadisiyya and al-Anbar became by necessity household names in Ba'athist Iraq' (Baram 1990: 425). Sixth and finally has been the production of government supported intellectual work on Iraq's Mesopotamian heritage in literary and academic journals, although it appears that by the late 1970s the Ba'ath party made a decision to 'arabize the ancients' (Baram 1983b: 439).

In seeking to broaden the context for the cultural campaign of the Ba'ath Party, Baram draws attention to the politics of both Reza Shah Pahlavi in Iran and Ataturk in Turkey as two other examples of the endeavour to create an 'intimate relationship between the people and the territorial pre-Islamic history of its existing state' (Baram

1990: 427). Yet beyond noting the negative connotations that all such Pagan cultures have in the 'Islamic tradition' as species of *jahiliyya* (ignorance), Baram does not dwell on the implicit *relativization* of Islamic identities, whether Sunni or Shi'a, entailed in the project to present pre-Islamic Mesopotamian civilizations as cultural ancestors of the Iraqi people. By contrast, of course, Sayyid identifies these attempts to disestablish and reinscribe Islam as the very essence of Kemalism. On the other hand, where Baram is enlightening is in his discussion of the tension not between Islamism and Mesopotamianism in Iraq, but between the Mesopotamianism of the cultural campaign and the Ba'ath Party's continuing pan-Arab nationalism. In other words it was not religious opposition to praise of the pre-Islamic status of the Mesopotamian heritage that caused the radical modification of the cultural policy, but concern over the non-Arabic character of the Sumerian, Babylonian and Assyrian civilizations to whom the Iraqi people were represented as cultural heirs.[19] The 'problem' was resolved, as noted above, by the Arabizing of the ancients and, by implication, of the entire Iraqi people, including the Kurds:

> To untangle this ideological knot, under the explicit instructions of Saddam Husayn, since the late 1970s Iraqi politicians, ideologues and historians endeavoured to establish an Arab pedigree for the ancient Semitic peoples who inhabited Mesopotamia from Akkad through Chaldea. This they did by invoking the well known 'wave theory', according to which all the Semitic peoples of ancient Mesopotamia emerged in successive waves from the Arabian peninsula from remote antiquity to the last such wave of Muslim Arabs under the prophet's successors. Having all emerged from Arabia ... [and] despite the great disparity between Akkadian, Assyrian and other ancient Semitic languages in Mesopotamia on the one hand and Arabic on the other, the Semites should be regarded as Arabs. (Baram 1990: 426)

One explicit aim of the cultural campaign then – the creation of a common Mesopotamian (i.e. non-Arab) past for all Iraqis – was rendered unattainable by the refusal of the Ba'athist Kemalists to de-Arabize the historic Iraqi nation. As we have seen, the theory of the historic civilizing role of the Arab people has had long roots in Iraqi Kemalism, going back at least to the writings of al-Sabri. How effective the cultural campaign was by itself in facilitating for Iraqi Kurds, Arabs and others a new realization of their historic common origins is difficult to judge. Indeed this question, on the efficacy of Kemalist cultural and social campaigns in relation to the agency of their intended targets, is a problem we will need to address after our discussion of similar policies in Iran and Turkey.

---

19. In keeping with his restrictive model of Kemalism and its focus on secularization, Sayyid does not mention the Arab nationalist counter-attack on the cultural campaign, despite citing the Mesopotamianism of the Ba'ath Party as key evidence of their Kemalism.

Kemalism in Iran

As with Iraq, it should be admitted that in Iran too there is a certain arbitrariness in dating the onset of Kemalism to 1926, given a longer pre-history of Kemalist discourse and practice. There is also of course a rich and complex history of the 'modernizing' of Persian governmental institutions (see for example Cronin 1996 on the modernization of the military). But these modernizing reforms did not involve as their vital corollary the attempted constitution and mobilization of citizens through a particular combination of Persianization and secularism (the state's disempowering of religious groups and its politicized appropriation of Islam). Nor were they able to be effectively carried through.[20] Accordingly the onset of the absolute rule of Reza Shah Pahlavi is an appropriate event to date Iranian Kemalism because of the centralization of modern power in Tehran under his control.[21] Further, it is Reza Khan

---

20. On the other hand, we could also date the origins of Kemalism as a structured political programme to 1921, with the military coup in Tehran that brought Reza Pahlavi himself to political prominence as commander of the army. Thereafter he progressively dominates Iranian politics, becoming Minister of War (in 1921), Prime Minister (in 1923) and Shah (in December 1925). According to Zirinsky, the secular reformers clustered around Reza from 1921 onwards 'aimed at erasing ethnic diversities and autonomist movements and ... sought to create a powerful central government that would introduce reform from above. Their program for national strength included the following policies: creating a well-disciplined national army and an honest professional bureaucracy, ending capitulations, settling the nomadic tribes, expanding Western-style state-supported schools (including girls' schools), opening careers to talent, encouraging Iranian capital development, separating religion and politics, and making Persian the national language' (Zirinsky 1992: 648).

21. Given the considerations in note 20, there is a crucial issue here pertaining to the constitution of a broader modernist elite empowered by and spearheading Kemalist 'revolutions' in Iran and Turkey. History of ideas' approaches often trace the origins of this class back to earlier Qajar or Ottoman groups or intellectuals retrospectively positioned as antecedent producers of ideological theories and practices enacted by the post-imperial state. A generation later this expanding if numerically weak class distinguishes itself through its adaptation and transmission of new scientific knowledges (in medicine, administration and statistics, education, engineering, economics), originating in a Europe intent on continuing its colonial domination. In this context, their appropriation of new knowledge is also driven by a nationalist or developmentalist urgency. Kemalist states and their military-politico elites 'capture' these groups and their discourses, incorporating them into their revolution (or otherwise marginalizing them). On the other hand, 'capture' is hardly the right word: there is a clear affinity between these groups, the application and legitimation of their new expertise, and dictatorial state power. Le Corbusier's dedication to *The Radiant City*, his influential statement on modernist architecture, might be taken to be without much exaggeration the motto of many experts empowered by new disciplines or scientific paradigms in Iran and Turkey: 'To Authority'. Schayegh's work provides a useful model for analysing the relationship between this emerging *modern* middle class and the Kemalist State in Iran (and Turkey). For him

> The initially frail institutional and legal bases of modernist professionals' use of modern scientific knowledge were strengthened by Reza Shah's autocratic modernizing state that, for example, expanded institutes of higher education, built more hospitals, founded secular courts, and promoted

who explicitly sought to emulate his friend and contemporary Atatürk, as seen most strikingly in his cabling of instructions whilst visiting Ankara in 1934 to his Prime Minister in Tehran, decreeing the wearing by Iranian peasants of a hat with full rims similar to that with which people were dressed in Turkey (see Perry 1985, Chehabi 1993). Other Reza initiatives closely indexed to Kemalism in Turkey included the 1928 and 1931 reforms of the legal code, the consolidation and expansion of existing colleges in Tehran into the new University of Tehran in 1934, the introduction of music education in the school curriculum, the confiscation of *waqf* land, the banning of political parties, the enforcing of universal male conscription, the programme of language purification formalized by the appointment of an 'Iranian Academy' in 1935, the instituting of a national bank in 1930 and an *etatist* economic policy of industrialization.

Despite the many innovations of 'cultural' Kemalism in Iran facilitated or initiated by the Pahlavi state, lack of space dictates that we focus on a restricted number of themes only, in this case on policies pursued in the area of language reform and of women's 'development'. As with the various proposals for Turkish language or alphabet change made by intellectuals and writers in the latter half of the nineteenth-century Ottoman empire, in Iran too debates over the necessity, motivation and extent of language purification had a long Kemalist prehistory. According to Kia (1998), as early as the 1830s a group of poets and writers at the Qajar court sought to write in a simplified Persian and the Prince Jelal o-Din Mirza constructed a purified Persian in his 1871 text *The Book of Kings*, produced by resuscitating old Persian words no longer in use. He also refused to use words of Arabic origin, pointing to what he called the Arabs' invasion of Iran and their destruction of the Persian language in the seventh century. The resulting text was difficult to read, its 'imagined' Persian criticized even by other advocates of language reform as arbitrary and artificial. One counter suggestion, proposed by the intellectual Mirza Aqa Kirmani, was that reformers collect the languages, literatures and vocabularies from tribes and villages of the country. In evolutionary fashion, he posited an isolated rural area of ideal and uncontaminated purity that made it the living repository of a pure Persian culture.[22] As with many other late nineteenth-century intellectuals, both Mirza and

---

infrastructural engineering projects. Together with his modernist politics and the administration's need for professional and technocratic expertise, this highlights the intertwined nature of state and class formation... Indeed, the modern middle class used the fact that its professional practice and culture was based on modern science to justify its claim to steer modernization. (Schayegh 2005: 168, 169)

22. The same conviction informs Kemalism's interest in both peasant music and folklore. Remote areas (speaking the 'right' language) provide the possibility of a national purity lost in the syncretism of urban or cosmopolitan life. They also promise the prestige of origins, if the knowledge of their inhabitants can be incorporated into an evolutionary and spatial map that models simplicity with original creation and increasing complexity with diffusion or later ornamentation. In his research for the Ankara People's House into folk music in Turkey in 1935, Bela Bartok took great pains to ascertain

Kermani conceived of the pre-Islamic period as constituting the supreme expression of Persian culture and history, in the process inscribing Islam as both foreign and responsible for Iranian weakness vis-à-vis European modernity.

Formalizing such conceptions, Reza Shah made celebration of the pre-Islamic (pre-Arab) history of Iran in general, and of the Achaemenid empire in particular, the official state policy. In claiming an essential cultural continuity between ancient Persia and the reawakened Iranian nation, he also intended to legitimize authoritarian monarchism as a native institution. Persianization of a very multicultural and multi-lingual population was pursued in the first instance through a new school curriculum, with its emphasis on Persian language, literature and history. Language policy there-fore became a central strategy of both regime consolidation and nation building. As Matthee argues, 'the decision to promote Persian as the uniform and exclusive language in the school system was expressly designed to enhance the centripetal effect of a single language as the official medium of expression' (Matthee 1993: 324). But what type of Persian was to be taught in the new linguistically unified education system? The question was to dominate language reform throughout Reza Shah's reign.

The first state-organized language purification initiative began in 1924, when Reza Shah ordered the Ministry of War to form a committee to replace loan words (of Arabic, Turkish or European origin) with Persian-based neologisms in the fields of warfare, transportation and military administration. Their deliberations were highly successful: 'In the first year of its existence, the committee produced three to four hundred new words which are still used in the everyday language' (Kia 1998: 20). Thereafter linguistic engineering continued apace, with developments in Iran and Turkey closely related to each other. In both countries, heated theoretical debates over purity versus readability accompanied the reforms. Similarly the Kemalists established a centralized language institution in both countries, firstly in Iran to standardize the word manufacture being undertaken by enthusiastic commit-tees in the military, education and other ministries, in Turkey to continue the work of the committee established in 1928 to Latinize the alphabet. Personally founded by Atatürk in 1932 and Reza Shah in 1935, the stated aims of the two institutions – the Türk Dil Kurumu[23] (Turkish Language Society) and the Farhangestan-e Iran

---

whether the rural singers he was recording were itinerant musicians or not: 'it is ... necessary to check whether the improvisators are truly permanent village residents or are wandering troubadours. In the latter case one must consider their improvisations with suspicion, with distrust' (Bartok 1976: 9). Following Soviet ethnomusicology he also assumed that the pentatonic scale was the earliest mode from which all other modal structures developed (see Stokes 1992: 51ff). As for Kermani's suggestion, a 'word-mobilization' campaign oriented to the recovering of the original language occurred not in Iran but in Turkey in the 1930s.

23. Its original name was Türk Dili Tetkik Cemiyeti (Turkish Society for the Study of Turkish) but *tetkik* and *cemiyeti* are words of Arabic origin. One of its first initiatives was to translate (from Arabic to Turkish) and prescribe a new call to prayer (*ezan*) in November 1932.

(Academy of Iran), appropriately both neologisms formed from Turkish and Persian roots – were extremely similar. In Turkey the society's goals were:

> (1) to collect and publish Turkish vocabulary from the popular language and old texts, (2) to define principles of word formation and to create words from Turkish roots in conformity with them, and (3) to propose and propagate genuine Turkish words to replace foreign terms in the (written) language…

The charter of the Academy in Iran

> committed it … to standardizing the derivational morphology – i.e., setting rules by which to coin new terms; proposing necessary neologisms; and pruning Persian of unsuitable foreign words. (Perry 1985: 299, 302)

As for the question of the two institutions' relative successes, at least in terms of transforming the targeted language, most critics conclude that the purification movement in Turkey has been more effective, although obviously not as effective as some of its most ardent proponents desired. A recent poster pasted on the walls at many of Istanbul's universities was headed: 'bye bye' ne demek? 'What does "bye bye" mean?'

It goes on to explain:

> Say NO to English affectations [counterfeits] and show respect for Turkish! Protect Ataturk's legacy and our future. SPEAK TURKISH!!! 'To say Turk is to say Turkish, and to say 'How fortunate are those who can claim to be a Turk!' 'The Turkish nation, which knows how to protect its independence and territory, should liberate its language from the yoke of foreign languages' M.K. ATATÜRK. (my translation)

The origins of the expressions used by the poster are revealing: the words used for independence (*bağımsızlık*) and affectations (*özentilik*) are neologisms, coined by the TDK in the 1930s. By contrast, the words asking readers to 'protect Ataturk's legacy' (*Ata'nın mirasına sahip çık*) are Ottomanisms.

Clearly, as the poster shows, language reform is not in essence a mere linguistic exercise or a matter of practicality. By contrast it is intimately connected to a wider Kemalist project of nationalist autonomy and self-institution. The perceived need to purify the language from the words of other peoples expresses a nationalist imaginary that particular nations dwell not only in an identified territorial space but also in a bounded space of language as well. The nationalist conception is seen in the very designation of the category of 'loan-words': they are the expressions of someone different and of somewhere else – each people to the genius of its own mapped language. Rather than being productive of new meanings that extend the possibilities of social action and self-expression, for nationalists the promiscuity of loanwords, especially those associated with a conquering nation, makes them suspect as carriers of others' claims to sovereignty. The claim to sovereignty exerted by loanwords is not just a claim to territorial ownership. Much worse, it is a claim to sovereignty over the nation's own worldview, as loanwords carry an insidious perceptual mentality that threatens the integrity of the indigenous system. In brief, the sovereign territory of the nation demands the hegemony of the language of that sovereign nation and language purification ensures a culturally authentic (yet modern) worldview as well.

For the more radical of the language purists of Iran and Turkey, then, Arabic in particular was not merely a foreign imposition. The cosmology that it brought with it was also an imposition of an anti-modern mentality, most pronounced in the religion of Islam. Persian culture before its period of decline was already 'modern', if by modernity is meant rationality and progress. As Schayegh argues in his analysis of what he calls the *modern* middle class associated with the Kemalist regime in Iran, their acquisition of new Western scientific knowledge (in the fields of biomedicine, sport, nutrition etc) was accompanied by a claim that the 'authentic, non-corrupted core of Iran's medico-scientific culture [was] congruent with Western science, if not its precursor' (Schayegh 2005: 169). Explaining, for example, the introduction of modern sports into Iranian schools and society, nationalists posited that a similar training of physical and mental faculties had been a basic aspect of ancient Persian education. The same argument was made to justify the state adoption of the boy-scout movement, membership in which was made compulsory in 1939 for all boys from fifth to ninth grades (Matthee 1993: 326). In other words, 'postulating that its own particularistic national culture had originally been rational and imbued with discipline, [the Kemalist elite] concluded that at the time of its authentic Self – i.e. in the pre-Islamic period – Iran had ... partaken in the unilinear universal history of progress only at present led by the West' (Schayegh 2001: 364). As we have seen in Chapter 1, Turkish Kemalism too similarly indigenized political modernity, arguing for example that in pre-Islamic Turkish society women were equal with men, or that, in the famous words of Atatürk now draped over the side of Istanbul's new Galata Bridge in huge type, 'Republicanism is the most suitable form of governance for the Turkish character'.

Disregarding what we might call the partisan's understanding of nationalism, which posits it as a natural 'instinct' of every legitimate national group, can we identify a dominant model of nationalism at work here which both critics and defenders of the language reforms in Iran or Turkey use to analyse its structure and origins? Nationalism in the colonized world has always been contextualized and often sympathized with as a politics of anti-colonialism. In more recent work inspired by Benedict Anderson's metaphor of the nation as an imagined community and even more so in postcolonial theory, the crafting of national selves by the nation-state and its modernist elites is analysed as intimately connected to Western knowledge about the colonized (or orientalism). As political project nationalism aims at the raising of the subaltern's self-esteem debased by orientalist discourse through the imagining of its special virtues. As economic project it seeks the prosperity of the national territory against exploitation by foreign governments and their businesses through developmentalist policy. Nevertheless, the work of Chatterjee and Prakash on India points to a central ambiguity in this enterprise: the very elements imagined as defining the authentic uncorrupted (pre-Islamic) national self – in this case Iran and India's indigenous sciences – are judged by their conformity to Western modernity. For this reason nationalism as anti-colonialism is described as a 'derivative discourse' (Chatterjee 1986). Schayegh's description of Iranian Kemalism is a good example of this type of analysis:

> With this 'authenticizing' of modern science, the modern Iranian middle class killed two birds with one stone. It inscribed Iran into the unilinear history of the world and of science in which the West's present dominance formed but a small instant in time and was described as the continuation of previous efforts rather than as a radical departure... Moreover, the modernists accentuated explicit critique of traditional modes of knowledge – that is, its social bearers – through the more explicit claim that they were themselves resuscitating Iran's 'authentic' past, or its scientific knowledge and practice, thus undercutting the clergy's entrenched sociocultural position in Iranian society. (Schayegh 2005: 182, 183)

But overlooked in this widespread model is an analysis of Kemalism that gives proper due to the third bird 'killed' by its nationalism. Given that for Kemalists the value of authentic Persian or Turkish national culture inhered in its modern-ness (as most apparent when counterposed to those corrupting carriers of anti-modernity, the Arabs), it followed logically that other non-Persian and non-Turkish ethnic groups within the national territory were marked (like the Arabs) by the absence of these same unique qualities. Kurdish society was declared incapable of taking this leap back to the future. Accordingly any internal movement for regional autonomy against centralizing Kemalist regimes made in the name of ethnic Muslim minorities was readily explained away as an 'outbreak' of reactionary forces, an expression of primordial loyalties dominated by traditional and/or foreign interests. The idea that the new Kemalist regimes could also seek to purify the Kurdish language from compromising loanwords in the name of the modernity of the authentic Kurdish self was unthinkable.[24] In brief, the third bird killed by the 'authenticizing' of modern science by Persian and Turkish Kemalism was any equivalent imagining of a Kurdish national self.

This same incomplete theorizing of nationalism can be seen in many analyses of the language revolutions in Iran and Turkey. In the most influential classic accounts of

24. As counterpoint, as we have seen in Chapter 1, Kurdish monopolists' discourse on the defining contribution of Mesopotamian Kurds to world civilization posits a similar pre-conquest modernity for indigenous Kurdish culture.

Turkish modernization, alphabet reform and language purification are nearly always explained as an understandable (if not always judiciously applied) facet of nation building and of the embrace of modern civilization. Bernard Lewis for example sees the romanization of the alphabet as a praiseworthy aspect of secularization, in which Atatürk was 'slamming a door on the past as well as opening a door to the future' (Lewis 1961: 273). For Lewis, this future was 'the final incorporation of Turkey into the civilization of the modern West' (Lewis 1961: 273).[25] Further, 'the main and really significant change [of the language reform] has been to bring the written language closer to the spoken' (Lewis 1961: 430). In fact, the exact opposite is true: the language revolution forced the spoken language to conform to the written. In an earlier passage Lewis acknowledges this to be the case. And the very language he uses to describe the language purification process, in the form of a shocking extended analogy made between linguistic and ethnic cleansing, betrays the violence of the Kemalist assault upon the plurality of actually existing spoken languages:

> The radicals of the Linguistic Society were opposed to Arabic and Persian words as such, even those that formed an *essential* part of the vocabulary of *everyday spoken* Turkish. On the one hand, the Society prepared and published an index of *alien* words, condemned to *deportation*; on the other *search parties* collected and examined purely Turkish words, from dialects, from other Turkic languages, and from ancient texts, to serve as *replacements*. When no suitable words could be discovered, resuscitated, or imported, new ones were invented. This *planned exchange* of *lexical populations* reached its height during the years 1933–34... (Lewis 1961: 428, my emphasis)

Other classical accounts imply that bridging the undemocratic 'gap' between the language of the educated elite and the proverbial humble peasant – naturally assumed to speak Turkish – was a main cause for the reform. Heyd for example blithely asserts as justifying background to the reforms that 'the vernacular of the common people and the language of popular literature preserved a more genuine Turkish character, but were despised by the educated as a barbarous and uncouth jargon' (Heyd 1954: 10). Finally in more critical vein attention has been drawn to the infelicities of the language revolution, in terms of its impoverishing impact upon speakers and writers of the new Turkish. The best example of this is also the most interesting book (in English) on the Turkish language changes, Geoffrey Lewis' *The*

25. Lewis' cluster of terms here – civilization, modern, West – is important. 'Civilization' and 'West' are words that suggest cultural formations of particularity, different but not necessarily superior to other cultural constellations. By contrast 'modern' carries with it the implication of universality and even inevitability, unless one wishes perversely to turn away from the future. Tellingly, Lewis (1961: 431) writes a few pages later that 'modern civilization rest[s] very largely on its scientific achievement'. Lewis' overall approval of Kemalism then is that it is a political programme seeking to attune itself to a civilization (the modern West) that for Lewis has transcended the particular in becoming universal. Anthropologically speaking, Lewis has ventriloquized the narrative of Kemalist ideology and its informants rather well.

Turkish Language Reform: A Catastrophic Success (Lewis 1999). For Lewis the catastrophe lies in the loss of Ottoman Turkish's 'natural development' (Lewis 1999: 4), so that something written in the 1940s in Istanbul is now unintelligible to present-day readers. Its end result has left 'the Turks with virtually no choice of levels of discourse' (Lewis 1999: 144), by which he means that with the purging of old words (and with their inadequate replacements) the new Turkish has diminished the ability of speakers to make fine distinctions or express subtleties with it. Yet puzzlingly, Lewis never properly discusses the motivations of the language reformers, except to note that their linguistic engineering was done 'for nationalistic reasons' (Lewis 1999: 2). But what were these? Nor does he inquire as to whether the linguistic impoverishment experienced by speakers in Turkey has been evenly distributed across the country. Indeed, apart from Ottoman Turkish, one would not know from his study that in the revolutionary period (or even today) any other language than Turkish was spoken there. In accordance with a model of nationalism that residually positions it as a project of anti-colonialism, the ban on the speaking and writing of Kurdish that occurred at the very same time is not mentioned, a prohibition that was, of course, the most complete example of how the spoken language was to be replaced by a (new) written one.[26]

Assessment of the Iranian case is often similar. Perry hopes that his comparison between the Turkish and Iranian language reforms might help explain 'why on balance one 'succeeded' while the other failed' (Perry 1985: 295), while Kia (1998), despite admitting in her introduction that the Persianization campaign could proceed only by denying the existence of non-Persian identities, is interested thereafter in the campaign's historical development and in assessing its overall impact upon the Persian language.

But is this all that is significant? In none of these analyses are the language policies of the Kemalist states dissected in terms of their *creation* of linguistic minorities and their continuing *exclusion* of them thereafter within the new monolingual territory. But what happens to speakers of languages who do not have a state sponsoring their language's transformation, or enforcing reading and listening in it? In other words, what of the twofold strategy of Kemalist language revolution, not just its *amplifying* of a purified Persian and Turkish but its *silencing* of Kurdish (and other languages)? Language reform is not primarily an exercise in literary rationalization, for example in better reconciling the sounds and writing systems of languages, or bringing the

---

26. Similarly, one recent and very interesting analysis of the 1930s Turkish language revolution focuses on 'the examining of the works of the amateur nationalist grammarians who were associated with the Turkish Language Society in the 1930s, to understand why in these works the West's linguistic tradition was labeled as racist, imperialist and Christian, and to show both their rejecting of this biased Western knowledge, and the various solutions that these amateur grammarians produced to bring the Turkish language into its proper worthy place' (my translation) (Aytürk 2006: 95). Again, nationalism is contextualized in the first instance as a movement of Turkish anti-colonialism and not simultaneously as a movement of Turkish chauvinism.

written language into closer conformity with the spoken one. Spoken languages in Anatolia and Iran were legion. It is, however, an exercise in social engineering. Clearly, radio and print domination intends that certain languages should not be reasoned with or imagined in. But not only this: Kemalist language reform was a key aspect of its aural politics. Just as with its attempted muting of certain genres of music, the sonic censorship of the period endeavoured to assure that the *sounds* of other languages would not be *heard*. The opposite applies to the purified language of course, whose sound is now heard everywhere. Given this desire, language revolution should be studied as an aspect of Kemalism's organization of space as much as of its linguistics. It was intended to produce the acoustic dimension of the new nationalist built environment, to compose a proper soundscape to complement its design of public buildings, its parks to promenade in, its monolingual military zones, courthouses and concert halls (see Chapter 5). In brief, to the extent that the drowning out of minority languages continues in Turkey and Iran as official policy, the language revolution of Kemalism is a project to soundproof the institutions of modernity from the logical and humane political consequences of heteroglossia.

Alongside its project to classicize (simplify) and rescore (augment) a sonorous purified Persian, women, too, became objects of the Pahlavi regime's social engineering. As we have already seen in the Ba'ath Party's publicizing of statistics in Iraq, women's progress is for Kemalism one key index of national development, although the connection made between the progress of the nation and an improved status of women – however defined – well predates the rise of Kemalist states in both Iran and Turkey. As with the late Ottoman and Qajar-period debates over language reform, a discourse on the 'woman question' can be seen in the writings of many pre-Kemalist modernists, as well as in the novels of the period. In Kemalist Iran, too, the transformation of women emerged as one central social policy of Reza Shah's government. According to Amin (2001), the many initiatives of the Pahlavi State that aimed at renewing women and their relations with their families and with the broader national society, culminated in the Shah's 'Women's Awakening' project, begun in 1936. The project coincided with the spectacular forced unveiling of Iranian women, which was reinforced by selected measures to hasten the sexual desegregation of cultural life. (Legislation targeting men's appearance had commenced much earlier, in 1927.)[27] Newly fostered recreational skills such as dancing or sports accompanied

27. Although hardly remarked upon by historians, sartorial reform for men legislating a brimmed hat and European suit was aimed not only at the cities but also at the country's 'tribal areas'. Citing the Governor of the province of Azerbaijan in 1929 (but without commenting upon it), Chehabi mentions that 'Kurds, in particular, seem to have clung to their costume longest' (Chehabi 1993: 214). Typically, his critique of the legislation concentrates on its intention to make everybody look European and not also on its determination to make the ethnic minorities look Persian. The fact that clothing reform had to be decreed for Persians as well was attributed by nationalists at the time to the baleful influence of Arab Islam on Persian society, given the shared ancestry (and dress sense!) of ancient Aryan Iranian and European cultures.

the compulsory unveiling, as did the encouraging of changed habits of pleasure such as official or domestic parties for married partners.

Less theatrically, women's awakening was pursued through the simultaneous censure and scientific improvement of existing social practices, most significantly in the reconfigured fields of education,[28] mothering/domesticity and what we might call kinaesthetics or body techniques (often glossed in the historical literature as unveiling). Characterizing all three fields was both the modern elite's dissemination of science-based knowledge and skills and their appropriation by women as new embodied abilities. The development of women that reformers and experts in each field of discourse and action sought to achieve was intimately connected to the nationalist concerns of the state, as the voluminous recent research on Iranian women's history stresses. It was no coincidence that Reza Shah chose to speak at the combined graduation ceremony of a number of girls' schools (which was held at the opening of a new teachers' college) on the day that the compulsory unveiling legislation was to be inaugurated and policed by state authorities. The emancipation of women from Islam for the nation (and not for individual frippery) is nicely demonstrated in the Shah's speech through his articulation of the triad of national development, women's education and home management (which includes appearance):

> I am exceedingly pleased to see that as a result of knowledge and learning, women have come alive to their condition, rights, and privileges. Being outside of society, the women of this country could not develop their native talents. They could not repay their debts to their dear country, nor serve it and sacrifice for it as they should... We should not forget that one-half of the population of this country was not taken into account... I expect you learned women who are now becoming aware of your rights, privileges and duties to serve your homeland, to be content and economical, and to become accustomed to saving and to avoid luxuries and extravagance. (cited in Chehabi 1993: 218)

Yet becoming educated for the nation is not necessarily an imposition, especially in a context where women's education and professional life thereafter was still opposed by many men. Writing about the debate in the official Iranian press in 1934

---

28. Figures give some sense of the special attention given to female education. According to Matthee (1993) there was virtually no state education in 1921, most schools being privately organized. By 1930 girls comprised 35,000 of the 150,000 students at primary and secondary levels. The vast majority of schools were not co-educational: the number of state-funded girls' schools rose from 14 in 1923 to 2000 by 1941. Education reform in 1928 saw secondary education concluded with a national examination, which allowed access to the various institutions of science, commerce, law and politics. Given its difficulty, graduate numbers from secondary schools were low for both boys and girls: in 1931–2 the numbers were 3, 716 and 1,346 respectively. Women's entrance to tertiary education (in the form of Teachers' College) was facilitated in 1936, and entrance to the new University of Tehran a few years later.

over whether women should enter higher education, Amin notes that the majority of readers' letters were against it (Amin 1999: 375). Even in 1939, the different curric-ulum for male and female secondary students meant that, as in Turkey, girls devoted a third of their schooling to aspects of home economics (Amin 1999: 366). The strict injunctions under which academic education was extended to women, which reveal the regime's intense anxiety that desegregating work and school should not threaten male guardianship, is seen in the propaganda accompanying the 'Women's Awakening' project. On the one hand there existed a discourse on the necessity of women entering and contributing to society. On the other this entrance into civil life required women's chaperoning by modern male protectors – most powerfully symbolized in the Shah himself, the 'Great Father'. And there was a disciplinary discourse too about abuse of one's new privileges, in either neglecting home duties or even in falling prey to immorality (see Amin 1999, 2001).

Less controversial perhaps, education for modern domesticity and attempted expert supervision of pregnancy, mothering, hygiene, sexuality and nutrition were a second group of state initiatives that shaped the experience of women in Kemalist Iran. Kashani-Sabet calls this an ideology of maternalism, which 'promoted motherhood, childcare, and maternal well being not only within the strictures of the family, but also in consideration of nationalist concerns' (2006: 2). Maternal ignorance produces unhealthy children, and as with ignorance of sexual hygiene and venereal diseases, ultimately endangers the population rate. Related to this was the importance placed upon the health of the female body through new school programmes of physical education and sport. Again, the numerous reforms aimed at modification of women's cultural practices, self-perception and embodied skills were not intended to facilitate women's independence from men. They were intended to legitimize the state as the liberator of women from the counterfeit Islam preached by reactionary *ulema*, and to enable women to serve the greater 'family' of the nation, at home and in public.

For this reason there has now been a debate several decades old in both Iran and Turkey about the motivations and insufficiencies of this state-sponsored 'feminism', especially given that in establishing their own women's organizations the Kemalists in both countries (as in Iraq) suppressed independent women's associations and journals. Drastically simplifying the discussion, the *emancipatory thesis* maintains that the Kemalist reforms of the Islamic legal code liberated women by abolishing or severely curtailing polygamy, equalizing inheritance and legally recognizing the nuclear family as the building block of the nation. Further, in giving women the right to vote and in opening educational institutions to women, equality between the sexes is made possible through women's working in the public domain. By contrast, the *patriarchal antithesis* argues that the Kemalist reforms were not made with the intention (or even in the name) of guaranteeing women's rights but were primarily articulated with the interests of the secularist regime. Being state-gifted, Kemalist 'emancipation' is a form of patriarchal bargain, made between women and the State (or its main representative in the nuclear family, the husband) in which education is granted so that women might be better mothers and wives. Further the new family law entrenched the husband's dominance over his wife in a host of areas, in divorce, remarriage, virginity, rape in marriage and in legislating the sexual division of labour.[29] Thirdly and intimately associated with the patriarchal critique is what we might call a *partial synthesis*, an assessment that focuses on the ambiguities at the core of Kemalism's development of women, noting both the controlling intent of the reforms *and* the agency of women in their very fleshing out. This ambiguity is seen to extend to professional women too, posited to be the prime beneficiaries of Kemalist women's development. Synthetic accounts then also pay attention to divisions among women, noting the classed dimensions of women's experience of Kemalist reforms.

Najmabadi's analysis of the changing discourse on the 'educated housewife' in Qajar and Pahlavi Iran is illustrative of this synthetic stance. She is concerned to explore the relationship between the state's self-interested investment in educating females and women's own reasons for responding favourably to such advances. She concludes that women in the 1930s

> having been entrapped by the very discourse that had opened up education to them in the first place ... now opted to enlarge their notion of 'domestic duties' to mean national service. The new home to whose management they now began to lay claim was no longer their conjugal home but the national home, Iran ... [O]ne can see both disciplinary and emancipatory dynamics in this scenario: appropriation of the notion of servant of the state enabled women to claim their right to higher education and professions while subjecting those rights to regulations, demands, and agendas of the state. (Najmabadi 1998: 114, 115)

Although Najmabadi is extremely sensitive to the simultaneously liberating and regulatory impacts on women's lives of Kemalist women's development in Iran, her argument is inattentive to the relationship between women's emancipation and the *ethnic* agenda of the proffered education. Perceiving the ambiguity of the modern educational regime vis-à-vis women to reside in its seemingly contradictory discourse on gender, she ignores the Persian chauvinism of the curriculum. Yet the modern educational regime sought to craft not just educated housewives or female professionals, but educated *Persian* housewives and professionals. As with female emancipation in Turkey, the conditional liberation offered women did not extend to minority ethnic subjects, unless they first became Persian. Her analysis of Kemalist education illuminates the 'difference gender makes' (Najmabadi 1998: 97). But it obscures the difference nationalism produces amongst these gendered subjects. It

29. See both Z. Arat (1994) and Sirman (2004) for a critique of 'state feminism' in the Turkish context.

reiterates how important it was for the nation state to mobilize women but overlooks the complex relationship Kemalism engenders between emancipated women and ethnic minorities. Almost by definition, Kemalist women's associations have been unsympathetic to 'non-sovereign' nationalism. In brief, for Najmabadi too, nationalism as a state project of anti-colonial economic development is assumed. Nationalism as a cultural project for reconfiguring 'orientalized' and perjured non-Western identities is stressed. Nationalism as a political tool of regime consolidation is understood. But nationalism as the simultaneous internal generation and exclusion of gendered ethnic subjects, or nationalism as the process of actively and often violently undermining other emergent national groups is persistently downplayed. As we have seen with the analyses of language reform, this tendency is not hers alone.

Turkish Kemalism

Throughout this chapter I have tried to illustrate how Kemalism, defined as a dual political project to nationalize the bodies and perceptions of the populations circ-umscribed by its new territorial boundaries and to reform Islam for service to the nation-state, is best seen as a trans-regional practice. Accordingly the cultural dom-ains created or marked out for regulation by Kemalist states are reminiscent of one another, notwithstanding, of course, the different superior ethnicities projected through them. As we have already seen in this and earlier chapters, the imagining and narrating of national origins and characteristics, the emancipating of women for service to the family of the nation, and the engineering and censoring of language have been and continue to be common practice to Iraqi, Iranian and Turkish Kemalism. Similarly, each state suppresses or has rejected Kurdish self-description of their national difference. Whereas in Iraq Kurds and other minorities were encouraged to trace their origins back to the Arabs, in Iran they were told they were Persian and in Turkey that they were Turks. The examination of Iraq and Iran has contributed I hope to the building of a cumulative tableau of Kemalism and its typical politico-cultural institutions.

Rather than repeat myself here by discussing Turkish Kemalism's variations on these themes, in this final section I want to branch out and briefly describe Kemalist initiatives in Turkey in what we might define as the realm of 'aesthetics.' By this I mean the area of the arts in general. Nevertheless for the sake of brevity we will discuss theatre, folklore and music only.[30] By focusing on the arts I am not suggesting of course that the work of Kemalist activists in Turkey in the formative single party period (1923-50) was primarily devoted to aesthetic

---

30. I explore Kemalist uses of architecture in the next chapter.

creation.[31] Rather as in Nazi Germany, the Soviet Union and in fascist Italy (three political formations admired by the Turkish Kemalists), the ruling elite in Turkey 'cared about … the arts to the extent that they could be used, first for general political purposes and second for compensating for the ideological gaps and ambiguities concerning national culture' (Köksal 2004: 93). These general political purposes included the use of art for propaganda and indoctrination. But it is important to examine the performing arts for another reason, because participation in them (as in sport) involves not only the imbibing of ideological precepts but also the learning of embodied skills, the experience of pleasure and the development of judgement/taste. The roles of performer and 'critic' are not mutually incompatible: art education intends that people become both skilled practitioners and connoisseurs. Kemalist discourse (including censorship) on music, dance and theatre etc. sought then to stabilize the cognitive meaning of the new artistic or performance genres developed and popularized by the state. Arts education in the broadest sense served Kemalism's attempted transformation of individuals' selves by constituting through the emotional experience of performance an affective dimension of the newly posited national/ ethnic community. This occurred at the time when Atatürk had outlawed collective associations such as the Islamic brotherhoods (*tarikats*), whose embodied practices of worship were influential in constructing affective dimensions of a different and potentially rival imagined community, the Muslim *ummah*.

More than one recent analysis has pointed out the importance of the 'People's Houses' (*Halk Evleri*) as key institutions of the Kemalist regime's patronage and mobilization of the arts. Established by the Republican People's Party (CHP),[32]

31. Indeed, since the 1990s much historical research on the Kemalist state's wide-ranging educational initiatives in its foundational period has noted and analysed the thoroughness of its attempt to manufacture a new society (see for example Salmoni 2003; 2004). This reforming zeal was not limited to the Kemalist pedagogy dominant in schools. As in Iran, in Turkey too Kemalist campaigns in the areas of maternal and child health linked change in such practices to the development of a rational and ordered modernity, intimately connected to Turkish national values. See Navaro-Yashin (2000) for analysis of Kemalist sciences of household management, Yenal (1999) on the Girls' Institutes, and Libal (2000) on the nationalist motivations inspiring welfare in the case of the Children's Protection Society. Beyond formal pedagogy, Kemalist ideals and discipline concerning the bodies and health of both men and women were seen in all aspects of its 'body politics', not just in the hat law (1925) or in women's unveiling but even in the outcome in 1934 of Turkey's first beauty contest: the initial winner was later disqualified as it was discovered that her physical dimensions did not conform to the European average.

32. Throughout the single-party period, but especially after 1930 the sole legal political party and administrative backbone of the State was the CHP. Italian fascism provided the model for emergent state/party relations in the 1930s, under the catchcry of 'unifying the forces'. According to Keyder, in essence this meant the shutting down or incorporation of every non-state institution within the party-state nexus. By 1936 the Prime Minister could declare 'full congruency between state administration and party organization. With this declaration all state officials in the administrative field became local party officials' (Keyder 1987: 100).

People's Houses were first opened up in fourteen major urban centres in 1932. By 1939 there were 373 all over Turkey (Öztürkmen 1994: 163). Most immediately the People's Houses were envisioned as adult education centres through which the Kemalist revolution might be disseminated to the people. But they were also concerned, at least in theory, with mediating artistic creation and education deriving from more formal institutional settings (new colleges and university departments) with the 'art' of the peasants or *halk* (people). This aim accounts for their serious interest in ethnographic research. In a speech given by Recep Peker, Secretary-General of the CHP, at the opening of the first and the most important People's House in Ankara in 1932, the raising up, training or fostering – the Turkish word is *yetişmek* – of a *milli* (national) society by the state via its educational institutions assumes prime importance. It was less commonly expressed, but not denied either, that this also meant 'Turkifying' the sensibilities of the population, including those who spoke Turkish:

> Friends, the classic institutions and instruments to raise up [*yetisip*] a nation and prepare them for the future are the schools. But in order to develop a well organized national existence, modern nations see that schools in themselves are insufficient instruments through which to order this task. It is true that fully-conscious and committed citizens can be brought up by schools with good, proper programmes and methods with practical application. But alongside school education and after it we need to establish a system of adult education and a place where people can meet and work together that will produce a national mass society that in turn would facilitate this true nation. Even the richest countries with their army of well-trained teachers, the most influential and appropriate lessons and their many school buildings do not neglect to develop the people, to raise the people into a mass movement and finally to form a nationalized population.
>
> Friends, youth are the light of the future. Youth should be facilitated to live in an environment that continually develops them and allows their development. (Peker 1933: 6, from the first edition of *Ülkü*, the journal of the Ankara People's House) (my translation)

In order to establish a People's House in their town, party members were directed to structure its social and cultural activities according to at least three of nine possible divisions. These were 1. Language, History and Literature, 2. Fine Arts, 3. Theatre, 4. Sports, 5. Social Assistance, 6. Public Classes and Courses, 7. Library and Publishing, 8. Village Development, 9. Museums and Exhibitions.[33] Öztürkmen goes on to explain the activities that various of the sections incorporated:

---

33. I have combined the lists of Öztürkmen (1996) and Karaömerlioğlu (1998), who translate the Turkish section terms in different ways. Note the similarities between the activities of the People's Houses and the cultural campaign organized by the Ba'ath Kemalists to fabricate Mesopotamian identity.

The 'Language and Literature' section, for instance, pursued studies on modern Turkish, its grammar and literature; organized commemoration days for Turkish intellectuals, artists and heroes; and published the results of such studies in their periodicals. The 'Fine Arts' section played an important role in mediating the Republic's image of a contemporary society, forming new choral ensembles and orchestras in the modern style, offering musical training and organizing painting and photography exhibitions and competitions. Similarly, the 'Theatre' section claimed among its new duties the organization of drama courses, the training of public speakers, emphasis on women's roles in theatrical pieces, the promotion of domestic arts and support for the art of the cinema... As for the 'Village Development' section, it would establish cordial relations between the village and the city... The 'Public Classes and Courses' section was responsible for running literacy courses, stimulating interest in science, opening laboratories and supporting folk art... (Öztürkmen 1994: 164)

According to Ari, theatre was both the preferred and the only effective non-literate medium of mass communication of the new regime.[34] Outside of Istanbul, which in fact already possessed a rich theatrical tradition including a number of professional companies, theatre as an integral aspect of the activities of the People's Houses was conceived as pedagogical art directed at the peasants. Ari cites the 1933 annual report of the Aydın People's House, which states the agenda clearly:

The theatre is the most practical tool for the transmission of messages to the people, and it is the best cultural school... In the past, actors were not able to surpass the level of improvisation... Among the obstacles confronting the arts were religious fanaticism that even accused artists of heresy, and the hollow heads of the disciples of Sufi and religious schools that were not able to digest the role of Turkish men and women in the theatre... The infrastructure for change was set up ... by the Republic that created a space for stage life. (Ari 2004: 44)

Yet Ari also notes that despite all best intentions, the majority of those exposed to the transmission of messages via the stage did not live in the villages but in the urban centres. It was the urban middle classes who most enjoyed the affective charge generated through attendance and participation in theatrical performance and who most often animated and interpreted the educative content of the characters' speeches and actions.

By contrast, Ahıska argues that both actors and Turkish broadcasters believed radio drama (rather than stage drama) was more efficient in presenting its message to the larger mass of people. She cites Kemal Tözem, Head of Drama Department at Ankara Radio in 1942, brilliantly describing the performative dimensions of state

---

34. Ari (2004: 34). But this claim is greatly exaggerated in view of the importance given to both music and architecture in the single-party period and beyond.

radio theatre: 'If people get used to listening to radio plays, then there would be a *modern stage in each living room*, which is rich in its *settings and props* to the extent of *richness of imagination*' (my emphasis) (Ahıska 2000: 34). The living room *mise en scene* of Tözem's imaginative audience however assumes a certain class setting, which is not in the first instance either public (i.e. the People's House) or rural. Ahıska herself argues that an audience 'attributes meanings more freely to what is heard compared to what is seen' (Ahiska 2000: 32). Wherein lies the affective power of the aural imagination? Listening in one's private room to the sounds of a unified nation facilitates an emotional bond to its fantasized public reality, in the same way that hearing the daily weather reports from the country's various regions encourage us to think the rain stops at the border. This emotional and spatial perception is reinforced of course by state dictates creating the 'unhearable' in radio drama: two of the prohibitions governing radio production were that 'segregationist thoughts cannot be included' and that 'the political climate of the country cannot be reflected' (cited in Ahıska 2000: 36).

How successful the People's Houses were in attaining their identified goals – the dissemination of the principles and new cultural practices of Kemalism to the people, the development of the 'social, medical and aesthetic dimensions of villages' (Karaömerlioğlu 1998: 70) and the creation of a national artistic culture – is difficult to assess. Ari (2004) notes that it was the expanding bureaucratic class and urban elites that operated the People's Houses and took most advantage of their programmes, a group of people already sympathetic to the civilizing project of the pedagogic state. Somewhat similarly, Karaömerlioğlu argues that what he calls the 'peasantist ideology' of the ruling Kemalist elites influenced its propagandists in the People's Houses much more than the peasants or their villages. Despite the fact that the village development division of the Houses was the most active, 'life in rural Turkey remained largely unchanged by the People's Houses', because whilst desiring to raise the cultural level of the peasants 'there was a virtual consensus on preventing the dissolution of the rural social structure' (Karaömerlioğlu 1998: 72, 85).

But where the People's Houses do seem to have had a lasting influence is in the creation or standardization of a number of artistic genres, or on what Öztürkmen (1996: 161) calls the form and content of a 'national art repertoire that still prevails.' Thus

> what is now called the 'Turkish national culture' follows, in large measure, the generic structure laid out by the People's Houses in the thirties and forties. The 'Theatre' sections ... promoted both the *Karagoz* and *Ortaoyuna* as Turkey's 'national drama.' The 'Language' sections compiled pioneering collections of local dialects, proverbs and folk narratives, working in cooperation with the TDK [Turkish Language Society]. The 'Fine Arts' sections collected folk songs... Folk costumes and other folk art material were collected to be exhibited ... as national costumes and national art. (Öztürkmen 1996: 164, 165)

Although she doesn't draw out the connections, the regular research trips by urbanites and Kemalist intellectuals to rural areas to collect and document 'peasant life', so as to produce new synthetic forms of Turkish national culture, attests once more to the common theoretical heritage shared by anthropology and nationalism in the heroic period of each (the 1920s and 1930s). It also shows how it was state-related agencies that executed the anthropological quest. In the process rural *Anadolu* (Anatolia) was claimed as the pure heartland of living Turkish culture, in contradistinction to the cosmopolitanism and anti-nationalism of the urban Ottoman past. Not just the material (*madde*) culture (from rug weaving to handicrafts) but the spiritual (*manevi*) culture (particularly folklore including proverbs, folk songs, riddles, folk tales, word games, poems and rhymes) of the different regions of the Anatolian peasants were construed as variegated local manifestations of a single ethnic genius.[35] They were taught as such thereafter in university Turkish Language, Literature, History, Geography and Ethnography departments. Forcibly included within this inventory of the Turkish *halk* (people) were 'Kurdistan' and 'Kurds', renamed and constituted as Eastern Anatolia and lost Turkish tribes respectively. Forcibly excluded from this Anatolian inventory were Greeks. Even so, the difference of Kurdistan and other areas was problematic, as N. Köymen, one of the most influential writers of the peasantist ideology had to confess (in 1935): 'there are some villages in which a foreign language is spoken although they are often racially Turkish and have been living in this country for centuries; and there are even some villages in which people speak Turkish but do not adhere to Turkism sufficiently' (Köymen cited in Karaömerlioğlu 1998: 89).[36] The urgency invested in folklore by the Turkish Kemalists as the discipline intimately connected with the new Division of Culture's 1924 charter to 'conserve our national culture and to raise our youth within the national culture' (cited in Ülkütaşır 1972: 46) is seen in the almost immediate founding of an Ethnographic Museum in Ankara in 1925. Indicative of the importance of the nationalist mission entrusted to ethnographic research, it was

35. The distinction is made by Hamit Zübeyr Koşay in his 1939 book *Etnografya ve Folklor Kilavuzu* (*Guide to Ethnography and Folklore*) and repeated in 1972 in Mehmet Ülkütaşır's survey *Cumhuriyet'le Birlikte Türkiye'de Folklor ve Etnografya Çalışmaları* (*Together with the Republic: Folklore and Ethnographic Studies in Turkey.*) In his foreword, Ülkütaşır (1972: 5) notes that 'Folklore is a scientific discipline that in our country only received the importance and appreciation it deserves in the Republican period. [It is] the branch of science that researches the society's spiritual (*manevi*) culture…' (my translation).

36. Without wishing to be too critical, it is a puzzle that Özturkmen's otherwise informative article on the People's Houses' production of a Turkish national culture ignores Kurdish claims about the simultaneous denial and appropriation of Kurdish dance, music and folklore. To cite just one example, the famous epic poem *Mem u Zim*, written in Kurdish in 1695 by Ehmedi Xani was claimed to have been a Turkish creation. It was immediately banned in 1968 when it first appeared in a latinized Kurdish and Turkish translation. For a discussion of Kurdish nationalism and its interpretation of *Mem u Zim*, see van Bruinessen 2003.

also in the Ethnographic Museum that Atatürk's body was laid for the first 15 years after his death, until the completion of his mausoleum in 1953.

Within this emerging field of ethnographic knowledge, music too became of prime concern for the Kemalist ethnographers. Hamit Koşay, one of Turkey's first musicologists and an expert on Anatolian music, accompanied Bartok on his trip to Adana to record local songs and melodies in 1936.[37] In the section on *Halk Musikisi* (Folk Music) in his *Guide to Ethnography and Folklore* Koşay makes a distinction between Anatolian and Greek modal melodies, as well as establishing, through a sleight of hand, a connection between Anatolian and Turkish/Central Asian music. In this he follows Ziya Gökalp, who in his 1923 work *The Principles of Turkism* described Ottoman music as both Eastern *and* Byzantine, as well as 'depressingly monotonous' because it was based on modal quarter tones (cited in Tekelioğlu 1996: 201). The result is that Koşay 'de-indigenizes' Greek, Ottoman and Arab history in Anatolia, making it native no longer:

> Anadolu is the country of the Hittites, Phrygians, and the Lydians who gave birth to its civilization. Anadolu is the country of the Turks. Anadolu has been the passage-way of countless streams of people. For this reason Anadolu possesses a folk art and a treasury of folklore that is limitless and innumerable in its richness. By binding its soul to these incomparable colours and endless changes Anatolian folk music has developed on a different path to the music of other countries: the Greeks incorporated within their own systems the [musical] modes (*makamlar*) that had accumulated in the two thousand five hundred years previously and established the theory of Anatolian folk modes...
>
> Can the existence of these two modes give us the idea that ancient Greek music continues its life in Anadolu? No. Here we have to remember that the Greeks accepted only the Dorian as their national mode; because the other modes were exported to Greece from different countries they acquired the reputation of being the 'barbarian modes' in comparison to the national mode. Now what place of origin can be agreed on for these modes? We can give an answer to this question easily: Anatolia, the country of the Phrygians and the Lydians; these civilizations exercised a powerful influence over Greek art, not only in music but in sculpture and literature too...
>
> Therefore Anadolu uses its own modes and its own music. In this matter the subject under discussion can only be Anatolian music, not Greek music. (Koşay 1939: 55, my translation)

Koşay's disinterring of the history of musical modes in Anatolia to nationalize certain series of notes and rhythmic intervals gives some inkling of the tremendous importance ascribed to music by the Kemalists. Yet the recording, notating and nationalizing of peasant music was only one aspect of an even more fundamental concern, the making of a music revolution (*musiki inkalıbı*). Indeed according to

---

37. Collection and notation of rural songs began in the period of the Young Turks. The first work representing peasants' songs and melodies was printed in 1915 (Ülkütaşir 1972: 30).

Tekelioğlu, 'from the moment the Republic was formed, music was given pride of place in policies relating to culture and art, a kind of "target" as leaders sought to fashion a new sort of citizen and a new nation-state' (Tekelioğlu 1996: 195). In this process certain existing musical genres and performance practices were censored, while new musical fields were developed and approved as authentic performance genres in the wider cultural revolution.

The first music targeted for muting was *tekke* music, or the music of the religious orders, with the closing down of their lodges and rooms in 1924. Tekelioğlu notes that with the exception of the music of the *Mevlevi* order, the 'mystical' music of the brotherhoods has now essentially disappeared.[38] The music of the Ottoman palace too, 'Classical Turkish Art Music', was as we have seen denigrated as Byzantine and twice even prohibited, briefly in 1928 and for a longer time in 1934, when the ban on its playing on the radio lasted two years. Positioned as simultaneously both Eastern and Byzantine, Ottoman music and its teaching at the *Dar-ül-Elhan* (House of Tunes), the conservatorium in Istanbul founded in 1917, were abolished in 1925. The Turkish Kemalists also sought to reduce to silence anything sung in Kurdish, including the music of religious worship of Sunni and Alevi Kurds, as well as of Kurdish popular songs.

If musical sounds constructed as 'eastern' or voiced in Kurdish were censured, their replacement sounds were composed of a number of new aural forms, organized by the triad West/Origin/East. The classification 'gave the elements with which union was sought (the West and the origin), while also referring to the territory with which unification was absolutely taboo, the East' (Tekelioğlu 1996: 195). Thus the newly identified folk music of Anatolia, when combined and scored with the harmonic devices (polyphony) of Western music, would produce the new synthetic *milli* (national) music. By contrast, as late as the 1980s musical styles such as *Arabesk* (meaning Arab-like) were constructed as eastern and banned. Other forms of Western-origin musical synthesis were composed and taught as well, including martial music. Üstel draws attention to the desire of the Kemalist educators to have every Turkish citizen sing 'march' music. Marches were written for the different sectors of society, including the Agricultural March, the Economics March, the Artists March, the Farmers March and the Teachers March (Üstel 1993: 43ff.). March music of course is particularly attuned to parades and processions, as the people walk and sing on national days. Thirdly, along with new institutions teaching Turkish Folk Music and Dance, Western classical music too was introduced, with

38. There is some logic to why the Mevlevi and Hacı-Bektaş orders were spared. Both were deemed capable of being nativized as Anatolian, Turkish and progressive, in distinction to more conservative or 'foreign' orders. Today most existing Islamic orders are careful to work within the parameters established by the state: the present name of the Mevlevi Lodge in Karagümruk in Istanbul is Türk Tasavvuf Musikisi ve Folklor Araştırmaları ve Yaşatma Vakfı (The Foundation for the Research and Revival of Turkish Folklore and Sufi Music).

German composer Paul Hindemith invited to Ankara in 1935 to supervise the founding of the new Ankara School of Music. 'His task was to oversee the establishment of a western-style conservatory, producing a symphony orchestra, soloists and composers' (Stokes 1992: 38). Even before this, the General Director of the People's Houses had commissioned three operas, including the first opera written in the Republican period (*Özsoy*-True Race) for the visit of Reza Shah to Ankara in 1935. Üstel (1993: 52) notes that the work, based on a Persian legend, celebrates the 'friendship' between the two peoples, while according to Tekelioğlu (1996: 205) Mustafa Kemal personally reviewed the libretto.

Let me conclude this section by referring briefly to a fascinating round table discussion on 'Music and the Republic', published in *Defter* journal in 1993. The participants wonder why the Kemalists sought a *revolution* in *music* (and not in literature or painting etc.). They propose a number of answers. The first is Atatürk's famous declaration in 1928 that Eastern music causes apathy, sluggishness, numbness and grief, while Western music brings joyfulness and liveliness. Implicit in Atatürk's statement, although not mentioned in the discussion, is a theory of music's *affectivity*, or its power to engender listeners' moods and behaviour. Eastern music was heard as a tranquilizer that kept the East in its backwards slumber, march music as conducive to courage and activity. We might say then that the music revolution intended to change the emotional temper of the population. The second reason mooted is the Kemalists' intuition that music is the key to social process. Thus discussant Ayvazoğlu cites early Republican intellectual Ahmet Tanpınar saying that 'because the musical understanding possessed by any culture is the most exalted expression of its intelligence, it is very difficult to change. Until a change in our music happens our attitude towards life won't change' (Ayvazoğlu *et al.* 1993: 9). As politics, a revolution in music then was strategically calculated, based on a conviction of the intimate relationship between music and a society's ties to its past. Thirdly, Ayvazoğlu makes an equation between the *music* and the *language* revolutions, arguing that the two most perfect channels through which any society expresses itself are music and its spoken language or mother tongue (Ayvazoğlu *et al.* 1993: 9). The implication is that both the new language and the new music were intended to transform cultural and self-expression. In brief, by creating new sounds *and* the educational institutions required to teach their 'proper' hearing or perception, the music revolution was directed towards changing the emotional, historical and expressive disposition or ethos of the population.

Finally, in Kemalist Iran too similar processes involving the banning of certain musical forms and the nationalizing of others were pursued. Youssefzadeh writes that Reza Shah prohibited the performance of *t'avieh*, 'the "singing" play depicting the martyrdom of Imam Hosein and his family' (Youssefzadeh 2005: 422). Likewise he sponsored the collecting and Persian language publication of village songs, the first volume appearing in 1938. As in Turkey, this notation and printing of what were named regional (not ethnic) styles has been continued throughout the century, including after the Islamic Revolution. Paralleling the festivals and musical events organized by the Ba'ath Party in the Mesopotamian cultural campaign, cultural politics during the 'White Revolution' of Muhammad Reza Shah (1969) took centre stage, including the completion of an opera house begun but never finished by his father Reza Shah in the 1930s.[39]

Crafting National Selves

To conclude, in this chapter I have defined Kemalism as a dual political practice and have claimed it to be the generic governing project characterizing state politics in Iraq, Iran and Turkey. Chauvinist against ethnic minorities and modernist against non-authorized Islamic practice, Kemalism has also underwritten the sovereign national identities of the citizens of all three states by what Vali calls a violent denial of Kurdish identity in particular (Vali 1998). Further, the attempted cultural revolution of the Kemalist elites in each country extends far beyond the restricted number of fields described above. As we have already seen, the historians' politicized reconstructions of the vital features of Ottoman society examined in Chapters 1 and 2 were all written after the institution of Kemalist states in the former Ottoman territory. Indeed, the intellectual cadres of these Kemalist regimes have been the chief interpreters of the Ottoman legacy. Similarly, the classical ethnographic representations of Kurdish society discussed in Chapter 3 were all produced in the foundational period (or after) of these Kemalist states. Turkish anthropology's representation of Kurds in the single-party era and its constitution of folklore as its major object of research might be summarily described as Kemalist ethnography.

Given this history, readers will no doubt be wondering about the status of Kemalism in Iran after the Islamic revolution. Sayyid's definition of Kemalist politics – the attempt to de-Islamize society in the name of Islam's retardation – would suggest that Ayatollah Khomeini's revolution in Iran heralds the failure and rejection of the Kemalist vision. And Sayyid argues just this of course, positing a strong distinction between Kemalist and Islamist political orders (Sayyid 1997: 150ff). On the other hand and as I have claimed earlier in the chapter, Khomeinism and Kemalism can be analysed as having certain central features in common, principally their revolutionary elites' pursuit of radical self-institution, in giving to themselves their own law and their own cultural forms. Furthermore although the linguistic and

39. Youssefzadeh's rather naïve approach to the sponsoring of a musical 'national tradition' by official institutions, including most importantly the Ministry of Culture and the National Iranian Radio and Television, is reflected in her comment that 'Iranians from my generation, who were teenagers in the 1970s, were introduced to our culture's musical heritage via the numerous public performances that were organized and presented during this decade' (Youssefzadeh 2005: 429). Again, one wonders at the model of nationalism informing her essay. Or rather should we say that the model of nationalism informing her analysis is connected to the Kemalism of the Pahlavi State?

institutional autonomy of the ethnic regions in Iran have been recognized in the new constitution, according to Khosrokhavar 'these articles have been systematically ignored by successive governments since the Islamic revolution' (Khosrokhavar 2004: 80). And it should have been sobering for Sayyid to remember that both Reza Shah I *and* the Islamist regime began their rule with military campaigns designed to crush autonomist movements in the province of Kurdistan (for Reza Shah's military campaigns, see Abrahamian 1982: 120). Lastly we could note the evolving legacies of both Ataturk and Khomeini in competitive, if restricted, electoral politics, which connect to overlapping trajectories in emerging religious-secular relations (Nafissi 2007: 47).

In sum, the question of the similarities and differences between Kemalism and Khomeinism is an open issue. Of course, the explicit endeavour of the Islamic regime to subordinate politics to religious rule reverses one key aspect of Kemalism, making Islamist Iran a post-Kemalist polity. Nevertheless in contemporary Iran Kemalism, to cite Arnason out of place, has an afterlife, 'possessing specific legacies and resources that can be reactivated in inventive ways' (Arnason 2006: 52).[40] One of the ways that the Islamist regime has reactivated its Kemalist legacy is through the censorship of cinema, common under the Shah. Another way is in its own music policies, with the sponsoring of music festivals by the Music Division of the Ministry of Culture and Islamic Guidance and the Arts Division of the Islamic Propaganda Organization. Among the most significant of these has been the Festival of Regional Music in Iran, established in 1999, which includes awards to researchers in ethno-musicology (see Youssefzadeh 2005: 431ff). Again, the revolution's amplification of approved sounds has been accompanied by its muting of disapproved sounds. Immediately after the revolution Western classical and pop music were banned, in the name of re-sounding the cultural heritage of Iran muffled by the Westernizing cultural policies of the two Shahs. A third reactivation of the Kemalist legacy has been the use of archaeology to demonstrate materially how Islam is an integral aspect of Iranian identity, as we will see briefly in the next chapter. If for Kemalist and Islamist politics the imagined authentic Iranian self is different, the project of gratuitous self-institution through cultural revolution is the same, as the forced veiling or unveiling by Islamists and Kemalists illustrates.

Being projects of self-institution then – Nilüfer Göle describes the Turkish case as 'voluntary modernization' (Göle 2002: 175) – Kemalist (and Islamist) projects need finally to be thought about in terms of their *efficacy*. How successful have

40. Arnason's quote refers to the inheritances that *civilizational complexes* (he talks of the Indian, Chinese, Islamic, Greek and Western) make available to modern actors, including states, governments, social movements and their intellectuals. His stress here is on the multiple possibilities that the 'distinct socio-cultural patterns', 'divergent cultural frameworks' or 'structures of consciousness' of different civilizations *open up* to agents in the present, and not on the dead weight of tradition that supposedly reasserts itself in variants of modernity such as Kemalism, Communism, and Islamism etc.

these attempts to craft in citizens a new ethic and self, as well as a new embodied knowledge been? In each field of state-supervised cultural production, there appeared a belief in the power of visual signs to generate reality for those to whom they were addressed, whether the iconic sign be in word, image, architectural form, musical sequence, bodily bearing or clothing. The endeavour itself is an indication of the Kemalists' belief in the sign's efficacy to constitute its carrier or audience as the desired subjects intended by the composers of the sign. It might be described as a commitment to make a 'concordance between the objective structures [the new physical organization of space for example] and the cognitive structures, between the shape of being and the forms of knowledge' (Bourdieu 2001: 9). Yet these new practices and symbols of nationalized modernity were propagated in polemical relationship to what were constituted as 'traditional', 'reactionary' or 'culturally alien' practices and symbols. Their very vilification helped to keep such signs in circulation as alternative cultural possibilities. As the example of the music revolution heralds, Kemalism is at one and the same time a sensuous politics of coercion and seduction, intent on suppressing existing pleasures while fostering the enjoyment of new. Even the prohibiting of the speaking of Kurdish, for those forced to learn a second language, is potentially productive of new competencies that impact upon the possibilities of social action and self-expression. But the pains and pleasures of these projects have been differentially distributed (if that is the word), regionally and ethnically, materially and psychologically. Kemalist cultural revolution has also been intrinsically undemocratic and, being sponsored by military vanguards, has been accompanied by the calculated exercise of violence.

According to Ahıska, in this attempt to mobilize the population for regime-determined goals, 'the mediation of ... reception was not acknowledged' (Ahıska 2000: 36). (Neither was it tolerated, if it led to counter practices.) Yet as much as the Kemalist elites produced nationalized modern symbols to be emotionally identified with, the programmes of cultural revolution focused also on transforming through performance individuals' use and experiences of the body. Indeed in the teaching of a range of new physical skills – ballroom dancing, sports, physical education, gymnastics, folk dance, marching, music playing, and military service – we see a Kemalist state project to craft *new* male and female bodies as well as selves. How successful has this enterprise been? In becoming both skilled performers and discerning spectators at the same time, the subjects of reform became well versed in interpreting the meaning of the spectacle. But perhaps they also became potentially cynical about its organizers' intent, precisely because they knew it was a performance. In relying on the 'theatrical' not merely to represent but to constitute the desired future over against the past, Kemalist regimes also drew attention to the performance's quality as a copy, to its mimicking of some posited cultural essence. In the performance's signifying of reality, the Kemalists were unable to control not only the mediation of individuals' reception but the consciousness of performers as well.

In brief, it is hard to make a definitive judgement on the efficacy of these cultural projects in transforming the ideas, sensibilities and bodies of citizens. How would it be assessed? On what grounds, and over which period of time? Does change happen once for all or does the revolution need to be continually enacted? Most importantly my claims above can only be substantiated through ethnographic research. Citizens of Kemalist regimes can and do imagine themselves differently to the way they are assembled in state-sponsored performance. And on another level, the pleasures that performance incites in them may also be cognitively understood in ways different to that suggested by their arts educators. This leads us on to our final chapter, where we will briefly explore Kurdish inhabiting and contesting of another semiotic system, the 'Kemalist City'.

–5–

Kurdish Inhabitation of the 'Kemalist City'

Kemalist regimes are great city-builders. In this final chapter I hope to extend our understanding of Kemalism by describing its creation of what I will provisionally name the 'Kemalist City'. Here we will explore how Kemalism, as the dominant political practice in countries with a large Kurdish minority, embeds in the built environment its governing narratives of Turkish, Persian or Arab nationalism. In order to put bricks and mortar to their imagining of nations and national identities Kemalists in all three states pursued the 'creation of new spaces as places of [nationalist] memory' (Kolluoğlu-Kırlı 2002: 4), accompanied by the de-Islamization of urban sites. To illustrate this construction of Kemalist cities, we will briefly describe the spatial organization of Ankara, Tehran and Baghdad, the emergent capitals of the new nation-states of Turkey, Iran and Iraq.

Indeed, it is strange that there has been so little interest in comparing the transformation of these three cities since the First World War by their respective Kemalist states, as well as how their spatial re-organization expresses and enforces those states' denial of Kurdish claims to a separate national identity. Yet emphasis on the programmatic or semiotic political power of architecture and urban planning needs to be complemented by a more phenomenological take on the built environment, which explores how buildings and spaces are intersubjectively and sensually experienced, remembered and transformed by their users. Again, this is a task for fieldwork. How are these cities reckoned with by their inhabitants, in particularly Kurds, in order to act in and upon them differently? In our last section we will briefly describe the production of (self-)knowledge by Kurds through their engagement with the 'Kemalist City', as experienced for example in their use of music. Self-consciousness about Kurdish identity leads to a diasporic experience of the Kemalist City. But before doing any of this let me make a few brief comments about Kemalism's *translatio imperii* (transfer of rule), effected in particular through the founding or re-modelling of cities, and about the power of architecture more generally.

The Power of the Built Environment

In her article on the Turkish republic's rebuilding of the fire zone that had once been Izmir's Frank quarter, wiped out in the great blaze that occurred in the course of the Turkish army's assault on the city in 1922, Kolluoğlu-Kırlı observes that the recent literature on nationalism has been dominated by analysis of the constructing and imagining of nations, focusing on the formation of a nationalist 'state of mind'. Lost in such accounts is how 'nationalist projects acquire materiality through the reconfiguration of cityscapes' (Kolluoğlu-Kırlı 2002: 3). In much the same way, narrative histories retelling the final days of the great Byzantine city of Constantinople and the fear of its residents have been of much greater popular interest than studies detailing the transformation of Constantinople's built environment by its conqueror, Sultan Mehmet.[1] The prospect of being witness to the end of an age has outweighed curiosity about reorganization of the city's symbols and landmarks thereafter. And yet what was lost or gained is seen most clearly in this spatial transformation. Minimally spatial organization directs and constrains movement, routes approach or facilitates shortcuts, sponsors contact or prompts avoidance, allows and denies perspective. Further material objects and environments generate in part their inhabitants' physical bearings and their kinesthetic abilities – what Mauss (1992) called a society's 'techniques of the body'. A sari allows a baby to be rocked in a certain way and not in another: pants do the same.[2] Macro and micro, the urban environment is planned and put together by architects and designers on behalf of states, corporations and institutions and is limed thereafter with their intentions. In the process built environments become social 'actors' in themselves, essential influences over our lives and relationships:

> I came upon that city
> And saw it being built.
> I too was built with it
> Amidst stone and earth.

>   (Hacı Bayram Veli)[3]

Limed, then, with the builder's intentions, the massing and apportioning of stone, earth and space, especially in the form of a city, crafts more than its houses, streets and workplaces. It makes those who make it. But the poet also affirms that those so arranged within and according to the city's spatial arrangements have a degree of

---

1. The very latest account (in English), Roger Crowley's (2005) *Constantinople: The Last Great Siege, 1453* lists more than 120 sources in its bibliography. It notes that the fall or conquest, depending on one's perspective, was a fulcrum moment in the period, and that news of the event spread 'with astonishing speed' (p. 261) over the Christian and Muslim worlds. Yet the news spreads still, if the constant production of media about the end of Byzantium over the past 200 years and up to the present is any guide – news made always to connect with or evoke the prejudices and hopes of the tellers and listeners. These hopes and prejudices are personal and collective at the same time, as are interpretations of the fall.

2. Thanks to Kalpana Ram for this example.

3. Cited in Kafadar (1995).

knowing about the city's power of constructing them. We are not oblivious to our assembling. On the basis of such knowledge, we may neutralize the city's power, insinuating alternative versions of ourselves amongst the nooks and crannies of its urban structure.

Zeynep Çelik (1999: 379) noted how urban history scholarship of 'non-Western' cities and societies is now interested in 'reading the nationalist penchant for the modern against the background of 'Islamic' fabrics [exposing] unforeseen resistances and contestations that transform the spatial and social structure of cities'. Yet obviously the 'Islamic fabrics' of these cities, which includes their non-Muslim quarters, are similarly the products of historic processes of urban transformation. In his brilliant analysis of the spatial re-configuration of Byzantine Constantinople and Ottoman Istanbul by their 'founding genii' and 'daemonic personalities' Constantine the Great and Mehmet the Conqueror respectively, Speros Vryonis makes a particularly sophisticated analysis of the architectural and social processes involved in turning those cities into the prime receptacles of power for their far-flung imperial domains. The puzzle is why he doesn't complete his analysis to examine the founding act of Ankara – or more accurately its similarly conscious re-founding, given the city's remodelling of Islam – by its equally 'daemonic' creator Mustafa Kemal.[4] As the very building of their respective cities show, Constantine, Mehmet and Atatürk each perceived that the organization of urban space and the construction of the built environment produced much more than neutral frames in which inhabitants lived out their daily affairs.

In the founding of what he calls Constantine's and Mehmet's 'super-cities', Vryonis speaks of their 'momentous drama of *translatio imperii*' or transfer of rule (Vryonis 1991: 18). One strategy through which the transfer of rule is engineered – from Pagan to Christian, from Christian to Islamic, from Islamic to Kemalist – is through a fundamental reorientation of the city's existing material infrastructure, 'both the urban structure as a whole and the relative disposition and deployment of its various component parts' (Preziosi 1991: 7). Each super-city subsumes the existing historically composed and sedimented urban fabric within its own new structures.[5] More specifically Vryonis sees political power amassed and integrated in the super-city through a nine-fold process. The first two of these processes are *imperialization* and *sanctification*. Imperialization – *dictatorization* in the Kemalist instance – entails the 'specific centralization of power about the person of the ruler' (Vryonis 1991: 19). The city's sanctification is closely related, sacralized by the 'tombs of martyrs, saints, şeyhs, and divinized rulers' (Vryonis 1991: 19). This translates, in the 'Kemalist

4. By contrast see Meeker (2002), who explicitly compares Mustafa Kemal's and Mehmet the Conqueror's political prescriptions for constituting their projects of modernity, in particular their identical formation of what he calls a *state-people* (Meeker 2002: xviiff.).

5. For example, Kemalist de-Ottomanization of Istanbul involved the transformation of long-standing symbolic or sacred sites into museums, such as Aya Sofya (Hagia Sophia).

City's' case, as the increasing density of nationalist monuments, mausoleums of its presidents or notables, martyrs memorials and statuary that cover the new capitals. Amazingly, in the high republican period (1923–50) no new mosques were built in Ankara. *Mandarinization* or the creation of a vast bureaucracy 'with its intricate networks of bureaus, clientele, and memory system (archives)' (Vryonis 1991: 19) is the third process whereby political power is concentrated in the city. Mandarinization brings with it *literatization*, 'as [it] could function only through the written word' (Vryonis 1991: 19). We have already seen how the Kemalist regimes of Turkey and Iran developed a new literary style as an integral aspect of the transfer of rule. Fifthly the presence of the ruler[s] in the city necessitates its *militarization*, so much so that in the new Kemalist capitals the buildings of the military 'mandarins' dominate the parliamentary complexes. *Demographization* follows with the building up of the city's population, not merely through the recruitment of workers, artisans, soldiers and bureaucrats but through the instituting of academies, national libraries and artistic companies (Presidential Orchestras, State Folk Dance Troupes etc), all with their cadres' specialized skills. These six processes entail the city's *thesaurization*, 'the accumulation and centralization of the [nation's] economic wealth' (Vryonis 1991: 21). Taxes flow into the super-city for its building, loans and investments out. Finally, the *translatio imperii* needs to be concretized, procured through the super-cities' *monumentalization* and *ceremonialization*. Architecture and ritual sanctify the city, periodically revivifying its sacred dead.[6]

6. The mausoleum of Atatürk in Ankara is the site of the most carefully orchestrated state ritual. Beyond the inscription of 'message-bearing units of composition' (Preziosi 1991: 106) in the design details of *Anıt Kabir*, it is the regular commemorative ceremonies at the site of Atatürk's tomb that infuses the memorial with its social power. The rituals facilitate an inter-subjective encounter between Atatürk and participants. Necdet Evliyagil's poem *In the Presence of Atatürk*, printed in a special edition of the journal *Culture and Art* for the celebration of the seventieth anniversary of Ankara in 1993 as the capital of the new republic, re-presents the meeting thus:

In Ankara once again this morning/We were at *Anıt Kabir*,/Once again we were together with you./Once again we refreshed and renewed our bonds,/Our trust in you.// You never died nor passed on,/Your presence never left us,/Because you make your voice heard/Each time our anxieties whelm/We rejoiced believing from our hearts.// Once again in your presence/We gave our word/ Your principles will ever be upheld,/Our hearts made an oath/As we passed by you, trembling.// Atam [My Atatürk],/Kneeling down we bound ourselves/To *Anıt Kabir*,/When we left your side/At last we were at ease// Because you were not sleeping:/Your blue eyes/Were fixed on the Motherland from *Anıt Kabir*,/As if standing straight and tall/You were waiting for us. (Evliyagil 1993: 22, my translation)

The historic stripping from Istanbul of its imperial sanctity and the sacralization of republican and nationalist Ankara in its place is echoed in the poem's divinizing of Atatürk as eternally living guide and inspiration. The encounter narrated in the poem has a broader context: as master of ceremonies, the state attempts to induce and control inter-subjective experience, to nationalize the inter-subjective consciousness.

In brief, the newly founded or transformed capitals of Ankara, Tehran and Baghdad are usefully seen as Kemalist super-cities, their urban form constituted through their antagonistic re-ordering of the infrastructure and iconography of discredited predecessor regimes, their political power consolidated and integrated through historic processes of *dictatorization*, *sanctification*, *mandarinization* and so forth. In the next three sections I want to briefly discuss each of these cities in turn.

Ankara

What was achieved on a grand scale in the new Kemalist capital of Ankara was reflected in urban environments to a greater or lesser extent the whole country over. We can describe this spatial politics through the category of the 'Kemalist City', a heuristic ideal type that in the first instance focuses attention on the generation of Turkish nationalism through the built environment. The last section of this chapter explores how Kurdish identity is experienced within this formal and sensory *animating* of cities as Kemalist.

Let me first clarify what I mean by both the 'Kemalist City' and its *animating* of urban space. In his book on the architecture and everyday life of Brazil's monumental new capital Brasília, James Holston notes how the Brazilian state desired and designed the city and its parts to initiate a political revolution, through the transformation of its inhabitants' daily practices and social relations. He traces this intention to the utopianism of modernist urban planning and architecture and to their critique of the industrial city, seen as captive to the irrationality and partiality of the bourgeois political economy (Holston 1989: 41ff). Accordingly, modernist architecture (as well as the regimes that applied its ideas) justified their spatial regimes by asserting that intervention in the built environment was necessary in order for inhabitants to perceive anew, so as to transform inculcated schemes of cognition that were themselves reproduced in and by the existing organization of (Islamic) space. The assumed efficacy of spatial intervention was predicated on a doctrine of environmental and (as we have seen) semiotic determinism.

If in the single-party period the belief in architecture's revolutionary potential was strongly held, the target of republican spatial redesign in cities in Turkey was their 'de-Ottomanization' rather than the disorder and inequality of the bourgeois city. What did de-Ottomanization entail? Both Meeker and Bozdoğan describe a certain attempted spatial uniformity post-1923 to Turkish towns across the country. Meeker describes how the 'republican' town plan constructed a city centre built around the government building and central square, the 'administrative and ceremonial spaces of the Turkish Republic' (Meeker 2002: 8). More extensively, Bozdoğan notes the key architectural developments for this 'high modernist' period, particularly after 1930: the constructing of standard administrative, educational and other public buildings – for example, the People's Houses (*Halkevleri*), village institutes, hospitals, schools and post offices – over the whole country, regardless of differences in vernacular styles and without regard for climate and site; the making of new ceremonial and public spaces, including the formal square and municipal park, organized around a variety of Atatürk statues or busts always facing West; the fostering of new associational and spatial practices connected with the People's Houses, secular centres partially supplanting the mosque complex and its range of activities; and the building of new residential suburbs for the Kemalist cadres, particularly near the new provincial railway stations (Bozdoğan 1994, 2001). The proliferation of these prototype buildings and public spaces was accompanied by the dissemination of a prototype Turkish language, to be heard and spoken within them. The 'Kemalist City' was built in more negative ways as well, through the inscribing of signs of republican reform on existing urban structures, including the closing down or reusing of the sufi *tekke* (lodges) and *türbe* (tombs of revered sheikhs). But perhaps most importantly, de-Ottomanization also meant the 'project of reshaping the population within its territories by eliminating the non-Muslims who began to be considered as "excesses" in the spatial and discursive matrices of the nation-state' (Kolluoğlu-Kırlı 2005: 42). The official population exchange became a means to dissolve the Empire and many of its characteristic spaces, creating in their place a Turkified nation.

The core of Kemalist Ankara itself, laid out on land south of the old town and citadel, was planned by Hermann Jansen of Berlin, whose master plan won the competition to [re]design the capital in 1929. The new capital bears some resemblance to Le Corbusier's 1924 model in *The City of Tomorrow*, with its zoned separation of functions, and its organization around two boulevards (on one of which the public centre is located) 'running north and south, and east and west, and forming the two great axes of the city' (Le Corbusier, cited in Holston 1989: 32). Given that there were three experts invited to submit proposals, why was Jansen's plan chosen? One key reason reiterated by a number of writers is that Jansen's development plan appeared to achieve a happier medium between preservation and destruction, and more specifically between the old city and the new. Sarıoğlu for examples writes that

> unlike Jausseley who wanted to completely replace old Ankara, and unlike Brix who proposed to leave the traditional fabric alone as much as possible, Hermann Jansen sought more balance... To put it another way, Jansen did not discuss conservation of the old city like Brix, but worked to incorporate the traditional city without special provision into the frame of the plan. On this account, Brix was more conservative than Jansen, and Jansen a more realistic and measured architect than Jausseley. (Sarıoğlu 2001: 59, 60) (my translation)

Similarly Imga claims that when the work of the candidates was assessed

Brix's plan was eliminated because while conserving the existing situation and solving its infrastructural problems it did not foresee new developments. Jausseley's was not accepted for the reasons that he presented a project that disregarded the evolution of old Ankara and the New City, and because the project was utopian, contrary to the city's conditions, expensive and unrealizable. Jansen's work was selected first in the competition because it was realistic and compatible with both the principles of urban planning and local conditions. (Imga 2006: 91) (my translation)

These remarks, along with the original directive given to the architects asking that they clarify and order the relationship between the old city and the new (see Sarıoğlu 2001: 53–4), indicate how problematic the existing built environment of Ankara was for the emergent and transplanted Kemalist elite. At the very same time the shortage of housing and the resulting urban sprawl (in the period 1923–7) meant that key Kemalist distinctions between 'backward' and 'contemporary' social and spatial practices were potentially indiscernible in the rapidly expanding capital. In short, the confusion of urban forms in the border zone between the old and new city meant the legibility of the transfer of rule was threatened.[7] Jansen's disillusioned resignation in 1939 suggests that the difference of the new city was still an issue throughout the 1930s, as population growth and rampant land speculation overran the city plan. Nevertheless, despite the gap between the planners' intentions – in the first instance, the jurists who chose the Jansen plan[8] – and the plan's realization on the ground, visually and spatially the new city could hardly be confused with the old.

Given the Kemalist revolt against Ottoman precedents, it was not surprising that the new monumental state-buildings of the capital after 1929 were built in a minimalist central European international style. According to Bozdoğan, it was the 'most recognizable features of German modernism that became the trademark of republican Ankara – namely, flat roofs used partly as terraces, plain surfaces, borders around windows or continuous window sills, and the use of tall colonnades for entrances' (Bozdoğan 2001: 72). The logic of the cultural revolution was extended to the built environment, wherein both modernist architecture and Kemalism signified advancement and rationality: '[Kemalism] is a revolution, modern architecture is

7. Much of the material on the French 'colonial city' in Algeria and Morocco emphasizes the role of urban planning in generating a racial separation between the 'non-European' and 'European' populations, via both a spatial *cordon sanitaire* and the artificial preservation in the Arab city of specific building forms and selected signs and symbols signifying oriental difference. In its broadest sense modernist urban planning and architecture was a global discourse, available for application and modification by late-colonial and early nationalist regimes alike. Some of the same architects (such as Henri Prost) worked in both political contexts, first in French Morocco and then in Istanbul as chief urban planner during the single-party period.

8. Sarıoğlu rather coyly writes that 'according to some researchers, the Jury members were all close to M. Kemal and upon completing their work they arrived at a decision after speaking with M. Kemal' (Sarıoğlu 2001: 63).

revolutionary, therefore it must be the architecture of [Kemalism]' (Bozdoğan 2001: 61).

Yet *complementing* this nationalized modernist architecture was a second type of architectural unit or structure, with its own expressive or referential function. We might identify it by asking a question: can we discern some combination of modernism and nativism in public monuments in Ankara? As we have already seen, Turkish nationalist discourse elaborated a fictive kinship with Hittite and Phoenician forebears that pronounced illegitimate other potential ancestors, specifically the Islamic Ottomans. In so doing it also claimed the Hittite patrimony, an age-old relationship with Anatolia that partially assuaged the anxiety caused by other nationalist narratives mythologizing the migration of Turkish tribes from central Asia. This new national genealogy was given tangible presence by the embedding of collective symbols in the urban texture of the city: for example, the large Hittite Monument erected on the busiest intersection of Atatürk Boulevard, or the establishing of major state enterprises Sümerbank and Etibank – named after the Sumerians and Hittites respectively – in the 1930s. The nationalizing of space generated by referencing Hittite sculptural themes is seen most powerfully in the design of Atatürk's mausoleum (*Anıt Kabir*) on its hilltop, with its solemn corridor of stone lions presaging entrance to the complex's public square and classical temple that houses the dead body (see Vale 1992, Meeker 1997). Jansen's original plan specified that Ankara's historic castle should be so isolated that it be seen from every place in the city (Sarıoğlu 2001: 60). Similarly Atatürk's mausoleum, lit up on its hill by night, is in the line of sight of every resident in Ankara.

The 'Kemalist City's' antagonistic relationship to what it interpreted as the backwardness of old Ankara was produced through more than exemplary architectural statements. Cantek writes that the Governor of Ankara sequestered Atatürk Boulevard (Ankara's most prestigious street) from peasants and workers throughout the 1930s, barring their entrance (Cantek 2003: 219). Further, modern Ankara was central in the Kemalist endeavour to model new habits of entertainment for citizens.[9] Its broad avenues and parks became academies for consumption and display, and the city was the scene of the first Republican Ball, held in 1925. The balls became so popular that often 'certain items [of clothing] were sold out so they needed to be ordered from Europe, [while] in the last few weeks before a ball the price of women's dance shoes leapt threefold' (Şenol 1998: 95). Jansen's plan also included a large central park (Youth Park), which over time was filled out with an artificial lake, rose garden, café-tea house, amusement park, open amphitheatre and swimming pool. A similar but even more complex park was built in Izmir, on the fire zone.

In sum, my interpretation of contemporary cities in Turkey as 'Kemalist' assumes their historic and continuing sensory arranging and enlivening as sites signifying the Turkish nation, through the performing and disciplining of what we might call an

---

9. We might note in passing how Vryonis' scheme lacks the dimension of centralizing leisure.

excess – in the spatial sphere, a hypervisuality – of Turkish nationalist identity. Here I include the physical or directive design of public space, its symbols, its sensory order (sounds and smells), its rituals and its expected convivialities. I include also the more informal and temporary mobilizing of space via the practice and performance of nationalist Turkish citizens themselves. Last we should include the explicit prohibiting of all symbols, sensory orders, or performances that might be perceived as signifying or constituting any unauthorized ethnic difference. This censorship attains exaggerated proportions: *Yeni Şafak* newspaper recently reported on a lawsuit sent to the Yüksekova Public Prosecutor by an Army Brigade General against the school principal and folklore teacher of a primary school in Hakkari province, accusing them of dressing dancing children in the colours of the PKK (yellow-red-green) at a public ceremony in a local stadium celebrating Republic Day. Defending the performance, Yüksekova Mayor said that 70 per cent of the local people in the area wore such clothes (*Yeni Şafak* 20 December 2005). Or again, the thirteen directors of the Rights and Freedom Party (*Hak ve Özgürlükler Partisi*) received gaol sentences between six months and a year in 2007 for 'speaking Kurdish at the party congress and because invitations to State representatives were sent in Kurdish and Turkish' (*Radikal*, 15 February 2007). The Prosecutor of the Court of Appeal then closed the party down.

Tehran

At exactly the same time that Ankara was under construction, Reza Pahlavi was remaking Iran's urban centres, both its major towns and its capital, effecting in his turn what we have identified as the 'Kemalist City's' *translatio imperii*. Indeed, perhaps more clearly than the case in Ankara, where the new city was built alongside the existing settlement, Kemalist Tehran was built on and over the old city. Using the comprehensive Street Widening Act in the early 1930s, 'Reza Khan imposed on the old town of Tehran a geometric network of broad straight avenues, many of which ploughed through dense residential and commercial areas with utter disregard for pre-existing buildings and their inhabitants' (Mazumdar 2000: 331). This was not of course the destruction of some unchanging 'Islamic City'. As Zeynep Çelik (1986) has shown for Istanbul, Tehran too had already undergone a fundamental transformation in the nineteenth century.[10] Nevertheless both Khosrokhaver and Banini make the point that Reza Shah's autocratic urban redesign completely

10. The Qajar Shah Nasser al-Din decided to expand the city in 1868, demolishing the old walls and building new cobbled avenues on top of the filled-in moats. Replacement walls were built nearly two kilometers away, meaning that the city became four and a half times the size of the existing settlement. The new streets of the expanded area to the north were 'wide, straight and unroofed' (Madanipour 1998: 34), and bordered with footpaths. By 1882 'many of the major avenues had tramlines, and railways had been built' (Mazumdar 2000: 325).

changed the city. Khosrokhaver (2004: 71) writes that 'the capital – previously a small city, much less influential than Tabriz – had been made the political as well as economic and cultural centre of the country by the Pahlavis in the 1920s', whereas Banini simply says that 'the Tehran of 1941 bore no resemblance to the Tehran of 1921' (Banini 1961: 144).

By 1941, then, Tehran and other urban centres in Iran had been transformed into open matrixes, their new transportation networks cutting through existing communes, their major intersections characterized by roundabouts or squares decorated with statues of the monarch. As in Ankara, cities were redesigned around two great axes, named either Shah (Reza) or Pahlavi. Urban surgery involved in the first instance the creating of a grid of roads, squares and statues. In the process the communal heterogeneity of the residential quarters of the urban areas, their partial ability to obstruct movement of goods, strangers and troops, and their degrees of seclusion or faction were 'to be overcome by the imposition of a framework on the urban fabric to create physical, as well as social, homogeneity' (Madanipour 1998: 40). This 'imposition of homogeneity' on urban space was replicated analogously in national territorial space as well. The development of highway and railroad networks facilitated military movements to previously less accessible areas, while regional difference (faction), local power (control over access and resources) and ethnic autonomy (seclusion) were to disappear in the name of national unity. Closing down non-Persian printing presses and community schools, the Persianization of the 'tribes', was accompanied by 'extending army outposts into their regions, disarming their warriors, conscripting their youth, stirring up their internal conflicts, undermining their chiefs, restricting their annual migrations, and, at times, forcing them into "model villages"' (Abrahamian 1982: 141).

Dotted along the new avenues, the bulk of the monumental buildings for the Kemalist super-city were constructed, as in Ankara, in international style. Because pre-Islamic Persian culture was posited to be both 'rational' and 'functional' (exhibiting the qualities said to be characteristic of modern architecture), the new structures built to house the ten ministries apportioning the work of the Pahlavi state could be designed according to a stripped-down modernism. The 'national culture' was best represented through modern urban design and architecture. Most buildings then were 'adaptations of current European architecture featuring columns without bases or capitals' (Wilbur 1987: 350–1). Similar to architectural practice in Kemalist Turkey, architectural plans for the buildings of provincial towns were drawn up in Tehran.

And yet, as in Ankara, there was also a visual aspect to the architecture that conveyed the national heritage in 'indigenous' terms as well. Many of those very same ministry buildings were designed with exteriors that referenced ancient Persian empires. The 'police headquarters at Tehran displayed a long façade lined with copies of the columns of the *apadana* at Persepolis', whereas the façade of the *Bank-e Melli* (The National Bank) 'offered a portico with engaged columns which derived from one of the palaces at Persepolis' (Wilbur 1987: 350).[11] The primary function of the exteriors was to connote the antiquity of the Persian nation, but they served also to signify a separation. As in Ankara again, the transformation of Tehran involved the rejection, in the name of its imposition as a colonial and alien ideology, of any architectural style that might allude to the Islamic or Arab interregnum. In both Iran and Turkey the national vernacular was uncovered in the glories of an indigenous time, discernible in the faint but still persisting continuity of cultural traits with pre-Islamic Iran. Whereas the Kemalists in Turkey pronounced that republicanism was natural to the Turkish character, the Iranian Kemalists declared the institution of kingship to be the true hallmark of Persian identity. Regardless of the posited essential political sentiments of the respective peoples, as in much of Europe at the time, their experience was of dictatorship.

As the designs inspiring the facades make clear, archaeology played a key role in the crafting and exhibiting of Persian nationalism. Already in the constitutional period after 1906 Iranian parliamentarians were unhappy with the concessions granted to the French by the Qajar monarch to conduct archaeological excavations. In partial reaction to the French 'looting' of antiquities, the National Museum of Tehran was established in 1910. Reza Shah himself was a strong supporter of archaeology, sponsoring digs throughout his reign and opening the Department of Archaeology at Tehran University in 1937 (Abdi 2001: 62). The excavations at Persepolis (the ruined capital of the Achaemenid empire) were of particular significance for him and he visited there four times throughout his rule. His speech in Tehran in 1932 after one of those visits is instructive:

> In the magnificent ruins of Persepolis one can witness this splendor [of ancient Iran] without historians' bias, the ruins speak for themselves and tell you the glory of ancient Iranian monarchs... When I saw the structures of Persepolis, I was moved by those colossal monuments, but seeing them [in such impaired state] deeply depressed me. I was nonetheless delighted [to learn] that such great kings have ruled Iran and left these magnificent remains. Patriotism and national pride should be embedded in every Iranian soul. (Reza Shah, cited in Abdi 2001: 60)

11. Mina Marefat's article on the architects who shaped modern Tehran for Reza Shah is a conventional although extremely interesting account of the architectural styles of influential local and foreign architects. But beyond noting that the state was their major architectural client, she makes no attempt to articulate any relations between architectural art forms and the Kemalist political project. Her article confirms the European training of the first generation of Tehran's architects, but argues too that 'while enthusiastically embracing modernism, these architects were knowledgeable of the inherently traditional context in which they practiced' (Marefat 1992: 104). In other words Marefat interprets their style as commendably synthetic, 'at once modern and eclectic, Western and Persian' (Marefat 1992: 105). Her own garden-variety Persian nationalism is less commendable, in her blithe indifference to the coincidence between Kemalist regimes that demand 'an imagining of 'traditions' to resolve [their] identity crises' (Kusno 2000: 93) at the same time as their suppression of regional 'vernacular' architecture.

His son and successor Mohammad Reza Shah Pahlavi extended the dynasty's investment in Kemalist archaeology, increasing excavation at pre-Islamic imperial capitals and funding conservation and reconstruction work at Persepolis. His revival of Persian glory reached its zenith at a grandiose ceremony before the world's Heads of Government in 1971 to commemorate '2,500 years of continuous monarchy'. Standing before the tomb of Cyrus the Great, the 'Shah of Shahs' addressed him 'in a flat but emotional voice':

> To you Cyrus, Great King, King of Kings, from Myself, Shahanshah of Iran, and from my people, Hail! We are here at this moment when Iran renews its pledge to History to bear witness to immense gratitude of an entire people to you, immortal Hero of history, founder of the world's oldest empire, great liberator of all time, worthy son of mankind.
>
> Cyrus, we stand before your eternal dwelling place and speak these solemn words: Sleep in peace forever, for we are awake and we remain to watch over your glorious heritage. (Mohammad Reza Shah, cited in Abdi 2001: 69).

There is no need to stress the resemblance of the ritual to those that continue at the tomb of Atatürk. What is interesting is the fate of archaeology after the Islamic revolution, with the immediate closing down of Tehran University's Department of Archaeology and the indictment of the discipline as a pseudo-science 'in service of the court to glorify despotism' (Abdi 2001: 70). Its rehabilitation began some years later, and it may now be seen as a vital resource bequeathed by Kemalism for reactivation by the Islamist state. Reza Shah's strategies for transforming urban life are another: in Islamist Tehran the two great axes of the city have been renamed again, from Shah-Reza and Pahlavi to Enghelab (Revolution) and Vali Asr Boulevards.

Baghdad

In the midst of the Iranian-Iraqi war (1980–8), in a period of military-induced economic crisis, Saddam Hussein and the Ba'ath Party rebuilt the ancient city of Babylon, at an estimated cost of more than 100 million US dollars (Baram 1991). The city became the site for the Babylon International Music Festival but it also served as backdrop for numerous Ba'ath Party ceremonies stressing the 'nation's' common destiny, past and present, [and] the eternal enmity, stretching back to the dawn of history, between the aggressive Persians and the unified Iraqi people' (Baram 1991: 48). A new Nebuchadnezzar, Saddam Hussein, would bring the Persians back, chained, to Babylon.

As in Turkey and Iran, the animating of cities as 'Kemalist' has been a constant project of the Iraqi state. However, unlike the Kemalist regimes in those countries, the incorporation of a glorious pre-Islamic ancient past into both the Iraqi 'national pantheon' and into the cities' built environments was a relatively late development.

The 'proto-Kemalism' of monarchical Iraq insisted in the first instance on pan-Arab nationalism and unification and it did not seek to blur distinctions between the ancient dwellers of Mesopotamia and present-day Arabs. Indeed, the breathtaking findings of European excavations at pre-Islamic sites were relatively uninteresting for the government. Only in 1934 did the king appoint a non-European Head of Antiquities, none other than Director of Education Sati al-Husri himself – this long after British and German expeditions to the pre-Islamic cities of Nineveh, Khorsabad, Nimrud, Ashur, Babylon, Uruk, Ur and Eridu had commenced or been completed. In deliberate reaction to the European obsession with pre-Islamic civilizations, during his tenure al-Husri selected only Arab-Islamic sites for excavation by Iraqi archaeologists (Baram 1994: 290ff). This too of course was a form of Arab-nationalist de-Ottomanization.

The destruction of the monarchy in 1958 boosted Iraqi nationalism and weakened pan-Arab sentiments. To celebrate the institution of the Republic, General Qasim commissioned Jewad Salim in 1959 to sculpt the 'huge Liberty Monument in central Baghdad's Liberation Square, a work that stylistically and thematically incorporated artistic elements drawn from ancient Mesopotamia, Pablo Picasso, and Soviet socialist realism' (Baram 1994: 301). Thereafter and despite swings in official historiography related to the political ascent of different military or Ba'ath Party factions, promotion of the Mesopotamian ancestry of the Iraqi people through the manipulation of urban space continued until 2004, halted only by the invasion of Iraq by the 'coalition of the willing'.

Nevertheless, according to Samir al-Khalil, there is a world of difference between Salim's 'Monument to Freedom' and the gargantuan sculptures or massive memorials in newly carved out public space that dominate the Ba'ath Party's Kemalist Baghdad. Two pictures from al-Khalil's book on the monuments of Saddam Hussein that have restructured Baghdad stand out. The first (p. 97) is of the old Unknown Soldier Monument in Sa'adoun Square, a split-level large roundabout paved with white concrete slabs. Built in the 1960s on a demolished block of the city, the abstract design stands opposite a large mosque, whose dimensions have been brought to the fore due to the architect's opening up of space. The two structures address each other in roughly equal terms. 'No building within an urban fabric is perceived in a vacuum. Invariably, its formal and functional characteristics are understood in relationship to those of other structures, both contiguous and separate' (Preziosi 1991: 104). The second (p. 28) is a photo of the new Unknown Soldier Monument, built in 1982 on the very same site as the torn down former memorial. The height of the roundabout has been added to, and an enormous half-raised circular Mesopotamian shield erected on the artificial hill. Visible from everywhere, the new monument dominates its surroundings, shrinking the mosque and staking its claim for the ultimate purpose of life: to die for the nation. Such is its statement but the clearing away of other urban clutter makes it a sovereign ethical imperative, unrelieved by counter-arguments.

The most notorious of the capital's monuments is the gigantic 'Victory Arch', dedicated in 1989 in a vast new parade ground in central Baghdad. The invitation card sent to selected guests explains Saddam Hussein's design:

> The ground bursts open and from it springs the arm that represents power and determination, carrying the sword of *Qadisiyya*. It is the arm of the Leader-President, Saddam Hussein himself (God preserve and watch over him) enlarged forty times. It springs out to announce the good news of victory to all Iraqis, and pulls in its wake a net that has been filled with the helmets of enemy soldiers, some of them scattering into the wasteland. (al-Khalil 1991: 2)

The steel for the sword was made by melting down the weapons of fallen Iraqi soldiers; the 5000 Iranian enemy helmets were collected on the battlefield; the *Qadisiyya* sword symbolizes those other swords carried by the invading Arab-Muslims who defeated the army of the Sassanid empire and led to the Islamization of Iran; and the arms were modeled from plaster casts of the President's own arm. The monument appalls by its realism, despite its lies about the victory over Iran. It takes its place in a city that has been the target of massive urban redevelopment, a redevelopment pieced together by new ceremonial avenues, public spaces and their monuments. On their family outings Iraqis cannot remain heedless of their leader's labours.

Kurdish Encounters with the Kemalist City

Making and unmaking the urban environment, Kemalism as spatial practice animates cities in Turkey, Iran and Iraq. The constructing of Ankara, the demolition of Tehran, the monumentalizing of Baghdad: all are strategies of Kemalist urbanism and architecture through which Islam is ordered and controlled, and nationalism engendered and expressed.[12] In the process, any equivalent crafting of a Kurdish national self is disallowed.

Does my schematic description above of a shared architectural logic and an emerging spatial conformity in the cities of Turkey, Iran and Iraq indicate that the 'Kemalist City' is best understood typologically, as defined essentially by these new physical structures and the desired social relations they frame? Somewhat ironically, Eldem, Goffman and Masters give indirect support to such a possibility

---

12. Al-Khalil notes the power of architecture to impact upon character formation in Saddam Hussein's Baghdad: 'Nothing remotely like Haifa street has ever existed in Baghdad before. And insofar as the environment in which people live has any influence on their behaviour, or sense of whom they are as a community, it can safely be said that an Iraqi nurtured in the bosom of Haifa street will not resemble one nurtured in "old" Baghdad, however one wished to define that long lost city' (al-Khalil 1991: 22, 23).

in their book *The Ottoman City between East and West*. On the one hand their clear rejection of Weberian-type formalistic claims about the 'Islamic City' culminates in their considered conclusion that Ottoman cities were simply too divergent to be 'normatively' cast. But their study concludes pessimistically by noting the 'steam-rolling' of these singular Ottoman (and by implication Qajar) cities in the early twentieth century by their successor states, 'seeming to level them into a homogenous lump' (Eldem, Goffman and Masters 1999: 214). The implication is that in the present some variety of formal typology – the peripheral industrial city, the nationalist city, the Kemalist City – might be more appropriate.

However despite the attraction of thinking of cities and towns in Turkey, Iran and Iraq as materially uniform and thus 'Kemalist' on those grounds, such an inclination still leans towards the very environmental behaviourism embraced by Kemalist regimes themselves. Yet buildings change. 'Function reforms form, perpetually', as Brand (1994: 3) puts it. Buildings and the spaces created through site organization change not only physically but through people's transformative use, experience and related memory of them. Of course, architects and their patrons' intentions are seeded in design, along with appropriate ways of behaving. But users' changing actions and representations, necessarily related to the changing built forms, transcend such forms' guiding and constraining solidity.

Further, my privileging of the 'Kemalist City's' visual and spatial dimensions needs to be supplemented by due attention to its fostering of a transformed *sensory* landscape, with its creation not only of new buildings but also of new sights, sounds, smells and tastes. The 'Kemalist City' is animated and experienced through the senses. The acoustics and texture of modernist architecture and public space contribute to its sensory order as the city is organized not only to be seen and moved through but also to be heard and even touched and smelt. Tekelioğlu (1996: 195) notes that light Western classical music was played in selected public spaces such as on Turkish Maritime Line ships. And as we have already seen, language reform impacts on more than the mechanics of rational thinking. It is equally a politics of the senses, the construction of a new physical soundscape. The animating of cities as Kemalist includes their shaping of 'sense-scapes' to effect the never-ending *translatio imperii*. Yet this sensory order too is contested through people's production of different or counter sense-scapes. This is particularly important because visual challenges to the Kemalist City by Kurds are severely punished.[13] Accordingly their contestation

---

13. Would it be too strong to accuse the 'Kemalist City' of visual fascism? In Turkey, republican statues, Turkish flags, and innumerable portraits, photographs and sayings of Atatürk are displayed all over the city, in the fisherman's humble boat, the security guard's pillbox placed at the gated driveways of Bosphorus houses, the cell of every shop in any complex, even in the cemetery where flags fly over the super-sized graves of conscripts 'martyred' in fighting in the south-east. Sacred objects, they produce their own exterior and interior spatial division of the environment. Recently massive new flags and flagpoles have been planted all over Istanbul. In the midst of this visual overkill, the State

of how the city is to be experienced takes sonic form more easily. In brief, much work on the urban architectural environment has focused on the semiotic meanings embedded in physical structures that are intended to be communicated to users and sightseers. There has been less research on the Kemalists' production of a sensory environment, and much less again on bringing these multiple dimensions of the city into relationship with their interpreters' and users'. Yet as Preziosi has argued, individuals do not 'read' cities as if they were texts. Rather they *reckon with* them in the dual sense of that phrase – simultaneously coping and thinking with them, 'in order to fabricate a lived relationship to [their] affordances and constraints' (Preziosi 1991: 4).

In like vein our brief application of Vryonis' model to the 'Kemalist City' and its integrating practices of *sanctification, ceremonialization, monumentalization* etc. does not in itself give us a clue about how we might move beyond the power of the *daemonic* architects of cities, whether statesmen, states or corporations. Illuminating in its analysis of the 'transformation of older urban imagery into structures meant to be 'read' in strikingly different ways' (Preziosi 1991: 7), Vryonis' work is not interested in the *readers* of the new conditions of legibility of Ankara, Tehran or Baghdad, let alone in their *hearers, smellers* and *tasters.* Bernard Tschumi gives us a better way of proceeding, in terms of the 'violence' of architecture: he notes its dual aspect, in both the violence of design and the violence done (by users) to design. Tschumi calls this the 'intrusion of a human body into a given space' (Tschumi 1994: 123) but we can broaden his inquiry into the violence of architecture to include as many human relationships with the urban built environment and sensory landscape as possible. To properly grasp our focus of study then, we should comprehend the 'Kemalist City' as also constituted through the *violating* of its sensory order in the form of counter-sensory experience, understood too as a political project. Here alternative or 'counter-public' selves are crafted not only through oppositional discourses to the dominant nationalist ideologies, but through their production of counter-sensescapes.

A conscious Kurdish diaspora provoked by the 'Kemalist City' is one such violating counter-public.[14] The animating of cities as Kemalist in the very regions where

---

Security Court opened a case against 18 members of HADEP (People's Democracy Party), in which the prosecutor's charge concentrated on the use of symbols and sounds proscribed in public space and performance:

> At the congress, the Turkish flag was not displayed, nor was the national anthem sung. By contrast, the party's march was recited, slogans protesting the conditions in F-type prisons and supporting the PKK were shouted, the colours representing that organization – yellow, red and green – were present, as were people donning the *pesmerge* [guerilla] clothes worn by that organization's members in the countryside... (*Radikal,* 7 January 2003)

14. In Turkey a second is an Islamist counter-public, and a third (at least in its present nationalistic climate), a liberal (anti-Kemalist) one. These counter-publics are not necessarily exclusive to each other.

Kurds have been historically the majority of the population means Kurdish diaspora is created not principally through an act of mobility of migrants, forced, voluntary or refugee. On the contrary it is nation-states' sometimes murderous incorporation of such regions into Kemalist and (in post-revolutionary Iran) Islamist republics that has encouraged some Kurds to imagine themselves as a nation or *ümmet* under occupation, sedentary urban exiles in their own homeland. The diaspora experienced by many Kurds has not required their physical scattering from the places to which diasporic discourse binds them. To live in diaspora then involves the self-constituting of subjects as a group in connection to a homeland, mapped or imagined. It is the active constituting of that connection, as well as the narrativizing of its rending, that creates a Kurdish diaspora or counter-public in 'Kemalist cities' today.[15]

True, the Kurdish diaspora has been unable to exhibit its own visual or visible counter-space, unless illegally, through graffiti sprayed on park walls. Indeed, the 'Kemalist City' is visually surveilled and policed for signs of counter-ethnic publics. Where the visual animation of cities as Kemalist is painted over by Kurdish counter-publics is in the micro organization of home and in the organization of its acoustic-scape by banned Kurdish media such as Med TV. Yet even the home is not necessarily a safe haven: for two years and more of fieldwork in the mid-1990s I had a friend's rapidly decaying bag of prohibited books sitting in the corner of a damp and unused room in my flat. Equally importantly, the spectacle of spatial organization cannot easily be separated off from regulation of other realms of sensual experience. 'There is no power without the control of noise,' says Jacques Attali (2002: x). The Kemalist public sphere mutes and amplifies, just as its exposes and conceals. Sensorial organization thus produces insiders and outsiders. Kurds murmur

---

15. As we have seen in Chapter 3, the historic ethnographic literature on Kurds rarely encompassed urban issues. However, in Turkey in recent years there has been an increased interest in the forced migration and re-settlement of Kurds in urban centres, one result of the war between the PKK (Kurdish Workers Party) and the Turkish state. This more applied research on the problems of subjects undergoing 'urbanization' often focuses on real issues of social exclusion, cultural adaptation and the practical difficulties of settlement. Yet it underplays in the process the urban spatial order and built forms within which such experiences are articulated. Too often the built environment and spatial structure is considered as setting for the migrant experience, determining its contours in some ways but being understood as non-amenable to or beyond the scope of policy intervention. Yet social problems, once named, incite disciplinary management. The enigma becomes the Kurd, rather than the 'Kemalist City' and the complicity of its built environment with practices of power. Mooted policy responses might at best call for a widening of the scope for Kurdish cultural expression; but there is little interest in curtailing those aspects and use of space, buildings and the built environment intended to address and constitute citizens as Turks through Kemalist architecture. In brief, the focus on immigration contrives to ignore how Kurdish experience of the city is related to – but not determined by – the political intentions embedded in its design. The anthropological question is not whether, or how, people reproduce or even reassert existing habits or traditions that thwart the urban planner, the modernist, or the expert, but how built environments facilitate transformed spatial, social and sensual practices related to, but not foreseen or determined by, the master planner.

their disreputable tongue, sensitive to its insurgent sound. What of the everyday experience of hearing – in the ferry announcements, in the *spiel* of the potato seller, through the schools' PA systems – a language whose dominance is assured by the proscription of one's own? What meanings do such acoustic environments have for Kurdish speakers? How do they negotiate them?

Regardless, alternative soundscapes resound in the aural nooks and crannies of the Kemalist City. In Turkey Kurdish is taught at private educational foundations, half-disguised under names such as 'Mesopotamian Cultural Centre'. Their common rooms agitate with songs in Kurdish, their artists and listeners re-presenting the rhythm of being non-Turkish in cities moving to Turkish pop. The Kurdish counter-public in the 'Kemalist City' is sonically plural – the two-minute silence to remember PKK martyrs at meetings held by Kurdish nationalists; the sound of Islamic *hadith* recited in Kurdish in a basement in an illegal city *medrese*; the serious merriment of nationalist game shows in Kurdish transmitting via satellite into lounge rooms; the different dialects of Kurdish and the politics vibrating between them; the playing of regional and/or sectarian folk music newly scored or collected, the banned cassettes passed from hand to hand and re-copied, their sounds getting more distorted with every new taping – the same songs, in a hundred different versions. Music provides a sonic space of 'sovereignty without territoriality' (Appadurai 1996), an interval or a time in which both makers and listeners hear alternative identities in relation to Kemalism's aural dictates.

The multifariousness of 'Kemalist Cities' becomes more apparent when we attempt to incorporate into our discussion their realms of smell and taste. It is far easier to trace how political projects restructure cities spatially, ritually (via the programming of space, time and movement), visually and even aurally, than it is to discern their attempts at producing embodied subjects through their manufacturing of the smell of architectural artefacts or of their inhabitants' taste buds. Perhaps the inventors of society through the built environment see an olfactory politics as inefficacious, or as unmanageable? After all, up to a point smells refuse to stay in their place. By contrast, vision is inherently manipulable through angles, obstacles, corners, and the control of perspective.

Not to be daunted, what does a Kemalist City smell like? Certainly its scent is implicated in political economy and class habitat, as inhabitants know if they grow up by the beach, or next to a sewerage outlet, or beside a biscuit factory. The state capitalism of Kemalist regimes means investment and industrial development has always been an ethnic issue. But everything and everyone smells and the smell of others is often sensed and given meaning as a powerful embodied experience of cultural and class difference, more often than not negatively perceived and signified. Yet in my fieldwork experience, Kurds were rarely denigrated as 'smelling' different, although Kurdish writer Mehmet Pamak recalls being called a *kuyruklu Kürt* (a Kurd with a tail) at school growing up in Çannakale. What I think this reveals is that, notwithstanding massive class inequalities and ever present social distinctions, the

'Kemalist City' as producer of nationalist identity is essentially an assimilative, not a segregative, city.

Yet if Kurds don't smell differently from others, do those who create themselves as a Kurdish counter-public smell or taste different things? 'There is no perception [in the present] which is not full of memories' writes Bergson (cf. Feld 2005: 181). If this is true, and given the massive trauma lived by millions of Kurds since the 1980s in the wake of the notorious *Anfal* campaigns of the Iraqi military, and the forced migration policies of the Turkish state in response to the PKK rebellion, the embodied memories of many Kurds produce a different sensory experience of the 'Kemalist City.' Nor of course does suffering need to have been individually experienced to be collectively remembered. Taste too – what one likes, desires and appreciates – has a social and political dimension, as does distaste. Hann makes the claim that Black Sea (*Çaykur*) tea, described by him as the most appropriate symbol of the new Turkish society, was neither well distributed in 'Kurdistan' nor was its taste particularly popular (Hann 1990: 99). Smuggled tea was the preferred brew. This accorded with some of the more conscious (*bilinçli*) Kurds I met during fieldwork in the 1990s who refused to buy *Çaykur* tea.[16] The discriminating palate of certain Kurds was linked to the lack of that reciprocal influence between civil society and state in the south-east of Turkey that Hann argues has developed in the eastern Black Sea region. In Rize and other eastern Black Sea towns, the smell of the 'Kemalist City' precedes one's visual contact with it, as the sweet scent of the state-funded tea factories spreads out and insinuates the senses.

16. *Bilinçli Kurtler* was a term used by informants to describe more knowledgeable Kurds (of their own history or ethnic background in the face of Turkish assimilation). The term has a similar meaning to the term '*şuurlu Müslümanlar*' used by some Islamists to describe 'self-conscious Muslims'.

Conclusion

In the final pages of their study of Kemalist ideology in Turkey, Taha Parla and Andrew Davison (2004) call for the *de*-Kemalization of that country's political culture, as a necessary prelude to the instituting there of properly democratic processes. In this brief conclusion I want to affirm that demand. But unlike their analysis, which charts the contours of what they identify as the 'authoritarian corporatism' of Kemalism's political theory and orients their reform agenda to their critique of its ideological content, I want to ground my tentative proposals for the *de*-Kemalization of the region in Kemalism's cultural *practices*. More precisely, the various changes that I discuss below as possible strategies for *de*-Kemalization relate to the Kemalist political and social programme as described and analysed in the preceding chapters. Accordingly, I suggest that *de*-Kemalization requires selected reform in the fields of education, historiography and ethnography, as well as in those myriad enterprises grouped together under the category of cultural performance or art, including music and language policy. I end by exploring what the *de*-Kemalization of a 'Kemalist City' might incorporate.

So what might *de*-Kemalization consist of? I have argued that Kemalism as a trans-national dominant discourse constitutes a generic governing project character- izing state politics in Iraq and Turkey. Islamist Iran, too, has a long and still highly influential Kemalist history. Chauvinist towards ethnic minorities and modernist towards non-authorized Islamic practice, Turkish, Persian and Arab Kemalisms underwrite the sovereign or privileged ethnic identity of their populations through a suppression of Kurdish (and other groups') claims for their own ethnic particularity. At its simplest then, *de*-Kemalization entails the cessation of this dual politics. Kemalism's disciplining and instrumentalizing of Islam – on the assumption of its essentially reactionary tendencies, in Turkey still invariably attributed to Arab corruption of proper Islam – closes down space for social struggle through and over the religious field. As a result and ironically, religious interrogation of the legitimacy of the instituted power is denied, diminishing individuals' ability to put the conventions and forms of Kemalist society into question. At the same time, Kemalism's creation of an Arab-Islamic, Persian-Islamic and Turkish-Islamic synthesis in Iraq, Iran and Turkey respectively implicates state religious institutions in the nationalistic assimilation of ethnic minorities. At root, Kemalism issues in a shrinking of civil society's self-organizing capacities via democratic debate and conflict.

But this discussion is still too general, pointing as it does to transformation of the core 'social imaginary significations' that constitute Kemalist society. Further, change of this magnitude requires struggle against concentrations of power (most importantly the military) that are not inclined to relinquish their advantage. To put it bluntly, an appeal to goodwill is insufficient for the making of such changes. Given this reality, *de*-Kemalization via critique and radical reform of its instituting principles appears unlikely. For this reason change is better pursued through targeting the 'scaffolding' of Kemalism, as I demonstrate below.

Parla and Davison (2004: 292) argue for the necessity of a *de*-Kemalization not only in politics, culture and society but also in people's 'individual psychology'. What does this mean and how might it be achieved? As we have seen in both Chapters One and Four, one of the ways in which Kemalist states instil nationalist sensibilities in the psyche of their citizens is through the education system, both in its written and unwritten curriculum. Schools facilitate students' psychological absorption of sentiments pertaining to the superiority and singularity of the sovereign ethnic group. 'Ataturk's greatest achievement was first to make the people (*halk*) perceive that they are Turks, and then to trust this aspect of themselves', says the blurb on the back of Baykara (2006) (see Chapter 1). One wonders whether his claim doesn't in fact anxiously perceive, as constructionist critiques of nationalism have long argued, that 'national' culture and character is in reality a product of the state, while simultaneously suppressing such knowledge. 'If nationalism is denied, then Turkish existence will be terminated', says the current textbook *History of the Revolution of the Turkish Republic and Ataturkism for High Schools* (cited in Bora 2004: 53). The same worry has exercised the minds of Arab pedagogues of Iraqi Kemalism, as seen in Sati al-Husri. The fear recalls Foucault's famous conclusion to his book *The Order of Things*: if the identity of Turks, as generated by the discourse of nationalism, is not continuously asserted then Turks (understood in this way) 'would be erased, like a face drawn in sand at the edge of a sea' (Foucault 1974: 387). Baykara's conceit about Ataturk's achievement is extendable to Iraq and Iran too: before Kemalism, there were no 'Arabs' or 'Persians' – that is, agents acting out the perception and behalf of the unity and essential shared interests of a national group of people.

'If nationalism is denied, then Turkish existence will be terminated.' *De*-Kemalization, then, seeks the termination in citizens of the existence of a chauvinistic and militaristic national-self. Should it be replaced by a less self-aggrandizing and less paranoid definition of Turkishness, Persianess, or Arabness? Should political virtue be de-linked from devotion to the national interest? Or should the productivist bond between the state and its nation be cut, so that state institutions become 'nation-neutral'? Should the nation be left undefined? 'I include multitudes', says the poet Walt Whitman. Should imagined identities other than national – local, familial, professional, sexual etc. – be accorded an autonomous value?

In like vein, *de*-Kemalization of individuals' psychology can be partially effected through modifying the nationalist history taught in schools and universities. In

Chapter 2 we have seen how historians have nationalized the patrimony of the Ottoman empire, to be reviled by Iraqi Kemalists or Bulgarian chauvinists (for example) as an alien imposition, or selectively appropriated for the nation by Turkish Kemalists, even while indicted as the cause of its backwardness. The Islam of the Qajar empire has received similar treatment in the Kemalist historiography of the Shahs' Iran. For the nationalist ideologues of all three states, including Kurds as well, the history of the Kurdish provinces of the Ottoman empire in particular is read through a commitment to state building in Kurdistan. *De*-Kemalization then requires a new consideration of the Kurdish provinces within Ottoman history, one that neither assumes their occupied status nor disregards their possible exceptionality. What is needed is a de-nationalization of the dominant constructions of Ottoman Kurdish history, so that it might be re-politicized in other ways. If it is true that the violence of nation building in Turkey, Iran and Iraq has conditioned Kurdish memory and history, it is also true that a richer historiography of Ottoman Kurdistan (by Kurdish nationalists too), would provide additional resources for Kurdish political practice.

As with historical representations of Kurdish society, ethnographic representations of it too need reconsidering. Just as exploration of the colonial inheritance of anthropology has stimulated illuminating critique of anthropological history and practice, the influence of Kemalist nationalism over ethnographic discourse of Kurdish society should also be deconstructed. In the field of anthropology then, *de*-Kemalization requires freedom for Kurds (or anyone else) to generate an alternative self-knowledge, against the long political half-life of Kemalism's production of anthropological knowledge about them. In fact as Chapter 3 has shown, non-Kemalist anthropological representation of Kurdish culture and society (Leach, Barth and Beşikci) has both obscured yet contradicted the cultural revolutions made by Kemalist elites in Iraq, Iran and Turkey, including those revolutions' constituting of 'national' folklore as a major object of research.

What we have called 'Kemalist ethnography', then, is only the most literal of the projects of cultural creation produced in the foundational periods of nation-building in Iraq, Iran and Turkey. In the name of instituting society anew, Kemalist states and their modern elites have generated a phenomenal amount of new artistic work, much of it still well loved; much of it still enacted and elaborated as political interventions in the present. In Chapter 4 then we sketched out Kemalism's interest in the institution, formalization and signification of artistic fields. Theatrical, folkdance and musical performances, even the exhibition of handcrafts and sculpture have become 'lessons in national culture', as translocal or regional cultural and aesthetic practices are claimed for their respective nations by Kemalist states.

De-Kemalization of the cultural revolution in the first instance entails not the abandoning of such performances but the lifting of state sanctions against those denied the sense or right to constitute themselves through cultural creation. Because the creating and consuming of cultural performance both induces pleasure and facilitates the making of self-distinction, social movements and individuals need the freedom to institute, formalize and signify the meaning of artistic fields in their own terms. They also require the opportunity to make their art pedagogical for others. Again, perhaps this simply translates as an 'ethnic-neutral' state in its sponsoring of various fields of cultural creation and performance? Or perhaps it means allowing cultural production and its aesthetic rules and processes *autonomy* from the unceasing efforts of the state and its Kemalist elites to mobilize through them sentiment and emotional energy against external and internal 'enemies'? The *autonomization* of public art then would be one aspect of the *de*-Kemalization of the 'Kemalist City'. One thinks, on the contrary, of the cultural politics of the gargantuan sculptures commissioned by the Ba'ath Party for Baghdad, or the contemporary use of photography in Istanbul in the massive iconic reprints of Atatürk pinned up on many of the city's major thoroughfares by Kemalist councils.

What else should the *de*-Kemalization of cities in Iraq, Iran and Turkey involve? Perhaps it might be posited that *de*-Kemalization should take its cue from the Kemalists' own '*de*-Ottomanization' of society – that is, to pursue a grand new vision of urban planning and transformation as cure for the political ills of Kemalism, on the grounds of architecture's potential efficacy in challenging habituated Kemalist practice and perception? But as we have seen in Chapter 5 and its discussion of Ankara, Tehran and Baghdad, Kemalist urban transformation was spearheaded by the state. Executed in the name of a future imagined as a radical negation of existing society, it is in fact this continuing state vision that is so problematic today. *De*-Kemalization should not replicate its logic by seeking to establish in its turn a new antagonistic spatial order constructed in antithetical relation to the Kemalist present. Holston contrasts this utopian ideology of planning with what he calls its *ethnographic* mode, a form of planning that seeks to transform an unwanted present by including as 'constituent elements of planning the conflict, ambiguity and indeterminacy characteristic of actual social life', thus basing its critique of the status quo on the 'possibilities for change encountered in existing conditions' (Holston 1999: 166). Chapter 5 has discussed one new emergent aspect of metropolitan politics, the formation of an urban Kurdish diaspora, in relation to the built environment – the 'Kemalist City' – that both provokes and seeks to assimilate it.

De-Kemalization through the ethnographic mode of planning is aided by the fact that throughout the twentieth century modernist architecture has been made to represent even opposed political regimes and ideologies. No essential meanings in its architectural forms therefore appear to preclude its re-signification. Rather than a radical re-founding of the built environment then, what needs transforming are spatial arrangements that violently impose the will of architects (or their patrons) upon users of that space. *De*-Kemalization of the 'Kemalist City' can be achieved not through a new heroic architectural statement but through 'architectural graft', through the adding of fragments of built matter to existing sites that destabilize Kemalist semiology, through installing objects, colours and layers that might distract the user from the designer's intended line of sight or approach. Graft adds complexity to spaces, facilitating new users and uses. In keeping with this, it is the 'sensory' environment of the 'Kemalist City' that is both most in need of and most amenable to *de*-Kemalization. As we have seen in Chapter 4, the language revolutions pursued by Kemalist Turkey and Iran intended not only to make the nation monolingual but also to transform and simplify the *aural* environment of the city and its key institutions. In response, *de*-Kemalization would aim at a 'sonic' graft to the city as well, through adding to the soundscape the vibrancy of Kurdish (and other) languages and music, the noise of reasoning, imagining or entertaining in them. It seeks an end to Kemalism's censoring of people's production, through ritual, performance or political activism, of their own acoustic and built environments.

In brief, through its re-structuring of the city *de*-Kemalization intends not yet another *translatio imperii* (transfer of rule). Instead it calls for a pluralization of the political rules or grammar of Kemalist cities. *De*-Kemalization means rejecting the claim that it is *only* because 'the state recognizes certain rights that we can participate in the country's governance and form political parties' (*Citizenship and Human Rights Education 7*, cited in Gök 2004: 113). On the contrary, it values other sources of citizenship and asserts their legitimacy, emergent in the ethnographic present of Kemalist society itself.

References

Abdi, K. (2001), 'Nationalism, Politics and the Development of Archaeology in Iran', *American Journal of Archaeology,* 105.

Abou-El-Haj, R. (1991), *Formation of the Modern State: The Ottoman Empire Sixteenth to Eighteenth Centuries,* Albany: State University of New York Press.

Abrahamian, E. (1982), *Iran between Two Revolutions,* Princeton: Princeton University Press.

Abu-Lughod, J. (1987), 'The Islamic City – Historic Myth, Islamic Essence and Contemporary Relevance', *International Journal of Middle East Studies,* 19(2).

Ahıska, M. (2000), 'Gender and National Fantasy; Early Turkish Radio Drama', *New Perspectives on Turkey,* Spring, 22.

Akcura, J. (1912), *Üç Tarz-ı Siyaset,* Ankara:Türk Tarih Kurumu Basımevi.

Akgündüz, A. (1992), *Osmanli Kanunnameleri ve Hukuki Tahilleri: 4. Kitap Kanuni Devri Kanunnameleri,* Istanbul: Fey Vakfı Yayınları.

Aksoy, G. (1996), *Tarihi Yazılmayan Halk Kürtler,* Istanbul: Avesta.

Alakom, R. (1998a), *Eski Istanbul Kürtleri,* Istanbul: Avesta.

Alakom, R. (1998b), *Hoybun Örgütü ve Ağrı Ayaklanması,* Istanbul: Avesta.

Al-Khalil, S. (1991), *The Monument: Art, Vulgarity and Responsibility in Iraq,* Berkeley: University of California Press.

Allouche, A. (1983), *The Origins and Development of the Ottoman-Safavid Conflict,* Berlin: Klaus Schwarz Verlag.

Al-Sabri, S. (1961), Extract from 'Concerning Arab Nationalism', in K. Karpat (ed.) (1968), *Political and Social Thought in the Contemporary Middle East,* New York: Praeger.

Altınay, A. (2004), *The Myth of the Military Nation: Militarism, Gender and Education in Turkey,* New York: Palgrave McMillan.

Altınay, A. (2004b), 'Human Rights or Militarist Ideals? Teaching National Security in High Schools', in D. Ceylan and G. Irzık (eds), *Human Rights Issues in Textbooks: The Turkish Case,* Istanbul: History Foundation of Turkey.

Altınay, A. (2005), 'Who is a (Good) Turk?: The Ideal Student in Textbooks', in D. Ceylan and G. Irzık (eds), *How are we Educated?* Istanbul: History Foundation of Turkey.

Ambrose, C. (2003), 'The Autonomist Imaginary', unpublished PhD thesis, Department of Sociology, Anthropology and Polics, La Trobe University.

Amin, C. (1999), 'Propaganda and Remembrance: Gender, Education, and "The Women's Awakening" of 1936', *Iranian Studies,* 32(3).

Amin, C. (2001), 'Selling and Saving "Mother Iran": Gender and the Iranian Press in the 1940s', *International Journal of Middle East Studies*, 33(3).

Andrews, P. (1989), 'Conclusion' in P. Andrews (ed.), *Ethnic Groups in the Republic of Turkey*, Wiesbaden: Reichert.

Antoun, R. (2006), 'Fundamentalism, Bureaucratization, and the State's Co-optation of Religion: A Jordanian Case Study', *International Journal of Middle East Studies*, 38(3).

Appadurai, A. (1996), 'Sovereignty Without Territoriality: Notes for a Postcolonial Geography', P. Yaeger (ed.), *The Geography of Identity*, Ann Arbor: University of Michigan Press.

Arat, Z. (1994), 'Turkish Women and the Republican Reconstruction of Tradition', in F. Gocek and S. Balaghi (eds), *Reconstructing Gender in the Middle East*, New York: Colombia University Press.

Ari, E. (2004), 'The People's Houses and the Theatres in Turkey', *Middle Eastern Studies*, 40(4).

Arnason, J. (2006), 'Understanding Intercivilizational Encounters', *Thesis Eleven* 86.

Asad, T. (1973), 'Two European Images of Non-European Rule', in T. Asad (ed.), *Anthropology and the Colonial Encounter*, New York: Humanities Press.

Atalli, J. (2002), 'Introduction', in R. Burckhardt (ed.), *Music and Marx*, New York: Routledge.

Aytürk, I. (2006), 'Türk Dil Milliyetciliğinde Batı Meselesi', in *Doğu Bati* 38.

Ayvazoğlu, B., Behar, C., Savaşır, I., Sökmen, S., (1993), 'Müzik ve Cumhuriyet', in *Defter* 22.

Aziz Efendi (1632/1985), *Kanun-Name-ı Sultan li Aziz Efendi*, Boston: Harvard University Press.

Banini, A. (1961), *The Modernization of Iran*, Stanford: Stanford University Press.

Baram, A. (1983a), '*Qawmiyya* and *Wataniyya* in Ba'thi Iraq: The Search for a New Balance', *Middle Eastern Studies*, 19(2).

Baram, A. (1983b), 'Mesopotamian Identity in Ba'thi Iraq', *Middle Eastern Studies*, 19(4).

Baram, A. (1990), 'Territorial Nationalism in the Middle East', *Middle Eastern Studies*, 26(4).

Baram, A. (1991), *Culture, History and Ideology in the Formation of Ba'thist Iraq, 1968–89*, New York: St Martin's Press.

Baram, A. (1994), 'A Case of Imported Identity: The Modernizing Secular Ruling Elites of Iraq and the Concept of Mesopotamian-Inspired Territorial Nationalism, 1922–1992', *Poetics Today*, 15(2).

Barbir, K. (1996), 'Memory, Heritage and History: The Ottomans and the Arabs', in L. Brown (ed.), *Imperial Legacy: The Ottoman Imprint on the Balkans and the Middle East*, New York: Columbia University Press.

Barth, F. (1953), *Principles of Social Organization in Southern Kurdistan,* Oslo: Brodrene Jorgensen.

Barth, F. (1959), *Political Leadership among Swat Pathans,* London: Athlone Press.

Barth, F. (2005), 'Britain and the Commonwealth', *One Discipline, Four Ways: British, German, French, and American Anthropology,* Chicago: University of Chicago Press.

Bartok, B. (1976), *Turkish Folk Music from Asia Minor,* Princeton: Princeton University Press.

Baykara, T. (2006), *Atatürk ve XX. Yüzyıl Türk Tarihi Araştırmaları.* IQ Kültür Sanat Yayıncılık, Istanbul.

Bayrak, M (2002), *Türk Imparatorlukları Tarihi,* Istanbul: Bilge Karınca Yayınları.

Berkes, N. (1964), *The Development of Secularism in Turkey,* London: Routledge.

Beşikçi, I. (1969/1992), *Doğu Anadolu'nun Düzeni: Sosyo-Ekonomik ve Etnik Temeller,* Ankara: Yurt Kitap-Yayın.

Beşikçi, I. (1992), *Devletlerarası Sömürge Kürdistan,* Istanbul: Alan Yayıncılık.

Bıçak, A. (2004), *The Idea of the State in Pre-Islamic Turkish Thought,* Istanbul: Isis Press.

Bloxham, D. (2005), *The Great Game of Genocide: Imperialism, Nationalism and the Destruction of the Ottoman Armenians,* Oxford: Oxford University Press.

Bois, T. (1981), 'Kurds', 'Kurdistan', in *Encyclopaedia of Islam (New Edition),* Leiden: E.J. Brill.

Bora, T. (2002), 'Türkiye'de Siyasal Ideolojilerde ABD/Amerika Imgesi', in U. Kocabaşoğlu (ed.), *Modern Türkiye'de Siyasi Düşunce: Moderleşme ve Batıcılık,* Istanbul: Iletism Yayınları.

Bora, T. (2004), 'Nationalism in Textbooks', in D. Ceylan and G. Irzık (eds), *Human Rights Issues in Textbooks: The Turkish Case,* Istanbul: History Foundation of Turkey.

Bourdieu, P. (1977), *Outline of a Theory of Practice,* Cambridge: Cambridge University Press.

Bourdieu, P. (2001), *Masculine Domination,* Cambridge: Polity Press.

Bozarslan, H. (1996), 'Political Crisis and the Kurdish Issue in Turkey', in R. Olson (ed.), *The Kurdish Nationalist Movement in the 1990s,* Lexington: The University Press of Kentucky.

Bozarslan, H. (2003a), 'Kurdish Nationalism in Turkey: From Tacit Contract to Rebellion (1919–1925)' in A. Vali (ed), *Essays on the Origins of Kurdish Nationalism,* Costa Mesa: Mazda Publishers.

Bozarslan, H. (2003b), 'Some Remarks on Kurdish Historiographical Discourse in Turkey', in A. Vali (ed.), *Essays on the Origins of Kurdish Nationalism,* Costa Mesa: Mazda Publishers.

Bozdoğan, S. (1994), 'Architecture, Modernism and Nation-Building in Kemalist Turkey', *New Perspectives on Turkey,* No. 10, Spring.

Bozdoğan, S. (2001), *Modernism and Nation-Building: Architectural Culture in the Early Republic,* Seattle: University of Washington Press.

Boztemur, R. (2004), 'History Textbooks and Human Rights', in D. Ceylan and G. Irzık (eds), *Human Rights Issues in Textbooks: The Turkish Case,* Istanbul: History Foundation of Turkey.

Brand, S. (1994), *How Buildings Learn,* New York: Penguin.

Brown, L (1996), 'The Background: An Introduction', in L. Brown (ed.), *Imperial Legacy: The Ottoman Imprint on the Balkans and the Middle East,* New York: Columbia University Press.

Bulut, F. (1992), *Dar Üçgende Üç Isyan: Kürdistan'da Etnik Çatişmalar,* Istanbul: Belge Yayınları.

Cantek, S. (2003), *Yaban'lar ve Yerliler*, Istanbul: Iletism.

Castoriadis, C. (1997), 'The Imaginary: Creation in the Social-Historical Domain', in *World in Fragments*. Stanford: Stanford University Press.

Ceylan, D. and Irzık, G. (2004), 'Introduction', in D. Ceylan and G. Irzık (eds), *Human Rights Issues in Textbooks: The Turkish Case,* Istanbul: History Foundation of Turkey.

Chatterjee, P. (1986), *Nationalist Thought and the Colonial World: A Derivative Discourse?* London: Routledge.

Chehabi, H. (1993), 'Staging the Emperor's New Clothes: Dress Codes and Nation-Building under Reza Shah', *Iranian Studies*, 26(3).

Cole, J. and Kandiyoti, D. (2002), 'Nationalism and the Colonial Legacy in the Middle East and Central Asia', *International Journal of Middle Eastern Studies*, 34(2).

Copeaux, E. (1996), '*Hizmet*: A Keyword in Turkish Historical Narrative', in *New Perspectives on Turkey*, 14, Spring.

Cronin, S. (1996), 'An Experiment in Military Modernization: Constitutionalism, Political Reform and the Iranian Gendarmerie, 1910–21', *Middle Eastern Studies,* 32(3).

Crowley, R. (2005), *Constantinople: The Last Great Siege, 1453*. London: Faber & Faber.

Çayır, K. (2004), 'Consciousness of Human Rights and Democracy in Textbooks', in D. Ceylan and G. Irzık (eds), *Human Rights Issues in Textbooks: The Turkish Case,* Istanbul: History Foundation of Turkey.

Çayır, K. (2007), *Islamic Literature in Contemporary Turkey: From Epic to Novel,* New York: Palgrave Macmillan.

Çelik, Z. (1986), *The Re-making of Istanbul,* Washington: University of Washington Press.

Çelik, Z. (1999), 'New Approaches to the Non-Western City', *Journal of the Society of Architectural Historians,* 58/3, September.

Çem, M. (2005), 'Dersim: 1923–1938', in *Munzur 23/24*.

Çınar, A. (2001), 'National History as a Contested Site: The Conquest of Istanbul and Islamist Negotiations of the Nation', *Comparative Studies in Society and History,* 43(2).

Danık, E. (2005), *'Dersim'de Protestan Fırat Misyonleri'*, in Munzur 23/24.

Dankoff, R. (1990), *Evliya Çelebi in Bitlis. The Relevant Section of the Seyahatname,* Leiden: E.J. Brill.

Deringil, S. (1996), 'The Ottoman Twilight Zone of the Middle East', in J. Barkey (ed.), *Reluctant Neighbour: Turkey's Role in the Middle East,* Washington: US Institute of Peace.

Deringil, S. (1998), *The Well-Protected Domains: Ideology and the Legitimation of Power in the Ottoman Empire 1876–1909,* London: I.B. Tauris.

Deringil, S. (2003), '"They Live in a State of Nomadism and Savagery": The Late Ottoman Empire and the Post-Colonial Debate', *Comparative Studies in Society and History*, 45(2).

Eldem, E., Goffman, D. and Masters, B. (1999), *The Ottoman City Between East and West: Aleppo, Izmir and Istanbul,* Cambridge: Cambridge University Press.

Emecen, F. (1994), 'Kuruluştan Kücük Kaynarca'ya', in E. İhsanoğlu (ed.), *Osmanlı Devleti and Medeniyeti Tarihi*, (Vol. 1), Istanbul: Research Centre for Islamic History, Art and Culture.

Erdentuğ, E. and Magnarella, P. (2001), 'Turkish Social Anthropology since the 1970s', *The Oriental Anthropologist,* 1(1).

Evliyagil, N. (1993), 'Ata'nın Huzurunda', in *Kültür ve Sanat*, Eylül.

Faroqhi, S. (2004), *The Ottoman Empire and the World Around It,* London: I.B. Tauris.

Feld, S. (2005), 'Places Sensed, Senses Placed: Towards a Sensuous Epistemology of Space', in D. Howes (ed.), *Empire of the Senses,* Oxford: Berg.

Feuchtwang, S. (1973), 'The Colonial Formation of British Social Anthropology', in T. Asad (ed.), *Anthropology and the Colonial Encounter,* Atlantic Highlands: Humanities Press.

Findley, C. (2005), *The Turks in World History,* Oxford: Oxford University Press.

Finkel, C. (2005a), *Osman's Dream: The Story of the Ottoman Empire 1300–1923,* London: John Murray.

Finkel, C. (2005b), Review of Findley Carter's 'The Turks in World History' in *Times Literary Supplement*, July.

Fortes, M. and Evans-Pritchard, E. (eds) (1940), *African Political Systems,* Oxford: Oxford University Press.

Foucault, M. (1973), *The Order of Things: An Archaeology of the Human Sciences,* New York: Random House.

Fuccaro, N (1997), 'Ethnicity, State Formation and Conscription in Postcolonial Iraq: The Case of the Yazidi Kurds of Jabal Sinjar', *International Journal of Middle Eastern Studies*, 29(3).

Fuccaro, N. (2003), 'Kurds and Kurdish Nationalism in Mandatory Syria: Politics, Culture and Identity', in A. Vali (ed.), *Essays on the Origins of Kurdish Nationalism*. Costa Mesa: Mazda Publishers.

Gemalmaz, M. (2004), 'Evaluation of Data Concerning Human Rights Criteria Obtained from a Survey of Textbooks', in D. Ceylan and G. Irzık (eds), *Human Rights Issues in Textbooks: The Turkish Case,* Istanbul: History Foundation of Turkey.

Gerber, H. (1980), 'Social and Economic Position of Women in an Ottoman City, Bursa', *International Journal of Middle Eastern Studies*, 12(3).

Gibbons, H. (1916/1968), *The Foundation of the Ottoman Empire,* London: Frank Cass.

Goldberg, E. (1991), 'Was there an Islamic "City"?', in R. Kasaba (ed.), *Cities in the World-System,* New York: Greenwood Press.

Gök, F. (2004), 'Citizenship and Human Rights Education Textbooks', D. Ceylan and G. Irzık (eds), *Human Rights Issues in Textbooks: The Turkish Case,* Istanbul: History Foundation of Turkey.

Göle, N. (1996), 'Authoritarian Secularism and Islamist Politics: The Case of Turkey', in A. Norton (ed.), *Civil Society in the Middle East,* Leiden: E.J. Brill.

Göle, N. (2000), 'İslami Dokunulmazlar, Laikler ve Radikal Demokratlar', in *Melez Desenler,* Istanbul: Metis Yayınları.

Göle, N. (2002), 'Islam in Public: New Visibilities and New Imaginaries', *Public Culture,* 14(1).

Göktaş, H. (1991), *Kürtler İsyan-Tenkil,* Istanbul: Alan Yayıncılık.

Haj, S. (1997), *The Making of Iraq 1900–1963: Capital, Power and Ideology,* Albany: State University of New York Press.

Hann, C. (1990), *Tea and the Domestication of the Turkish State,* Huntington: Eothen Press.

Hassanpour, A. (1992), *Nationalism and Language in Kurdistan 1918–1985,* San Francisco: Mellon Research University Press.

Hassanpour, A. (2003), 'The Making of Kurdish Identity: Pre-Twentieth Century Historical and Literary Sources', in A. Vali (ed.), *Essays on the Origins of Kurdish Nationalism,* Costa Mesa: Mazda Publishers.

Hathaway, J. (1997), *The Politics of Households in Ottoman Egypt: The Rise of the Qazdağlıs,* Cambridge: Cambridge University Press.

Hesenpur, E. (2005), 'Türkiye'de Dilkırım Siyaseti ve Kürt Dili', in *Vesta,* Hejmar-Sayı 6.

Heyd, U. (1954), *Language Reform in Modern Turkey,* Jerusalem: Israel Oriental Society.

Hirschler, K. (2001), 'Defining the Nation: Kurdish Historiography in Turkey in the 1990s', in *Middle Eastern Studies*, 37(3).

Holston, J. (1989), *The Modernist City: An Anthropological Critique of Brasilia,* Chicago: University of Chicago.

Holston, J. (1999), 'Spaces of Insurgent Citizenship', in J. Holston (ed.), *Cities and Citizenship,* Durham: Duke University Press.

Houston, C. (2001a), *Islam, Kurds and the Turkish Nation State*, Oxford: Berg Press.

Houston, C. (2001b), 'The Brewing of Islamist Distinction: Tea Gardens and Public Space in Istanbul', *Theory, Culture and Society,* 12(1).

Houston, C. (2004), 'Islamism, Castoriadis and Autonomy', in *Thesis Eleven,* 76.

Houston, C. (2006), 'The Never Ending Dance: Islamism, Kemalism and the Power of Self-Institution in Turkey', *Australian Journal of Anthropology*, 17(2).

Humphrey, C. (2005), 'Ideology in Infrastructure: Architecture and Soviet Imagination', *Journal of the Royal Anthropological Institute*, 11(1).

Imber, C. (2002), *The Ottoman Empire, 1300–1650: The Structure of Power,* New York: Palgrave Macmillan.

Imga, O. (2006), *Siyaset ve Yerel Demokrasi,* Ankara: Dipnot Yayınları.

Inalcık, H. (1962), 'The Rise of Ottoman Historiography', in B. Lewis and P. Holt (eds), *Historians of the Middle East,* London: Oxford University Press.

Inalcık, H. (1973), *The Ottoman Empire: The Classical Age 1300–1600,* London: Weidenfeld & Nicolson.

Inalcık, H. (1996), 'The Meaning of Legacy: The Ottoman Case', in L. Brown (ed.), *Imperial Legacy: The Ottoman Imprint on the Balkans and the Middle East,* New York: Columbia University Press.

Irzık, G. (2004), 'Human Rights Issues in High School Sociology, Psychology, and Philosophy Textbooks', in D. Ceylan and G. Irzık (eds), *Human Rights Issues in Textbooks: The Turkish Case,* Istanbul: History Foundation of Turkey.

Islam Ansiklopedisi (1977), 6, Istanbul: Cilt. Milli Eğitim Basımevi.

Itkowitz, N. (1996), 'The Problems of Perceptions', in L. Brown (ed.), *Imperial Legacy: The Ottoman Imprint on the Balkans and the Middle East,* New York: Columbia University Press.

Jackson, M. (1998), *Minima Ethnographica: Intersubjectivity and the Anthropological Project,* Chicago: University of Chicago Press.

Joseph, S. (1991), 'Elite Strategies for State-Building: Women, Family, Religion and State in Iraq and Lebanon', in D. Kandiyoti (ed.), *Women, Islam and the State,* London: Macmillan.

Kafadar, C. (1995), *Between Two Worlds: The Construction of the Ottoman State,* Berkeley: University of California Press.

Kahn, J (1981), 'Marxist Anthropology and Segmentary Societies: A Review of the Literature', in *The Anthropology of Pre-Capitalist Societies,* London: Macmillan.

Kahn, J. (1995), *Culture, Multiculture, Postculture,* London: Sage Publications.

Kandiyoti, D. (1997), 'Gendering the Modern: On Missing Dimensions in the Study of Turkish Modernity', in S. Bozdoğan and R. Kasaba (eds), *Rethinking Modernity and National Identity in Turkey,* Seattle: University of Washington Press.

Karaömerlioğlu, M. (1998), 'The People's Houses and the Cult of the Peasant in Turkey', *Middle Eastern Studies*, 34(4).

Karpat, K. (ed.) (1968), *Political and Social Thought in the Contemporary Middle East*, New York: Praeger.

Karpat, K. (2003), 'Comments on Contributions and the Borderlands', in K. Karpat (ed.), *Ottoman Borderlands: Issues, Personalities and Political Changes*, Madison: University of Wisconsin Press.

Kasaba, R. (2000), 'Hard Time in Turkey', *New Perspectives on Turkey*, Fall, No. 23.

Kashani-Sabet, F. (2006), 'The Politics of Reproduction: Maternalism and Women's Hygiene in Iran, 1896–1941', *International Journal of Middle Eastern Studies*, 38(1).

Keyder, C. (1987), *State and Class in Turkey*, London: Verso.

Khosrokhavar, F. (2004), 'The Islamic Revolution in Iran: Retrospect after a Quarter of a Century', in *Thesis Eleven*, 76.

Kia, M. (1998), 'Persian Nationalism and the Campaign for Language Purification', in *Middle Eastern Studies*, 34(2).

Kiel, M. (2004), 'Ottoman Sources for the Demographic History and the Process of Islamization of Bosnia-Hercegovina and Bulgaria in the Fifteenth to Seventeenth Centuries: Old Sources – New Methodology', in M. Koller and K. Karpat (eds), *Ottoman Bosnia, A History in Brief*, Madison: Centre of Turkish Studies, University of Wisconsin.

Kılıç, O. (1999), 'Yurtluk-Ocaklık ve Hükümet Sancakları Üzerine Bazı Tesbitler' in *OTAM*, Sayı 10.

Kırzıoglu, F. (1963), *Kürtlerin Kökü*, Diyarbakır: Diyarbakırı Tanıtma Derneği Yayınları.

Kolluoğlu-Kırlı, B. (2002), 'The Play of Memory, Counter-Memory: Building Izmir on Smyrna's Ashes', in *New Perspectives on Turkey*, Spring, No. 26.

Kolluoğlu-Kırlı, B. (2005), 'Forgetting the Smyrna Fire', *History Workshop Journal*, 60(1).

Koşay, H. (1939), *Etnografya ve Folklor Kilavuzu*, Ankara: Cumhuriyet Halk Partisi Yayini.

Köker, O. (2005), *Armenians in Turkey 100 Years Ago. With the Postcards from the Collection of Orlando Carlo Calumeno*, Istanbul: Birzamanlar Yayıncılık.

Köksal, D. (2004), 'Art and Power in Turkey: Culture, Aesthetics and Nationalism during the Single Party Era', *New Perspectives on Turkey* Fall, 31.

Köprülü, F. (1935/1986), *Osmanli Imparatorluğunun Kuruluşu*, Istanbul: Ötüken.

Kuklick, H (1984), 'Tribal Exemplars: Images of Political Authority in British Anthropology, 1885–1945', in G. Stocking (ed.), *Functionalism Historicized: Essays in British Social Anthropology*, Madison: University of Wisconsin Press.

Kusno, A. (2000), *Behind the Postcolonial: Architecture, Urban Space and Political Cultures in Indonesia*, London: Routledge.

Kutschera, C. (2001), *Kürt Ulusal Harketi,* Istanbul: Avesta.

Larkin, P. (1964) *Selected Poems,* London: Faber & Faber.

Law, L. (2005), 'Home Cooking: Filipino Women and Geographies of the Senses in Hong Kong', in D. Howes (ed.), *Empire of the Senses,* Oxford: Berg.

Leach, E. (1940), *Social and Economic Organisation of the Rawanduz Kurds,* London: Percy Lund, Humphries & Co.

Leach, E. (1954), *Political Systems of Highland Burma*: *A Study of Kachin Social Structure,* London: Athlone Press.

Lewis, B. (1961), *The Emergence of Modern Turkey,* London: Oxford University Press.

Lewis, G. (1999), *The Turkish Language Reform: A Catastrophic Success,* Oxford: Oxford University Press.

Libal, K. (2000), 'The Children's Protection Society: Nationalizing Early Child Welfare in Early Republican Turkey', in *New Perspectives on Turkey* Fall, 23.

Lowry, H. (2002), *Fifteenth Century Ottoman Realities: Christian Peasant Life on the Aegean Island of Limnos,* Istanbul: Eren.

Lowry, H. (2003), *The Nature of the Early Ottoman State,* Albany: State University of New York Press.

Madanipour, A. (1998), *Tehran, The Making of a Metropolis,* Chichester: John Wiley & Sons.

Maksudyan (2005), 'Gauging Turkishness: Anthropology as Science-Fiction in Legitimizing Racist Nationalism, 1925–1939', unpublished MA thesis, Boğazici University.

Malmisanij (1991), *Said-I Nursi ve Kürt Sorunu,* Istanbul: Doz Yayınları.

Maqsud, C. (1960), Excerpt from 'Crisis of the Arab Left', in K. Karpat (ed.) (1968), *Political and Social Thought in the Contemporary Middle East,* New York: Praeger Publishers.

Mardin, Ş. (1993), 'Religion and Secularism in Turkey', in A. Hourani, P. Khoury and M. Wilson (eds), *The Modern Middle East,* Berkeley: University of California Press.

Marefat, M. (1992), 'The Protagonists Who Shaped Modern Tehran', in C. Adle & B. Hourcade (eds), *Teheran: Capitale Bicentenaire,* Paris/Teheran: Institut Francais de Recherche en Iran.

Marx, K. (1977), 'The Eighteenth Brumaire of Louis Bonaparte', in D.McLelland (ed.), *Karl Marx: Selected Writings,* Oxford: Oxford University Press.

Matthee, R. (1993), 'Transforming Dangerous Nomads into Useful Artisans, Technicians, Agriculturalists: Education in the Reza Shah Period', *Iranian Studies,* 26(4).

Matthee, R. (2003), 'The Safavid-Ottoman Frontier: Iraq-I Arab as seen by the Safavids', in K. Karpat (ed.), *Ottoman Borderlands: Issues, Personalities and Political Changes,* Madison: University of Wisconsin Press.

Mauss, M. (1992), 'Techniques of the Body', in J. Crary and S. Kwinter (eds), *Incorporations*, New York: Urazone.

Mazumdar, S. (2000), 'Autocratic Control and Urban Design: The Case of Tehran', *Journal of Urban Design,* 5(3).

McCarthy, J. (1997), *The Ottoman Turks: An Introductory History to 1923,* London: Longman.

McDowall, D. (2000), *A Modern History of the Kurds,* London: I.B. Tauris.

Meeker, M. (1997), 'Once There Was, Once There Wasn't': National Monuments and Interpersonal Exchange', in S. Bozdoğan and R. Kasaba (eds.) *Rethinking Modernity and National Identity in Turkey,* Seattle: University of Washington Press.

Meeker, M (2002), *A Nation of Empire,* Berkeley: University of California Press.

Meeker, M. (2004), 'Concepts of Family, State, and Society in the District of Of, Trabzon', in *Social Practice and Political Culture in the Turkish Republic,* Istanbul: The Isis Press.

Melman, B. (1992), *Women's Orient: English Women and the Middle East, 1718– 1918,* Basingstoke, Macmillan.

Minorsky, V. (1927), 'Kurdistan' and 'Kurds', in *Encyclopaedia of Islam,* Leiden: E.J. Brill.

Morrison, S. (2006), Review of 'Arab Nationalism in the Twentieth Century: From Triumph to Despair', *International Journal of Middle East Studies,* 38(3).

Nafissi, M. (2007), 'Before and Beyond the Clash of Civilizations', *ISIM Review,* 19.

Najmabadi, A. (1998), 'Crafting an Educated Housewife in Iran', in L. Abu-Lughod (ed.), *Remaking Women: Feminism and Modernity in the Middle East,* Princeton: Princeton University Press.

Navaro-Yashin, Y. (2000), 'Evde Taylorizm: Cumhuriyet'in ilk Yıllarında Evişinin Rasyonelleşmesi', in *Toplum ve Bilim,* 84.

Nezan, K. (1980), 'The Kurds under the Ottoman Empire', in G. Chaliand (ed.), *People Without a Country: The Kurds and Kurdistan,* London: Zed Press.

Nezan, K. (1993), 'Who are the Kurds?' in P. Kreyenbroek & C. Allison (eds), *Kurdish Culture and Identity,* London: Zed Books.

Nugent, D. (1982), 'Closed Systems and Contradiction: The Kachin in and out of History', *Man,* 17(3).

Nuri Paşa, I. (1955/1991), *Kürtlerin Kokeni,* Istanbul: Doz Yayınları.

Ögel, B., Yıldız, H., Kırzıoğlu, F., Eröz, M., Kodaman, B. and Çay, A. (1985), *Türk Milli Bütünlüğü İçerisinde Doğu Anadolu,* Ankara: Türk Kültürünü Arıştırma Enstitüsü.

Olson, R. (1996), *Imperial Meanderings and Republican Byways: Essays on Eighteenth Century Ottoman and Twentieth Century History of Turkey,* Istanbul: Isis Press.

Öz, M. (2003), 'Ottoman Provincial Administration in Eastern and Southeastern Anatolia: The Case of Bidlis in the Sixteenth Century', in K. Karpat (ed.), *Ottoman Borderlands: Issues, Personalities and Political Changes,* Madison: University of Wisconsin Press.

Özkan, R. (2001), '17 Mayıs 1638 Qesr-i Antlaşması', in *Özgür Politika* 18 May (downloaded 16 March 2006, www.özgürpolitika.org/2001/05/18/hab58b.html).

Özoğlu, H. (1996), 'State-Tribe Relations: Kurdish Tribalism in the Sixteenth- and Seventeenth-Century Ottoman Empire', *British Journal of Middle Eastern Studies*, 23(1).

Özoğlu, H. (2005), *Osmanlı Devleti ve Kürt Milliyetçiliği,* Istanbul: Kitap Yayınevi.

Öztürkmen, A. (1994), 'The Role of the People's Houses in the Making of National Culture in Turkey', in *New Perspectives on Turkey* 11, Fall.

Pamak, M. (1996), *Kürt Sorunu ve Müslümanlar,* Istanbul: Selam Yayınları.

Pamuk, O. (1994), *The Black Book,* London: Faber & Faber.

Parla, T. (1998), 'Military Mercantilism in Turkey, 1960–1998', in *New Perspectives on Turkey*, 19, Fall.

Parla, T. and Davison, A. (2004), *Corporatist Ideology in Kemalist Turkey: Progress or Order?* New York: Syracuse University Press.

Peker, R. (1933), 'Halkevleri Açılma Nutku', *Ülkü*, 1(1).

Perry, J. (1985), 'Language Reform in Turkey and Iran', *International Journal of Middle Eastern Studies*, 17(2).

Pesmazoglou, S. (1995), 'Turkey and Europe, Reflections and Refractions: Towards a Contrapuntal Approach', *New Perspectives on Turkey*, No 13, Fall.

Piterberg, G. (2003), *An Ottoman Tragedy: History and Historiography at Play,* Berkeley: University of California Press.

Preziosi, D. (1991), 'The Mechanisms of Urban Meaning', in I. Bierman, R. Abou-El-Haj and D. Preziosi (eds), *The Ottoman City and its Parts,* New York: Aristide D. Caratzas.

Rajagopal, A. (2001), *Politics after Television: Religious Nationalism and the Re-shaping of the Indian Public,* Cambridge: Cambridge University Press.

Robins, K. (1996), 'Interrupting Identities: Turkey/Europe', in S. Hall and P. du Gay (eds), *Questions of Cultural Identity,* London: Sage Publications.

Rodinson, M. (1978), 'Preface', in G. Chaliand (ed.), *People without a Country*: *The Kurds and Kurdistan,* London: Zed Press.

Rogan, E. (1999), *Frontiers of the State in the Late Ottoman Empire: Transjordan, 1850–1921.* Cambridge University Press, Cambridge.

Rohat (1991), *Unutulmuşluğun Bir Öyküsü Said-i Kürdi,* Istanbul: Fırat Yayınları.

Roy, O. (2005), 'A Clash of Cultures or a Debate on Europe's Values', in *ISIM Review,* 15.

Runciman, S. (1962), 'Byzantine Historians and the Ottoman Turks', in B. Lewis and P. Holt (eds), *Historians of the Middle East,* London: Oxford University Press.

Said, E. (1978), *Orientalism: Western Conceptions of the Orient,* London: Penguin Books.

Salmoni, B. (2003), 'Turkish Knowledge for a Modern Life: Innovative Pedagogy and Nationalist Substance in Primary Schooling, 1927–50', *Turkish Studies,* 4(3).

Salmoni, B (2004), 'Turkish Nationalist Educational Thinking in the Last Ottoman Decade: Run-Up to the Republic', *New Perspectives in Turkey*, Fall, 31.

Sarıoğlu, M. (2001), *Ankara Bir Modernleşme Öyküsü (1919–1945)*, Ankara: T.C Kültür Bakanlığı Yayınları.

Sayyid, B. (1997), *A Fundamental Fear: Eurocentrism and the Emergence of Islamism*, London: Zed Books.

Schayegh, C. (2001), 'Sport, Health, and the Iranian Middle Class in the 1920s and 1930s', *Iranian Studies* 35(4).

Schayegh, C. (2005), '"A Sound Mind Lives in a Healthy Body": Texts and Contexts in the Iranian Modernists' Scientific Discourse of Health', *The International Journal of Middle East Studies,* 37(2).

Seal, J. (1995), *A Fez of the Heart,* New York: Harcourt Brace.

Seufert, G. (1999), 'The Faculties of Divinity in the Current Tug-of-War', in *Les Annales de l'Autre Islam*, No 6. Paris: INALCO-ERISM.

Seufert, G. (2000), 'The Impact of Nationalist Discourses on Civil Society', in S. Yerasimos, G. Seufert and K. Vorhoff (eds) *Civil Society in the Grip of Nationalism,* Istanbul: Orient –Institut.

Simon, R. (1986), 'The Teaching of History in Iraq before the Rashid Ali Coup of 1941', *Middle Eastern Studies,* 22(1).

Simon, R. (1997), 'The Imposition of Nationalism on a Non-National State: The Case of Iraq during the Interwar Period, 1921–1941', in J. Jankowski and I. Gershoni (eds) *Rethinking Nationalism in the Arab Middle East*, New York: Columbia University Press.

Sinclair, T. (2003), 'The Ottoman Arrangements for the Tribal Principalities of the Lake Van Region of the Sixteenth Century', *International Journal of Turkish Studies,* 9 (1 and 2).

Singer, A. (1994), *Palestinian Peasants and Ottoman Officials: Rural Administration around Sixteenth-Century Jerusalem,* Cambridge: Cambridge University Press.

Sirman, N. (2004), 'Kinship, Politics and Love: Honour in Post-colonial Contexts – The Case of Turkey', in S. Mojab and N. Abo (eds) *Violence in the Name of Honour*, Istanbul: Bilgi University Press.

Spivak, G. (1999), *A Critique of Postcolonial Reason: Toward a History of the Vanishing Present,* Cambridge MA: Harvard University Press.

Stansfield, G. (2003), *Iraqi Kurdistan: Political Development and Emergent Democracy,* London: Routledge Curzon.

Starr, J. (1992), *Law as Metaphor,* New York: State University of New York Press.

Stokes, M. (1992), *The Arabesk Debate: Music and Musicians in Modern Turkey,* Oxford: Clarendon Press.

Sykes, M. (1915), 'The Kurdish Tribes of the Ottoman Empire', *The Caliphs' Last Heritage, A Short History of the Turkish Empire,* London: Macmillan.

Şahin, R. (1988), *Tarih Boyunca Türk İdarelerinin Ermeni Politikaları*, Istanbul: Ötüken.

Şenol, F. (1998), 'İktidar mücadelesinin savaş meydanı: Mekan Cumhuriyet'in ilk yıllarında Ankara'da eğlence mekanları', in *Toplum ve Bilim* 76, Bahar.

Şeref Han (1597/1990), *Şerefname: Kürt Tarihi,* Istanbul: Hasat Yayınları.

Strohmeier, M. (2003), *Crucial Images in the Presentation of a Kurdish National Identity,* Leiden: E.J. Brill.

Taneri, A. (1983), *Türkistan bir Türk Boyu Kürtler: Kürtler in Kökeni-Siyasi, Sosyal ve Kültüral Hayatları,* Ankara: Türk Kültürünü Arıştırma Enstitüsü.

Tapper, R. (1990), 'Anthropologists, Historians and Tribespeople on Tribe and State Formation in the Middle East', in P. Khoury and J. Kramer (eds), *Tribes and State Formation in the Middle East,* Berkeley: University of California Press.

Tekelioğlu, O. (1996), 'The Rise of a Spontaneous Synthesis: The Historical Background of Turkish Popular Music', in S. Kedourie (ed.), *Turkey: Identity, Democracy, Politics,* London: Frank Cass.

Todorova, M. (1995), 'Bulgarian Historical Writing on the Ottoman Empire', *New Perspectives on Turkey*, Spring, 12.

Todorova, M. (1996), 'The Ottoman Legacy in the Balkans', in L. Brown (ed.), *Imperial Legacy: The Ottoman Imprint on the Balkans and the Middle East,* New York: Columbia University Press.

Tschumi, B. (1994), *Architecture and Disjunction,* Cambridge: MIT Press.

Tucker, J. (2000), *In the House of Law: Gender and Islamic Law in Ottoman Syria and Palestine,* Berkeley: University of California Press.

Ülkütaşır, M. (1972), *Cumhuriyet'le Birlikte Türkiye'de Folklor ve Etnografya Calısmaları,* Ankara: Başbakan Basımevi.

Üstel, F. (1993), '1920'LI ve 30'LU YILLARDA "MILLI MUSIKI" ve "MUSIKI INKILABI"', in *Defter* 22.

Vale, L. (1992), *Architecture, Power and National Identity,* New Haven: Yale University Press.

Vali, A. (1996), 'Nationalism and Kurdish Historical Writing', in *New Perspectives on Turkey*, Spring, No. 14.

Vali, A. (1998), 'The Kurds and Their "Others": Fragmented Identity and Fragmented Politics', in *Comparative Studies of South Asia, Africa and the Middle East*, 18(2).

Van Bruinessen, M. (1988), *Evliya Celebi in Diyarbakır,* Leiden: E.J. Brill.

Van Bruinessen, M. (1989), 'The Ethnic Identity of the Kurds', in P. Andrews (ed.), *Ethnic Groups in the Republic of Turkey,* Wiesbaden: Reichert.

Van Bruinessen, M. (1992), *Agha, Shaikh and State: The Social and Political Structures of Kurdistan,* London: Zed Books.

Van Bruinessen, M. (2003), 'Ehmedi Xani's "Mem u Zim" and its Role in the Emergence of Kurdish National Awareness', in A. Vali (ed.), *Essays on the Origins of Kurdish Nationalism,* Costa Mesa: Mazda Publishers.

Vincent, J. (1990), *Anthropology and Politics: Visions and Trends,* Tuscson: University of Arizona Press.

Vryonis, S. (1991), 'Byzantine Constantinople and Ottoman Istanbul: Evolution in a Millennial Imperial Iconography', in I. Bierman, R. Abou-El-Haj and D. Preziosi (eds), *The Ottoman City and its Parts,* New York: Aristide D. Caratzas.

White, P. (2000), *Primitive Revolutionaries or Revolutionary Modernizers: The Kurdish National Movement in Turkey,* London: Zed Books.

Wilbur, D. (1987), 'Pahlavi, before World War II', *Encyclopedia Iranica,* London: Routledge & Kegan Paul.

Wittek, P. (1938/1958), *The Rise of the Ottoman Empire,* London: The Royal Asiatic Society of Great Britain and Ireland.

Wolfe, P. (1999), *Settler Colonialism and the Transformation of Anthropology: The Politics and Poetics of an Ethnographic Event,* London: Cassell.

Yalçın-Heckmann, L. (1991), 'Ethnic Islam and Nationalism amongst the Kurds in Turkey', in R. Tapper (ed.), *Islam in Modern Turkey,* London: IB Tauris.

Yavuz, H. (2000), 'Cleansing Islam from the Public Sphere', *Journal of International Affairs,* 54(1).

Yeğen, M (1996), 'The Turksh State Discourse and the Exclusion of Kurdish Identity', *Middle Eastern Studies,* 32(2).

Yeğen, M. (1999), *Devlet Söyleminde Kürt Sorunu,* Istanbul: Iletisim Yayınları.

Yeğenoğlu, M. (1998), *Colonial Fantasies: Towards a Feminist Reading of Orientalism,* Cambridge: Cambridge University Press.

Yenal, Z. (1999), 'State Forms the Market', *New Perspectives on Turkey,* Spring, 20.

Yildiz, K. (2004), *The Kurds in Iraq: The Past, Present and Future,* London: Pluto Press.

Yılmaz, H. (1991), *Aşiretten Ulusallığa Doğru Kürtler,* Istanbul: Fırat-Dicle Yayınları.

Youssefzadeh, A. (2005), 'Iran's Musical Traditions in the Twentieth Century: A Historical Overview', *Iranian Studies,* 38(3).

Yüksel, M. (1993), *Kürdistandaki Değişim Süreci,* Ankara: Sor Yayıncılık.

Zeki, M.E. (1947/2005), *Kürd ve Kürdistan Ünlüleri (Meşahire Kürd u Kürdistan),* Ankara: Özge Yayınları.

Zirinsky, M. (1992), 'Imperial Power and Dictatorship: Britain and the Rise of Reza Shah, 1921–1926', *International Journal of Middle Eastern Studies,* 24(4).

Zubaida, S. (2002), 'The Fragments Imagine the Nation: The Case of Iraq', *International Journal of Middle Eastern Studies,* 34(2).

Zürcher, E. (1995), *Modernleşen Türkiye'nin Tarihi,* Istanbul: Iletişim Yayınları.

Index

Abdi, K., 149, 150
Abrahamian, E., 136, 148
aesthetics, 126
Ahıska, M., 129, 130, 137
Akgündüz, A., 39n4, 40
Aksoy Gürdal, 17
Alakom, Rohat, 1, 63
Alevi, 103
 see also Kurds
al-Khalil, S., 151
Allouche, A., 46
Altınay, A., 25, 26
Amin, C., 122, 124
Anatolia, 10, 12, 22n11, 44, 46, 86, 131, 132, 146
Andrews, P., 65
Ankara, 97, 115, 128, 131, 134, 139, 141, 142, 142n6, 143, 144–6, 152, 162
anthropology, 5–6, 9, 31, 67, 92, 93, 94, 95, 101, 131
 and colonialism, 66, 67, 68, 71, 76, 77, 92, 94, 161
 and nationalism, 68, 92, 94, 95, 131, 135
 circuits of knowledge, 68, 74, 85, 94, 95
 dominance of English, 69
 historical perspectives on, 66–7, 81, 92, 93, 161
 segmentary lineage, 81–2, 83, 88, 93
Appadurai, A., 156
Arabs, 3, 5, 6, 10, 14n6, 16, 24n15, 25, 33, 35, 40, 49, 56, 63, 70, 72, 77, 102, 107, 108, 152, 159, 160
 Arabism, 108, 108n15, 109, 110, 111, 112, 113
 history, 15n8, 132
 historiography, 15n8
 Kemalism, 159
 pan-Arab, 110, 113, 151
 see also nationalism
Arat, Z., 125n29
archaeology, 112, 136, 148, 149, 150, 151

architecture, 114n21, 139, 142, 143, 145–6, 148, 149, 152, 152n12, 153, 155, 162
Ari, E., 129, 130
Armenian & Kurdish relations, 57, 60, 62–3
Armenians, 25, 34, 35, 55, 55n18, 56, 57, 59, 60, 110
 genocide, 57, 57n19, 59, 60
 uprising, 60
army, 114n20
Arnason, J., 136
arts,
 art education, 127, 161–2
 arts and crafts, 112, 126, 129, 130–1, 161
 dance, 133, 137, 146, 161
 folk art, 128, 130–1, 161
 performing arts, 127, 159, 161–2
 photography, 162
 state patronage of, 112, 127, 137, 161–2
  see also music, theatre
Asad, T., 77
assimilation, 104, 105, 157, 159
Assyrians, 55, 56
Atalli, J., 155
Atatürk, 16, 27n17, 28, 103n5, 112, 115, 116, 118, 120, 127, 132, 134, 136, 141, 145n7, 146, 153, 160, 162
 Mausoleum, 142n6, 146
Australia, 106
Ayatollah Khomeini, 135, 136
Ayvazoğlu, B., 134

Ba'ath Party, 104, 109, 110, 111, 112, 113, 122, 128n33, 135, 150, 151, 162
Babylon, 112, 150
Baghdad, 10, 41, 97, 139, 143, 152, 162
Banini, A., 148
Baram, A., 111, 112, 113, 150, 151
Barbir, K., 7
Barth, Fredrik, 65, 67, 76, 79–82, 85n15, 86, 87, 88, 90, 92, 93, 161

179